Smart Moves

Developing Mathematical Reasoning with Games and Puzzles

Michael Serra

Publisher	Copyeditor
Executive Editor	Designer
Project Administrator	Technical Artist
Production Manager	Compositor
Angela Snead	**Tamar Chestnut**

Editors
Dan Bennett
Tamar Chestnut

Cover Designer
Lumina Designworks

Printed in the USA
Lightning Source

Playing It Smart
PO Box 27540
San Francisco, CA 94127
mserramath@gmail.com
www.michaelserra.net
ISBN 978-0-9834-0990-8

Contents

Acknowledgements

Some of the puzzles and games appearing in puzzle books today can be traced back to Martin Gardner and H.E. Dudeney. *Smart Moves*, like many puzzle books, owes much to these two champions of recreational mathematics.

To the teachers Diane Garfield and Amber Lewis-Francis, thank you for letting me into your classroom to try the games and puzzles with your students. Your efforts in preparing students to think and explain their reasoning made my visits a learning experience for all of us. I am especially indebted to the students for their wonderful enthusiasm, creativity, and encouragement.

I am grateful to our adult field testers: Jack Abad, Paul Abad, John (Scott) Connors, and Matt DiMaggio for their help in identifying errors and points of confusion.

We greatly appreciate the support of Karen Coe, Josephine Noah, Christine Osborne, and Judy Anderson at Key Curriculum Press who patiently answered our questions and encouraged us along the path to self-publishing.

I wish to express my appreciation to our first round editor, Dan Bennett, who read the original manuscript and offered his input as an experienced math teacher and textbook editor.

A very special thank you to Tamar Chestnut for turning my manuscript into something I am proud to share. Tamar is our copy editor, designer, and compositor. Thank you Tamar, you are amazingly versatile.

Thanks also to Terry Lockman and Jill Zwicky of Lumina Designworks for their innovative cover design.

Finally, I want to thank my wife, Angie, who took my idea and turned it into a reality. To the executive editor, project administrator, production manager, publisher, puzzle tester—you name it—Angie, my love, this book is dedicated to you.

Introduction

With ordinary talent and extraordinary perseverance, all things are attainable.
–Thomas Foxwell Buxton

In high school I happened upon Martin Gardner's "Mathematical Games" column in *Scientific American,* and I still return to his games columns for classroom ideas. Mr. Gardner introduced the world to Polyominoes, the Soma Cube, and Racetrack (see Chapter 2). I later discovered that, in the world of recreational mathematics, Henry E. Dudeney was the master puzzle inventor. Dudeney's *The Canterbury Puzzles* begins with a puzzle that is an extension of what we now know as the *Tower of Hanoi* (see Chapter 1). Martin Gardner's monthly column of mathematical recreations and the puzzles of H.E. Dudeney have had an enormous influence on my classroom teaching and on this book.

As a high school math teacher, puzzles were a regular part of my *Problem of the Week* assignments, as well as interesting class openers and lead-ins to many curriculum topics. When we published my textbook, *Discovering Geometry,* I insisted that each lesson end with a puzzle. Puzzles are intriguing yet simple to understand, and they are an excellent way to introduce and reinforce mathematical ideas. Guided by rules that are easy to follow, students learn how to think mathematically and problem solve sequentially. And, because they are so much fun, games and puzzles help teachers with a big part of our job: motivation.

After *Discovering Geometry* was published, I received a lovely letter from Martin Gardner commending me on my selection of puzzles. In his letter, Mr. Gardner wrote, "I zipped through the pages last night with amazement at how judiciously you selected material that would not be either too hard or too easy for your readers..." Of course, I framed his letter and it now hangs in my office.

Throughout my career I have found the motivation of games and puzzles to extend far beyond the high school classroom. For instance, I recently taught a geometry class (at San Francisco State University) to prospective elementary school teachers. On the first day I sensed a great deal of fear, which would make learning mathematics impossible for these future teachers. I used puzzles to reduce that math anxiety and by the end of the course they had a new perspective on mathematics. You will find many of those puzzles in this book.

As another example, I currently volunteer once a week as a "mathemagican" in a fifth grade classroom. Fifth graders are curious,

Stanford psychologist Carol Dweck conducted studies with early adolescents. In these experiments researchers gave the students some difficult IQ test questions. After the IQ test some youngsters were complimented for their effort: "You must have worked really hard." The others were praised for their ability: "You must be smart at this." Students who were praised for their intelligence were more likely to turn down the chance to try a new exercise that they could learn from. "They didn't want to do anything that could expose their deficiencies and call into question their talent," Dweck says. However, of the students who were praised for their hard work, ninety percent of them were eager to try the new task.

enthusiastic, and fearless, and they love to play math games and solve math puzzles. Sometimes we even work through activities I did with my high school students. Again, I learned that games and puzzles are an important component to a successful math foundation, even as early as the fifth grade.

Through my many years of varied experience, I have established a few rules that assist in the successful use of puzzles in the classroom. First, it is very important to establish a safe classroom environment when using games and puzzles. Students need to feel comfortable asking questions and exploring ideas without the fear of being criticized or marked down for a wrong answer. Second, allow plenty of time for students to experiment and ponder these challenges. Third, nothing succeeds like success. Start with puzzles that everyone can accomplish to help boost confidence. Fourth, praise good effort rather than complimenting students for being brilliant. Finally, focus on games and puzzles that stress sequential reasoning and good old fashion "stick-to-it-ness." Puzzles that require flashes of insight or cleverness are occasionally solved by the rare, brilliant student, but these "trick problems" can turn off some of the mainstream students.

Smart Moves is a collection of games and puzzles that emphasize and strengthen sequential reasoning. The broad term, "sequential reasoning," is given to the type of thinking that is at the core of mathematics and everyday problem solving. Thinking sequentially leads to a solution or outcome through a series of steps and reasoning sequentially can take the following form:

I need 'X' to happen. In order for 'X' to happen, I need 'Y' to happen first. If I start by doing 'A' then 'B' results. If I have completed B then I get 'C' as a result. If I have 'C' in place then 'Y' is my result and I can get my final desired product, 'X'.

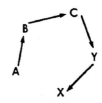

Good sequential reasoning is used in almost all activities, such as planning a vacation, remodeling a home, or solving logistical problems at work. Many daily tasks also require sequential thinking, which we often do unconsciously. If you live in a multi-level home you quickly learn to plan all the stops you need to make on the first floor before returning to the second floor. Preparing family meals, installing a new piece of software on your computer, or assembling furniture, all require sequential reasoning. This is true for any project you choose to undertake. If you carefully consider the project you will become better equipped at making a plan and working through the steps to achieve your goal.

It is not that I am so smart, it's just that I stay with problems longer.
   –Albert Einstein

One of the goals in this book is to encourage beginner-level puzzle solvers. At a time when complex mysteries are neatly solved in one-hour TV shows, perseverance is a quality that is sadly under-utilized. Thomas Edison said, "Genius is one-percent inspiration and ninety-nine percent perspiration." The puzzles in *Smart Moves* are not the type of puzzles that require the solver to "think out of the box" or to have a "Eureka moment." Instead, it is designed to strengthen your sequential reasoning, help you learn some mathematics, and have fun along the way. I sincerely hope you enjoy the experience!

Features of *Smart Moves*

Puzzle Solving Tips

Puzzle solving and mathematical problem solving share similar strategies. Here are a number of those strategies and their corresponding sections in this book:

1. Solve simpler or analogous problems first (Tower of Hanoi puzzle in section 1.4 and Coin Jump puzzles in Section 3.1).

2. Look for patterns (Coin Slide puzzles in Section 3.1 and Tour puzzles in Chapter 4).

3. Work backwards from the desired result to the given information (Square Route puzzles in Section 1.2).

4. Make a table (Container puzzles in Section 1.3).

5. Use manipulatives (Sequential Movement puzzles in Section 1.4).

6. Pay attention to detail (Robot puzzles in Section 1.6).

7. Plan ahead (Racetrack games in Chapter 2).

8. Check your answer to see if it is reasonable and accurate (all puzzles and games).

And remember, the time it takes to solve a puzzle has no relationship to how intelligent you are. Many ordinary people became great thinkers because of concentrated and deliberate effort. Perseverance is incredibly important to mathematics and puzzle solving.

Playing Boards

You will find 14 different racetracks for the game of Racetrack, in Appendix 1. I suggest you begin with the simpler tracks and gradually move up to more challenging ones. After playing with some of the supplied racetracks, I encourage you to create some of your own and share them with others. You will also find large playing boards for the coin slide puzzles, the sliding block puzzles, the Queen Bee puzzles, and the Mini Robot puzzles, in Appendix 2.

Algebra and Geometry Summary

You will find a short review of algebra in Appendix 3. In addition to solving equations in one, two, or three variables, you will need to recall order of operations, special products, and factoring. You will also need to be familiar with function notation and how to find a linear function given a table of values. Graphing is such a large and important topic that I have saved my games and puzzles, involving the coordinate plane, for my next book, *Buried Treasure* (working title).

Appendix 4 contains a short review of geometry, including: the properties of vertical angles, linear pairs of angles, the corresponding angles formed by parallel lines, properties of isosceles triangles, the sum of the measures of the interior angles of polygons, and a host of circle properties.

Hints and Answers

Many puzzles have hints to assist you in solving the puzzles. Look at the examples in the chapter, make a serious effort at solving the puzzles, and only if you need more direction, turn to the hints. Puzzles with hints are marked with an *h*. You will find the hints in Appendix 5. Answers to all the puzzles are found in Appendix 6.

Proof in Recreational Mathematics

Appendix 7 demonstrates some of the proofs of certain properties in *Smart Moves*, such as the proof that the 3×3 magic square is unique. Many of the techniques in solving the puzzles in *Smart Moves* are also common proof strategies. For example, you will find indirect proof techniques very useful in solving most puzzles. The angle chase puzzles in Chapter 7 are another way to practice with proof that I've found very successful in my geometry courses.

A Closer Look at *Smart Moves*

Chapter 1, *Warm-up Puzzles*, introduces seven different sequential reasoning puzzles. The chapter takes you through various puzzles and prepares you to "think ahead."

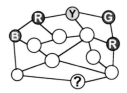

In Chapter 2, you will play the game of *Racetrack*. Planning ahead is the key to success in this game. After playing *Racetrack* on a variety of tracks, I encourage you to look at Section 2.2 Mathematical Connections: Vectors. Your moves in the game of *Racetrack* are actually vectors.

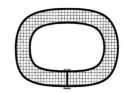

Chapter 3, *Movement Puzzles*, introduces six different movement puzzles. The objective is to move objects from an initial position to a final solution. Using manipulatives will help you discover the correct sequence of steps. To learn about other types of playing boards, take a look at Section 3.5 Mathematical Connections: Archimedean Tilings.

Chapter 4, *Tour Puzzles,* introduces three different types of tour puzzles. It is not necessary to know how to play chess to solve these puzzles but you will need perserverance. See Section 4.4 Mathematical Connections: Euler Paths to see how mathematical recreations have led to the development of a major branch of mathematics, Topology.

In Chapter 5, *Magic Square Puzzles*, your goal is to use sequential reasoning to complete magic squares. A Magic Square is a grid of distinct integers such that each row, column, and both main diagonals have the same sum. Be sure to look at some of the interesting proofs about magic squares in Appendix 7.

Chapters 6, *Sequential Reasoning in Algebra* takes Magic Square puzzles and Tour puzzles to new levels. Algebra skills are necessary to solve the puzzles in this chapter.

Chapters 7, *Sequential Reasoning in Geometry*, introduces Angle Chase puzzles. An angle chase puzzle is a network of lines and segments intersecting with some of the angle measures given. The goal is to use sequential reasoning to find the measures of the marked angles. You must understand the basic properties of geometry to solve the puzzles in this chapter.

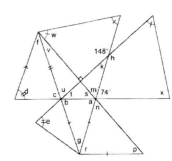

Using *Smart Moves*

Classroom Setting

Smart Moves can be used as part of a school mathematics curriculum or as extra curricular activities for students. The puzzles make excellent classroom openers, end-of-period thought provokers, or for students to work on during school holidays.

5th Graders Playing Racetrack

10th Graders Solving Coin Jump Puzzles

Using the puzzle solving tips and Mathematical Connections will engage the students in problem solving, help them discover strategies, and encourage mathematical thinking. The Mathematical Connections sections can be used as starting points for group or individual research projects.

The puzzles in *Smart Moves* are wonderful for cooperative problem solving activities in the classroom. I encourage teachers to post group solutions on classroom bulletin boards to showcase student work. Another great way to introduce a puzzle lesson is to use a document camera. You can project a puzzle worksheet onto a screen for the entire class to see and discuss. A student can write on the worksheet as the class solves the puzzle together. For a more dramatic effect, project a color PDF of the puzzles onto a white board and have students fill in the parts of the puzzle as they explain their reasoning to the rest of the class. The color PDFs can also be dropped into PowerPoint™ or Keynote™ to create presentations for classroom use or to share on "Back to School Night."

Home School Setting

Finding supplemental materials for the home school teacher can be challenging. Straight textbook instruction in mathematics can be very difficult if done in an isolated setting and drill-like manner. Integrating home mathematics instruction with games and puzzles creates a fun and playful environment for the students. I encourage parents to participate in these games and puzzles with the whole family. The Mathematical Connections can be used as starting points for your students to explore mathematics in their own way and pace.

Mental Gymnastics

Research has shown that both physical and mental activities help to keep the mind alert and strong. Besides helping develop a child's cognitive function, mental activities are an essential component for senior fitness. As the baby boomer generation approaches retirement, they find that keeping the mind active is just as important as healthy nutrition and a good night's sleep.

Any personal trainer will tell you that doing the same set of exercises is not as beneficial as varying the routines. The same is true of mental exercise. If you have become an expert at Sudoku puzzles, your brain is ready for a change. Playing the puzzles in *Smart Moves* will give you the variety needed, as Agatha Christie's Hercule Poirot once said, to keep "those little grey cells" humming along.

Chapter 1   Warm-Up Puzzles

Perseverance is not a long race; it is many short races one after another.
                                                              –Walter Elliott

Sequential reasoning is necessary for everyday living and problem solving. Planning your day or week requires thoughtful step-by-step thinking. Subjects you study in school, or research you do on your own, often require you to work through a series of steps. These warm-up puzzles will get your sequential reasoning muscles loosened up. Puzzles with hints are marked with an *h* and can be found in Appendix 5. Puzzle answers can be found in Appendix 6.

1.1   Color Network Puzzles

In Color Network Puzzle 1, you need to color each circle Red (R), Yellow (Y), or Blue (B). However, no two vertices of a triangle may be the same color. Which color goes in the circle with a question mark? In Color Network Puzzle 2, color each circle with Red (R), Yellow (Y), Blue (B), or Green (G), without coloring two vertices of a non-overlapping quadrilateral the same color. Which color goes in the circle with a question mark?

CN Puzzle 1   **CN Puzzle 2** *h*

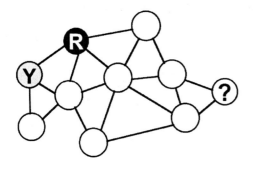   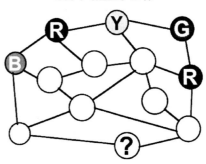

1.2   Square Route Puzzles

In the square route puzzles, the goal is to find a route or path that starts at 1, in the upper left corner, and ends at 100, in the lower right corner. You can move to an adjacent square horizontally, vertically, or diagonally, according to rules defined by given arithmetic operations. In Square Route Puzzle 1, you must add, subtract, multiply or divide the number in your square by 2 or 5 to move to a neighboring square. For example, from square 11, you could move to square 9 by subtracting 2 or move to square 55 by multiplying by 5. In Square Route Puzzle 2, you must add, subtract, multiply, or divide by 2 or 3 to move to a neighboring square.

SR Puzzle 1   **SR Puzzle 2** *h*

1	5	10	20	30
2	3	22	6	28
4	27	8	14	19
20	17	11	55	95
18	9	50	57	100

1	3	6	54	50
2	11	27	55	52
5	9	58	26	78
7	29	31	95	97
21	24	72	93	100

1.3   Container Puzzles

In each of the puzzles below, you have unmarked containers and an unlimited supply of water. You are trying to measure out a particular amount of water in the fewest moves. Let's look at an example.

Example

Given an unlimited supply of water and using an unmarked 5-liter container and an unmarked 3-liter container, how can you measure exactly 4 liters of water?

Solution

Steps 1-2: Fill up the 3-liter container and pour the water into the 5-liter container.

Steps 3-4: Fill up the 3-liter container again and pour as much of the water as possible into the 5-liter container. It will take 2 more liters to fill the 5-liter container, leaving 1 liter in the 3-liter container.

Steps 5-7: Empty the 5-liter container. Pour the 1-liter from the 3-liter container into the 5-liter container. Fill the 3-liter container. This gives a total of 4 liters (1 + 3 = 4).

The solution can also be demonstrated with a table:

	Start	1	2	3	4	5	6	Finish
5-liter	0	0	3	3	5	0	1	1
3-liter	0	3	0	3	1	1	0	3

Now it is your turn. Solve each container puzzle below. Record your solution in a paragraph or table, or represent it using diagrams or symbols.

Container Puzzle 1 *h* Using an 8-liter container and a 5-liter container, how can you measure 11 liters?

	Start	1	2	3	4	5	6	7	8	9	10	11	12
8-L	0												
5-L	0												

11 liters

Container Puzzle 2 Using a 9-liter container and a 4-liter container, how can you measure 3 liters?

	Start	1	2	3	4	5	6	7	8	9	10	11	12
9-L	0												
4-L	0												

3 liters

Container Puzzle 3 Using an 11-liter container and a 3-liter container, how can you be certain of getting 10 liters?

	Start	1	2	3	4	5	6	7	8	9	10	11	12
11-L	0												
3-L	0												

10 liters

What if you do not have an unlimited supply of water? What if you have three containers? Try these variations of container puzzles.

Container Puzzle 4 Using an empty 1-liter container, an empty 3-liter container, and a full 6-liter container, how can you get exactly 1 liter of water, 2 liters of water, and 3 liters of water distributed among the three containers?

Container Puzzle 5 *ħ* Using an empty 3-liter container, an empty 5-liter container, and a full 8-liter, how can you get exactly 4 liters of water in two of the containers?

Instead of moving water with containers, what if the task is to measure time with differently sized sand timers? Solve the timer puzzle below.

Container Puzzle 6 You have two sand timers. One is calibrated to measure 7 minutes and the other measures 11 minutes. How can you use these two timers to accurately measure 15 minutes?

1.4 Sequential Movement Puzzles

The classic sequential movement puzzle is the Tower of Hanoi (also called the Three-Peg Puzzle). It first appeared as a toy in France, and soon after in W.W.R. Ball's *Mathematical Recreations and Essays*. The puzzle consists of three pegs and a number of disks. The initial position has all the disks stacked on one peg so they are arranged from largest, on the bottom, to the smallest on top. No larger disk sits on top of a smaller disk. The task is to move the disks so they are arranged in the same order on another peg. There are three rules for moving the disks:

1. Only one disk may be moved at a time.
2. A move consists of removing only the top disk from one of the pegs and placing it onto another peg. The moved disk must be placed on top of any other disks that may already be present on that peg.
3. No disk may be placed on top of a smaller disk.

To solve the sequential movement puzzles below, you will need to either purchase a Tower of Hanoi puzzle or build your own Tower of Hanoi puzzle. To build the puzzle use wood dowels or nails for the pegs and secure them to a wooden base. Use different size washers for the disks or cut them out of cardboard. You can also eliminate the pegs and stack paper disks on three spots on a piece of paper.

SM Puzzle 1 *ħ*

Solve the Tower of Hanoi Puzzle with seven disks.

SM Puzzle 2 *ħ*

What is the fewest number of moves necessary to successfully transfer 64 disks from one peg to another?

Another classic sequential movement puzzle is Rush Hour®. It was created by Nob Yoshigahara[1] in the late 1970's and was a smash hit when it was first introduced in the United States, in 1996. Rush Hour is produced by ThinkFun, formerly Binary Arts. The goal is to maneuver a car (marked with an X in the example below) out of the playing grid through the one opening. In order to get the car out of the six-by-six grid, you need to move the other cars and trucks out of its way. Cars are 1×2 rectangles and trucks are 1×3 rectangles. Each vehicle can only move back and forth in a straight line.

For instance, in the example below, car E can move left and right, but not up or down. Truck C can move up and down, but not left or right. Use "U" for up, "D" for Down, "R" for right, and "L" for left in writing your solution. Try this example.

Example

Get the car (X) out of the 6×6 grid through the opening on the right side.

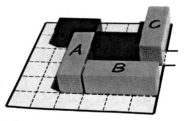

Solution

Truck C is blocking the path so it needs to be moved out of the way. But since truck B is blocking C's path, B needs to be moved first. However, B cannot be moved until truck A is moved. Truck A can be moved once car E is moved out of A's way. Therefore the solution: Move car E right 2 units or left 1 unit. Move truck A up 1 unit. Then move truck B left 1 unit. Next, move truck C down 3 units. Finally, move car X right 3 units and out! One solution written symbolically is: EL1 • AU1 • BL1 • CD3 • XR3.

To help you visualize your sequential reasoning for these puzzles, create your own 6×6 grid on a sheet of graph paper. If you can locate Cuisenaire® rods, you can use the red lengths for cars and the green rods for trucks. You can also cut out pieces of paper or break pieces of linguine or pappardelle pasta into lengths for your cars and trucks.

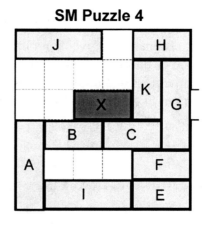

Try your sequential reasoning on these four movement puzzles.

SM Puzzle 3

SM Puzzle 4

SM Puzzle 5

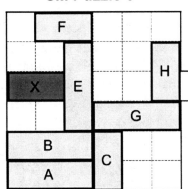

SM Puzzle 6 *h*

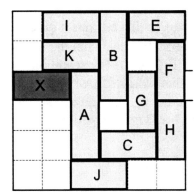

1.5 Cryptarithm Puzzles

Cryptarithms[2] are mathematical puzzles in which letters are substituted for numbers in arithmetic calculations. In each puzzle, every letter represents a different digit and each occurrence of a letter represents the same number. The left digit of a multi-digit number cannot be zero. Let's look at a few examples.

Example A

Find the value of each letter in this cryptarithm puzzle.

```
  A B
+ B A
-----
C A C
```

Solution

A + B is a two digit number (see the tens column), therefore C = 1. Since C = 1, then, from the units column, B + A = 11 (Figure 1). From the tens column, A + B + 1 (the carry) = 11 + 1 = 12 (Figure 2). Therefore, A must be 2 (Figure 3) and B must be 11 − 2 = 9. So C = 1, A = 2, and B = 9 (Figure 4).

```
   A B
 + B A
 -----
 1 A 1
```
Figure 1

```
    1
   A B
 + B A
 -----
 1 2 1
```
Figure 2

```
    1
   2 B
 + B 2
 -----
 1 2 1
```
Figure 3

```
    1
   2 9
 + 9 2
 -----
 1 2 1
```
Figure 4

Example B

Find the value of each letter in this cryptarithm puzzle.

```
      F 7
  x   6 A
  -------
    B D A
  B C B
  -------
  D E A A
```

Solution

First, notice that 6 times 7 gives a B in the tens position. Therefore, since 6 × 7 = 42, B = 2 (Figure 5). Since D is in the thousands position of the product, D is one greater than B, or D = 3 (Figure 6). The result of 7 times A gives a value of A in the units position. The only value that works for A is 5 (Figure 7). You now know that F7 times 5 = 235. Therefore, F = 4 (Figure 8). So, you can solve the entire problem: 47 x 65 = 3055 (Figure 9). The values are B = 2, D = 3, A = 5, F = 4, E = 0, and therefore, C = 8.

```
     4              4              4              4              4
   F 7            F 7            F 7            4 7            4 7
 x 6 A          x 6 A          x 6 5          x 6 5          x 6 5
 -------        -------        -------        -------        -------
   2 D A          2 3 A          2 3 5          2 3 5          2 3 5
   2 C 2          2 C 2          2 C 2          2 C 2          2 8 2
 -------        -------        -------        -------        -------
 D E A A        3 E A A        3 E 5 5        3 E 5 5        3 0 5 5
```

| Figure 5 | Figure 6 | Figure 7 | Figure 8 | Figure 9 |

Find the value of each letter in the cryptarithm puzzles below.

Cryptarithm Puzzle 1 *h*

```
  A B C
+ C B C
-------
C D E B
```

Cryptarithm Puzzle 2 *h*

```
  A B B C
+ A D E C
---------
C B B 6 E
```

Cryptarithm Puzzle 3 *h*

```
    B A
+   B A
-------
  R A A
```

Cryptarithm Puzzle 4 *h*

```
    A 4 C D
  x     E 3
  ---------
    7 4 F 4
  A 4 C D
  ---------
  3 A F D 4
```

Cryptarithm Puzzle 5 *h*

```
    7 A 8
    A 8 7
  + 8 7 A
  -------
  B C D E
```

Cryptarithm Puzzle 6 *h*

```
      7 B C
  x     B C
  ---------
    F E D C
    7 B C
  ---------
  B B F G C
```

When the letters in the cryptarithm make recognizable words the puzzle is sometimes call an **alphametic**. A popular alphametic was created by Henry Ernest Dudeney (1857-1930) and published in the magazine *The Strand* (yes, the same magazine where you would find the latest installment of *Sherlock Holmes* by A.C. Doyle). For a real challenge try Dudeney's classic alphametic: SEND + MORE = MONEY. Find hints to this puzzle in Appendix 5.

$$\begin{array}{r} \text{SEND} \\ + \text{MORE} \\ \hline \text{MONEY} \end{array}$$

1.6 Robot Programming Puzzles

You've heard the expression, "A picture is worth a thousand words." A drawing usually conveys information more quickly than a long written description. Many, if not all occupations rely on visual thinking. Architects create blueprints. Choreographers visualize and sketch dance steps. Composers—well, you get the picture. Research in educational theory strongly suggests that using visuals is one of the best strategies for teaching students how to think, reason, and problem solve.

One very useful visual thinking tool is a flowchart[3]. A flowchart shows steps in a process using different kinds of boxes. Arrows connecting the boxes demonstrate the flow or sequence of actions. Here is a simple example of a flowchart that describes one possible problem solving sequence for a flashlight that does not work.

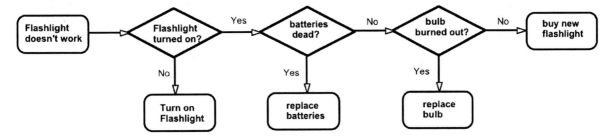

When you create a series of steps for a flowchart you are creating a program. In this section you will learn simple programming to move robots from a starting position to a desired endpoint.

We begin with two types of programming instructions for this very simple robot. One instruction tells the robot how far to move forward. The other tells the robot to turn right or left 90°. For example, F3 instructs the robot to move forward three squares and TR instructs the robot to turn right.

Example

Robot R is in the northwest room facing east as shown in the diagram. Program the robot to get to point A in the southeast room in the fewest moves. It must end up facing south. Remember, the robot can only move forward and can only turn 90° right or left.

Solution

TL - TL - F2 - TL - F5 - TL - F5 - TR
Or: TL - F1 - TR - F4 - TR - F5 - TR - F1 - TR

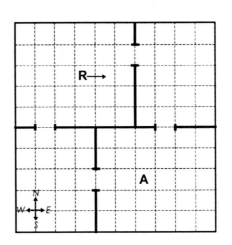

Now try your sequential reasoning skills on these five robot-programming puzzles.

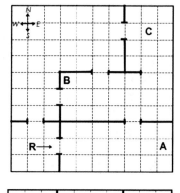

Robot Puzzle 1 In this puzzle the robot can only move forward and turn right (TR) or left (TL) 90°. For example, F5 instructs the robot to move forward five squares. Write a program with 12 or fewer steps that moves the robot to position A then to position B and finally to position C, and facing west.

Robot Puzzle 2 Using the same movement rules as Robot Puzzle 1, write a program with 16 or fewer steps that moves the robot to the three positions A, B, and C in any order. The robot may end facing in any direction.

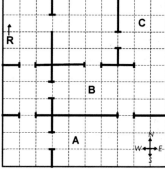

Robot Puzzle 3 In this puzzle, some paths are one-way and others are two-way. The robot may not move against the one-way directions. Write a program with 19 or fewer steps that moves the robot to collect the three items A, B, and C, in any order, and return to its starting square. To "collect" an item the robot must be programmed to stop at the item, then collect it, then proceed as needed. The programming symbol for collecting item B is CB. The robot may end facing in any direction.

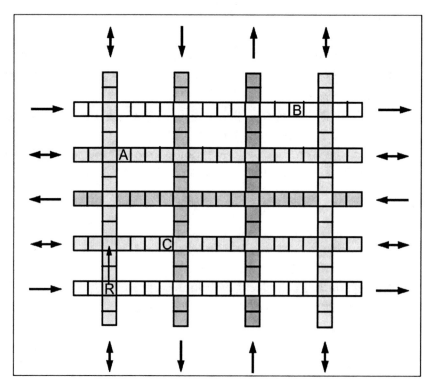

Robot Puzzle 4 In this puzzle the robot's right turn mechanism is broken so it can only make left turns (TL). If the robot attempts to make consecutive left turns without forward moves in between it automatically shuts down, so no consecutive left turns are permitted. Write a program with 33 or fewer steps that moves the robot through the maze and out of the exit.

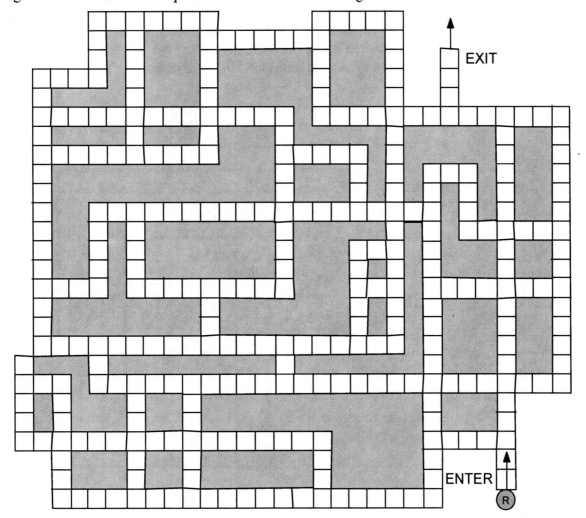

Robot Puzzle 5 In this puzzle the robot's task is to collect the treasure and get out of the castle. The robot needs to collect keys to the locked doors but it can only carry a maximum of three keys at any one time. Keys are locked within different cells of the castle dungeon. To collect key A write CA. To drop key B write DB. To open locked door D write OD. To collect the treasure, write C$. Write a program that moves the robot into the room containing the treasure and safely back out to its starting position in 92 steps or fewer.

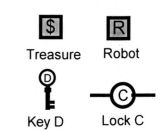

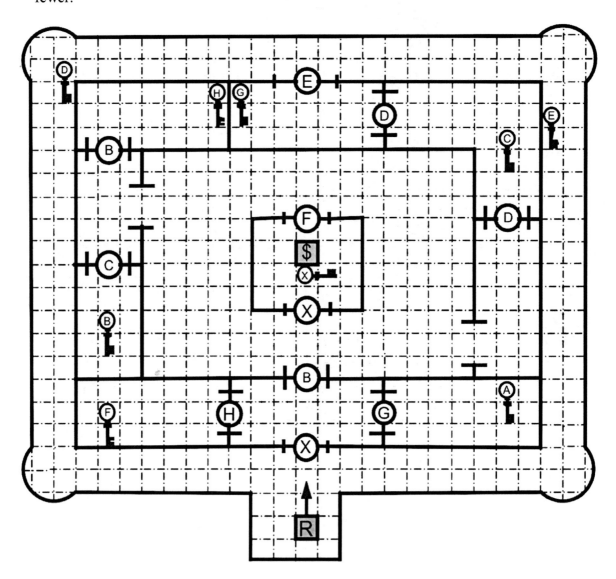

What is the relationship between fun math and serious math? When you play a game, if you learn to be good at it, you find what it is you should be thinking about... That is what we do in mathematics.
— John Horton Conway

2.1   Racetrack

Racetrack is a wonderful visual application of sequential reasoning. The game first appeared in the U.S. in Martin Gardner's *Mathematical Games* column of *Scientific American*. The origin of the game is unknown, but a computer scientist who saw it in Europe brought it to Gardner's attention. Le Zip, a racecar game very similar to Racetrack, appeared in *Le Livre des Jeux,* a French games book by Pierre Berloquin, published in 1971.

Martin Gardner[4] (1914 – 2010)

The Rules of Racetrack

Racetrack is played on graph paper with two or more players, each using a different colored pen or pencil. The players are racecar drivers attempting to maneuver around a track and across the finish line. Drivers take turns relocating their car to a new grid point according to the following rules:

Rule 1.   A move consists of an ordered pair that represents the racecar's move from one position to a new position. In this way the ordered pair also represents the speed of the racecar. At each turn, a car may maintain its speed or change its speed by one unit, in either or both directions.

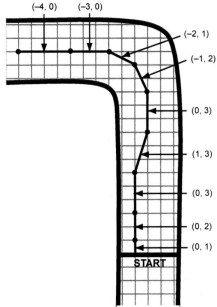

Example

If one move is (1, 2), then the next move can be the same speed, (1, 2); sped up in one or both directions, (1, 3), (2, 2) or (2, 3); or slowed down in one or both directions, (1, 1), (0, 2), or (0, 1). Your pre-game speed is (0, 0), so the first move for the track at right should be (0, 1), (1, 1), or (−1, 1). With moves of (−1, 0) or (1, 0) you would slide sideways. You could, but you wouldn't want to, put it in reverse and move (0, −1).

Rule 2.   The new grid point, and the segment connecting it to the preceding grid point, must lie entirely within the track.

Rule 3.   No two cars may occupy the same grid point at the same time —no crashes! A racecar whose path leaves the track or collides with another racecar is out of the race.

For a two-car race, the winner of a coin toss may choose either the starting position or the first move. The first car to cross the finish line after an equal number of turns is the winner of the game. If more than one player has crossed the finish line on the same move, the winner is the racecar that is farthest past the finish line.

Variations on the Game of Racetrack

Level 1

I recommend you begin by playing with a simple racetrack, such as the Beginners Racetrack (See Appendix 1). Use the basic Racetrack rules listed above.

Level 2

Use the basic Racetrack rules on a more advanced racetrack. See Racetracks 1-6 in Appendix 1.

Level 3

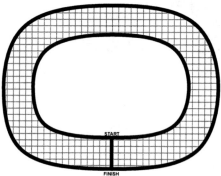

Use the basic Racetrack rules on an oval track. Now the race can take multiple trips or laps around the track. You might want to change pen colors after each lap to keep track of the number of laps. See Racetrack 7 in Appendix 1.

Level 4

Use the basic Racetrack rules on a racetrack with obstacles, hazards, or oil slicks. See Racetracks 8-10 in Appendix 1.

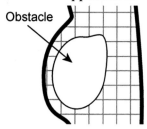

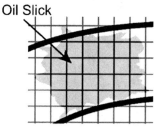

Level 5

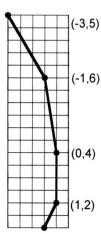

Use the basic Racetrack rules and add a new move rule:

Rule 4. A car can maintain its speed in either direction or increase its speed by a maximum of two units, in either or both directions. However, it can decrease its speed by only one unit distance, in either or both directions.
See Racetracks 9-10 in Appendix 1.

Level 6

Use rules 1-4 and add a new crash rule:

Rule 5. If a racecar runs off the track it may be allowed back as long as it reenters the track behind where it ran off. Once off the track, the car may reduce its speed by a maximum of two units per move, in either or both directions.
See Racetracks 11-13 in Appendix 1.

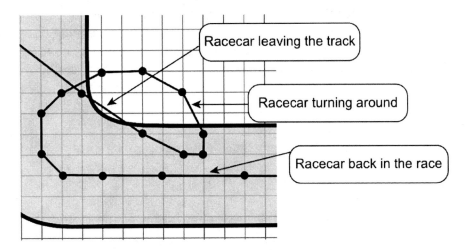

Level 7

Use rules 1-5 and play on an oval track with a pit stop. The racecar must come to a complete stop—a move of (0, 0)—within the pit stop area after each lap, or every other lap in a longer race. Remember to change pens after each lap to keep track of which lap you are on.

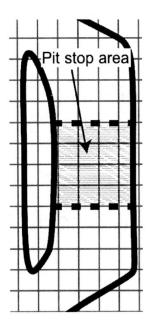

Level 8

Design your own track and define your own move rules. For example, you could permit no crossing of paths or, on an oval track, have one player race clockwise while the other races counterclockwise. Another idea is to permit "drifting" or "power turns" by allowing a player to switch the numbers in the ordered pair from one turn to the next. You could also set up "checkpoints" on the racetrack and if a player lands on one, they can earn points for more speed (see rule 4). Finally, you could create a ramp or overpass by looping the track over itself. There are infinite possibilities, so be creative!

To create your own racetrack you will need a sheet of graph paper and a pen. A wide track permits more than two players and allows obstacles to be placed in the racetrack path.

Racetracks

A full-size version of all racetracks can be found in Appendix 1. You should create a table, like the one on the right, to keep track of your moves. A table will also help remind you to change the horizontal and/or vertical directions by only one unit.

Team A	Team B
1.	1.
2.	2.
3.	3.
4.	4.
5.	5.
6.	6.

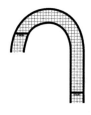

Beginner's Racetrack

I recommended that you begin by playing with a simple racetrack like this one. It is short and has only one turn. Then, as your understanding of the game increases and your sequential reasoning ability improves, move up to racetracks with more twists and turns. Make a copy of the racetrack and find a partner to play.

Racetrack 1

Use this racetrack for your first challenging game. Your racecar path must stay within the track boundaries.

Racetrack 2

Use racetrack 2 for this game. You will begin moving to the left, so your first moves will have a negative for the x-value. For example, your first move might be $(-1, 0)$. Discuss a fair way of determining where each person starts and the order of play for a 3-person race.

Racetrack 3

Use racetrack 3 for this game. This track has two very sharp turns so don't go too fast. There is room for a 3-person race. Discuss a fair way of determining where each person starts and the order of play.

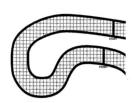

Racetrack 4

Watch out for the curves on this challenging racetrack!

Racetrack 5

Guide your car carefully on this narrow racetrack.

Racetrack 6

Narrow road and sharp curves ahead! Is the shortcut, really a shortcut?

Racetrack 7

Here is your first oval racetrack. Try playing on oval tracks with rule 4: horizontal and/or vertical speeds can increase by 2 units but only decrease by 1 unit.

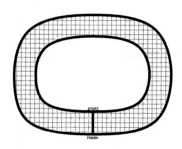

Racetrack 8
The three oval patches within the next track are barriers that cannot be touched or crossed by the racecars. To speed up the game, try using rule 4.

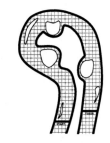

Racetrack 9
Watch for obstacles and barriers on this dangerous track.

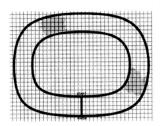

Racetrack 10
Here is a racetrack to use with Rule 5: if a racecar runs off the track it may be allowed back on as long as it reenters the track behind where it left off. Once off the track, the car may reduce its speed by a maximum of two units per move, in either or both directions.

Racetrack 11
Use Rules 4 and 5 with Racetrack 11. Before you draw each path, record your move in a table to help you follow the rules.

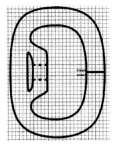

Racetrack 12
On this track you will encounter oil slicks that require careful driving. If you land in an oil slick region, you cannot change your speed or direction. Instead, you must repeat whatever move you made coming into the spill in order to leave the area. Use Rules 4 and 5 in this game.

Racetrack 13
This oval track has a turn-off for a pit stop. The racecar must come to a complete stop—a (0,0) move—within the pit stop area after each lap, or every other lap in a longer race. Use Rules 4 and 5 in this game.

Racetrack 14
This oval track has a pit stop, a hazard, and an oil slick. Review the rules for these obstacles and use Rule 5.

2.2   Mathematical Connections: Vectors

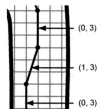

In the game of Racetrack, movement is simulated by an ordered pair rule (*x*, *y*). Using this rule, the *x*- and *y*-values represent the horizontal and vertical components, respectively, for any move. These ordered pairs are called **vectors**.

Vectors are quantities that have a magnitude and a direction. Some quantities have only magnitude. For example, time, temperature, and mass are quantities that have one measure. The time it takes you to eat an orange may be two minutes, the room you are in may have a temperature of 68 degrees Fahrenheit, or this book may weigh one pound. But some quantities, like velocity or force, have both a magnitude and a direction.

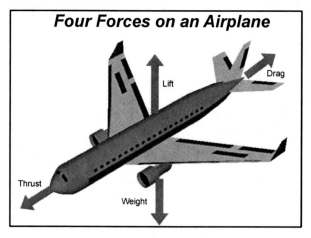

We use vectors to represent these quantities. The velocity of a car may be 35 miles/hour, heading northeast. The 35 miles/hour is its speed (or magnitude) and northeast is its direction. We use arrows to represent vectors because an arrow has a magnitude (its length) and a direction. There are a number of vector forces acting on an airplane.

Here are some examples of how vectors represent real-life situations.

In the vector diagram at right, an arrow is used to represent the velocity of an airplane moving at a certain speed and traveling in a particular direction. The diagram shows the velocity vector of an airplane that is traveling at 250 miles/hour with a southwest heading. The tip of the arrow is called the **head** of the vector and the other end is called the **tail** of the vector.

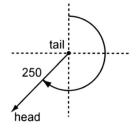

If you are rowing a boat at a right angle to a river current, will you go directly across the river? Probably not. Since the current is a force acting on the boat, it will push the boat at an angle, downstream.

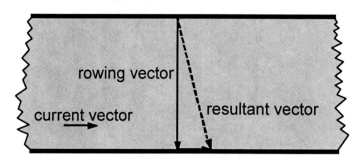

If you are in an airplane, heading due west, with the wind blowing directly across you from the south, what is your true direction of travel? It will be north of west.

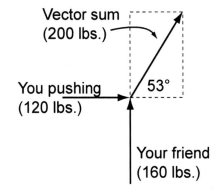

In both of these situations we are adding vectors to get their sum, called the **resultant vector**. Notice that adding vectors is different than adding numbers. When you add $2 and $3 you get $5. In football, a gain of 3 yards on the first play and a loss of 7 yards on the second play results in a net loss of 4 yards. We are all familiar with regular addition, but adding vectors is not as straightforward.

For example, say you are pushing a box straight in front of you with a force of 120 pounds and, at the same time, your friend pushes the box at a right angle to you with a force of 160 pounds. The resulting force on the box will be 200 pounds (not 280 pounds) and the box will be pushed in a direction approximately 53° from you.

The addition of two vectors becomes even more curious when the angle between the vectors is not 90°. For example, if your friend pushes the box at a 60° angle to you, the sum of the two vectors is a vector with a magnitude of about 234 pounds and the direction is approximately 34° from you.

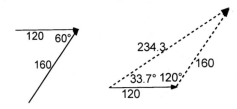

So how do we add vectors? The rule for finding the resultant vector is to translate one vector so that its tail is moved to the head of the second. Then the sum is the vector from the tail of the first one to the head of the second vector, as demonstrated in the diagram below.

Example

A pilot is planning a flight from Las Vegas, Nevada to Boise, Idaho. Boise is due north of Las Vegas and, at flight altitude, there is an expected wind of 26 mph, blowing due east. The pilot plans to fly at an average air speed of 130 mph, and needs to determine her heading so she can compensate for the wind. If she does not, she risks flying too far east of Boise. She knows her heading needs to be a bit west of due north, but by how much?

Solution

At what angle to the west of north should the pilot fly so the resultant vector has a heading of due north? The solution requires a bit of trigonometry (the law of cosines and the law of sines) and gives us the angle measure $a = \sin^{-1}(26/130) \approx 11.5°$.

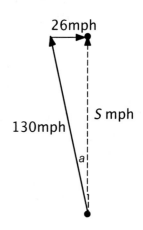

What is the resulting speed (the magnitude of the resultant vector)? We can use the Pythagorean theorem to determine this number.

$$130^2 = 26^2 + s^2$$
$$s^2 = 130^2 - 26^2$$
$$s^2 = 16224$$
$$s \approx 127.4$$

Note that the pilot's actual speed (127.4 mph) will be slightly less than her airspeed (130 mph), since she must fly with a heading that faces a bit into the wind. The distance from Las Vegas to Boise is 520 miles. How long will it take the pilot to fly there? Use the distance formula ($d = rt$) to try and calculate this yourself. For the answer, see Appendix 6.

Prior to the 1800's mathematics was essentially the study of two common ideas: number and shape. Geometry studied shape, arithmetic concerned numbers, and algebra explored the properties of numbers. But mathematical thinking began to expand in the 19th century and mathematics no longer needed to restrict itself to numbers and shapes. Mathematics could be about anything! A mathematical system can be created to consist of a set of elements with a set of logical operations.[5] Vector algebra is one example of a mathematical system. Instead of operating with numbers, vector algebra performs operations with vectors.

What properties do vectors have? When you represent vectors with arrows, you can arrange them anywhere in space as long as you give them the correct direction and length. Notice that $(a + b)$ and $(b + a)$ have the same sum, indicating that vector addition satisfies the commutative property. The associative property for addition is also true. Can you show this with diagrams? The associative property says: $a + (b + c) = (a + b) + c$. See Appendix 6 for one possible answer.

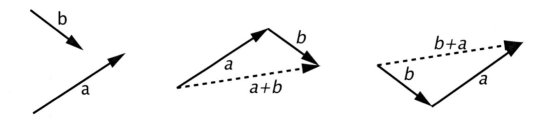

If two vectors have the same direction, the magnitude of the resultant vector is the sum of their magnitudes. When they are in opposite directions, the magnitude of the resultant vector is the difference between their magnitudes. When they are at an angle to each other, the magnitude of the sum of the two vectors is somewhere between the two extremes. If vector y has the same magnitude as vector w but has the opposite direction then their sum is the zero vector ($y + w = 0$).

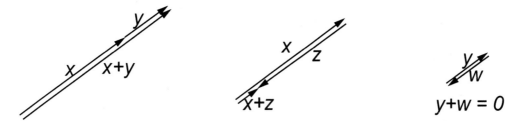

If v is a vector and you multiply it by a positive real number s, called a **scalar**, then the resulting vector sv, has the same direction as v but the magnitude has been multiplied by the factor s. Suppose you also multiply vector w by the same scalar s, then the resulting vector is sw. Is the vector sum $sv + sw$ the same as $s(v + w)$? Yes, $sv + sw = s(v + w)$, so vectors also obey a distributive property. Below is an example where the scalar is 3.

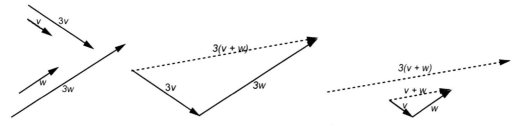

You have seen that two vectors can be added to find the resultant vector. Conversely, any single vector can be considered the resultant of two vectors. A pair of vectors—one horizontal and one vertical—that sum to a given vector, v, are called vector v's **component vectors**. This allows us to write every vector as an ordered pair. Vector v is written as the ordered pair $\langle x, y \rangle$, where x is the horizontal movement and y is the vertical movement, from the tail to the head of the vector. These ordered pairs are the directions, or movements, you make while playing the game of Racetrack.

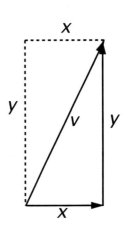

It is easier to perform the operations on vectors if we do not have to draw the arrows. If $v = \langle a, b \rangle$ and $w = \langle c, d \rangle$, then the sum of v and w is
$v + w = \langle a + b, c + d \rangle$.

If a vector has components $\langle 0, 0 \rangle$ then the vector is called the **zero vector** and is written $\boldsymbol{0} = \langle 0, 0 \rangle$. The magnitude of the zero vector is, not surprisingly, 0. The direction of the zero vector is any direction you wish!

If $v = \langle a, b \rangle$ is a vector, then **the opposite of v** is written: $-v = \langle -a, -b \rangle$.

With the definitions above and given that u, v, and w are vectors and a and b are scalars, we can create a vector algebra with the following properties:

1. If you add any two vectors the resultant is a vector.
2. $u + v = v + u$
3. $u + (v + w) = (u + v) + w$
4. $u + 0 = u$
5. $u + (-u) = 0$
6. If you multiply any vector by a scalar, the result is a vector.
7. $a(du) = (ad)u$
8. $(a + d)u = au + du$
9. $a(u + v) = au + av$
10. $1 \cdot u = u$
11. $(-1)u = -u$
12. $(0)u = 0$
13. $c0 = 0$

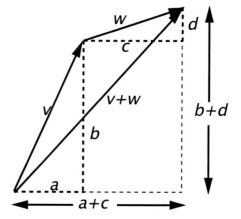

An interesting exercise (and good introduction to vector algebra) would be to demonstrate these properties using arrows or ordered pairs, as vector representations. I hope this brief introduction to vectors has whetted your appetite for more mathematics!

Chapter 3   **Movement Puzzles**

A good math puzzle, paradox, or magic trick can stimulate a child's imagination much faster than a practical application ... and if the game is chosen carefully, it can lead almost effortlessly into significant mathematical ideas.
—Martin Gardner

3.1   Coin Puzzles

Coin puzzles have been around since before there were coins. The objective of a coin puzzle is to switch a set of like coins (for example pennies) on the left side, with an equal number of different coins (perhaps dimes) on the right side. There are a variety of coin puzzles, but we will play with two types: coin slide puzzles and coin jump puzzles.

Coin Slide Puzzles

In coin slide puzzles (sometimes called shunting puzzles), the objective is to switch positions of the coins; you may move one coin into any adjacent empty space. These coin slide puzzles have an odd number of squares in a row and additional squares above or below the center square of the row.

A coin slide playing board is available in Appendix 2. Use coins, colored chips, or two different types of beans as markers with the playing board to solve the coin slide puzzles below. Use only the squares shown for each puzzle. Let W and B stand for white coin and black coin, respectively. Let r, d, u, and l stand for right, down, up, and left.

CS Puzzle 1

Switch position in 6 moves or fewer.

CS Puzzle 2

Switch position in 26 moves or fewer.

CS Puzzle 3

Switch position in 80 moves or fewer.

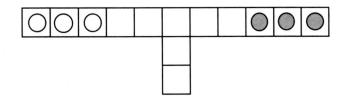

CS Puzzle 4 ♄

Switch position in 124 moves or fewer.

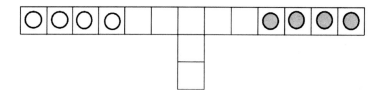

Coin Jump Puzzles

The playing board for coin jump puzzles is an odd number of squares in a row. In a coin jump puzzle, you may move one coin into an adjacent, empty space in either direction or jump one adjacent coin if there is an empty space on the other side to land. Again, the objective is to switch the positions of the coins.

In the previous set of coin slide puzzles, I gave you an easy puzzle (fewer squares/fewer moves) to start off. You then solved progressively more challenging puzzles. If you had started with the hardest one first, you may not have been as successful. This leads to a great problem solving strategy.

Problem Solving Strategy

If a puzzle appears to be too difficult, try to solve easier but similar (analogous) puzzles. Solving these puzzles may give you insight into solving the more challenging puzzles.

Try this very challenging coin jump puzzle. A coin jump playing board is available in Appendix 2. If you are trying easier puzzles first, use only as many squares as you need (use one more than your number of coins).

Coin Jump Puzzle 1 ♄

Switch positions of the five pennies and five dimes. To record your moves, it might be helpful to use symbols similar to those shown below.

R   ⌒L

Slide to the right   **Jump to the left**

Or perhaps, let D← and P→ stand for dime sliding to the left and penny sliding to the right, respectively. Then let D↖ stand for the dime jumping to the left and P↗ stand for penny jumping to the right. Or, create your own symbolic way of describing the moves.

You might try these puzzles first.

 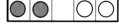 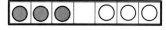 

3.2   Sliding Block Puzzles

The classic sliding block puzzle is the "15-Puzzle" often attributed, incorrectly, to puzzle master Sam Loyd[6] (1841–1911). This puzzle is a 4×4 grid consisting of 15 numbered squares and one blank. The task is to reposition the numbers from the starting position to the final position by sliding numbers one at a time into the empty space. The starting position for Sam Loyd's puzzle (also called the "14-15 Puzzle") is shown below left. The final position is shown to the right of it. This puzzle is impossible. Try your hand at the "3-Puzzle" below right. You should be able do it in four moves. Draw a grid of squares on a piece of paper for Sliding Block Puzzles 1-3. Use coins, tokens, or slips of paper with numbers on them, to solve the puzzles.

14-15 Puzzle

1	2	3	4
5	6	7	8
9	10	11	12
13	15	14	

Starting Position

1	2	3	4
5	6	7	8
9	10	11	12
13	14	15	

Final Position

SB Puzzle 1

3	1
2	

Starting Position

1	2
3	

Final Position

Next try the "8-Puzzle" below left. You should be able do it in twelve moves. Although the 14-15 Puzzle above is impossible, the "15-Puzzle" below right is possible.

SB Puzzle 2

1	2	3
4	5	7
8	6	

Starting Position

1	2	3
4	5	6
7	8	

Final Position

SB Puzzle 3 *h*

1	2	3	4
5	6	7	8
9	10	11	12
15	13	14	

Starting Position

1	2	3	4
5	6	7	8
9	10	11	12
13	14	15	

Final Position

Another sliding block puzzle, which is my personal favorite, is Lunar Lockout.® Lunar Lockout[7] is a set of 40 puzzles created by Hiroshi Yamamoto (with the assistance of Nob Yoshigahara) for Binary Arts, now called Thinkfun.® Here is the description from the Lunar Lockout box:

You're locked out of the Mothership – the computers have taken command! The oxygen in your Spacepod is running out… Thank the stars for those loyal Helper-Bots! They'll help maneuver your Pod to the ship's Emergency Entry Port so you can shut down those rebellious computers.

In the puzzles to follow, the objective is to maneuver the piece indicated by the letter Q to the shaded square in the center. You will need the help of the pieces, numbered 1–5. All pieces move according to the same two rules:

- All pieces move only horizontally or vertically.

- Once you move a piece it continues to move until its path is blocked by another piece (the other pieces are your only brakes). If there is no other piece to stop the moving piece it will continue on past the outer edge of the 5×5 grid into space—an illegal move! In other words, the outer edge of the 5×5 landing grid is not a barrier that stops pieces from moving.

Example A

How do you move the Q onto the shaded square?

Solution

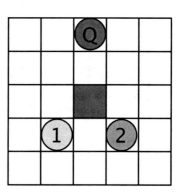

The Q-piece, cannot move straight down because there is nothing to stop it. However, if the 1-piece moves to the right it is stopped by the 2-piece. Then, Q can move down to the shaded, center square because it will be stopped by the 1-piece.

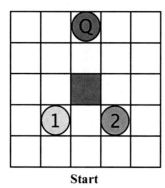

Start

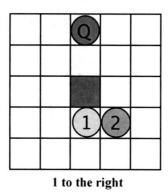

1 to the right

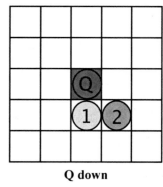

Q down

We will symbolize the movements up, down, right, and left by using arrows: ↑ ↓ → ← .

The solution is 1 to the right, then Q down. Symbolically it is written: 1→ Q↓ .

There is another solution: 2← Q↓ .

Examples B-D

Write the solution for these puzzles in symbolic form (using Q, the numbers, and arrows). The solutions are shown at the bottom of this page. Cover them up and try to solve the puzzles yourself. Each puzzle may have more than one solution. Can you find the others?

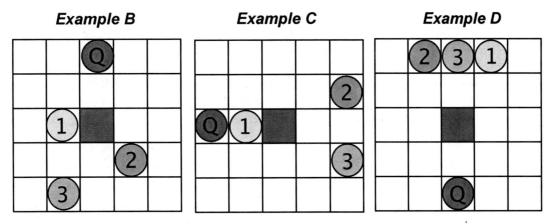

Are you ready? Solve these puzzles. The first three moves are given below.

(Note: In puzzle 4, for example, the 3 followed by an up arrow and a right arrow indicates that the 3-piece moves up and then to the right. The 2 followed by a down arrow indicates that the 2-piece moves down.)

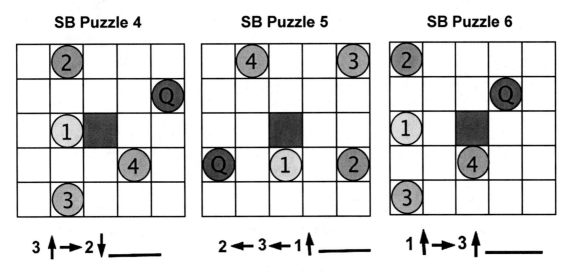

Solve these puzzles. The first two moves are given below.

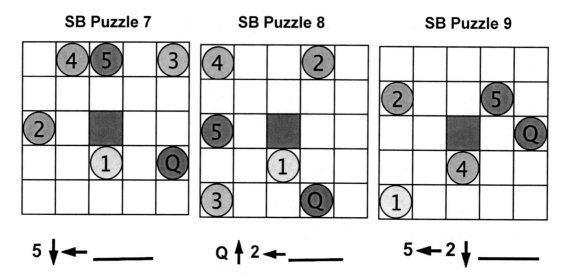

SB Puzzle 7

5 ↓ ← _____

SB Puzzle 8

Q ↑ 2 ← _____

SB Puzzle 9

5 ← 2 ↓ _____

Now it is your turn to solve puzzles completely on your own. To solve more complicated puzzles, such as those below, you will need six different colored or numbered pieces. These pieces can be game tokens, buttons, beans, multi-link cubes, dice, painted pennies, or whatever works on the large 5×5 grid. (See Appendix 2)

Once you have the necessary markers, place them on the grid according to the positions of puzzles 10-18. If you would prefer to play with the original Lunar Lockout puzzle, you might be able to find it online, but the set is currently unavailable at Thinkfun.com.

Solve these puzzles using your markers and the 5×5 grid. The answers are in Appendix 6.

SB Puzzle 10

SB Puzzle 11

SB Puzzle 12

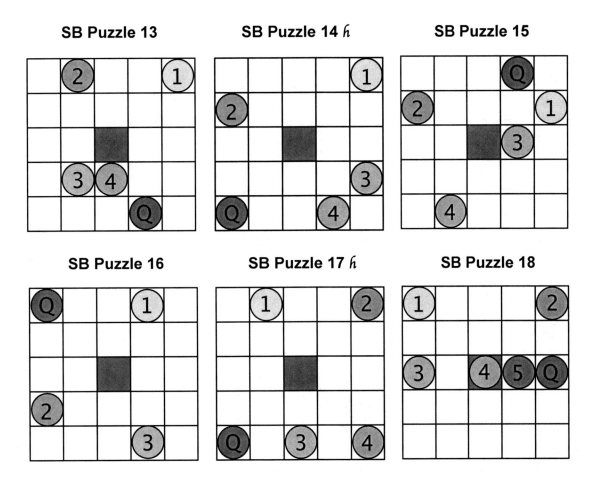

You can create variations on these puzzles by changing the size or shape of the playing grid and changing the location of the target square. Solve the following puzzles using your markers on playing grids that you create.

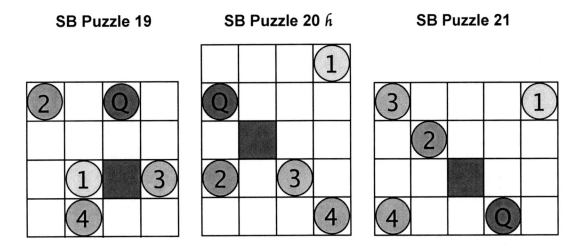

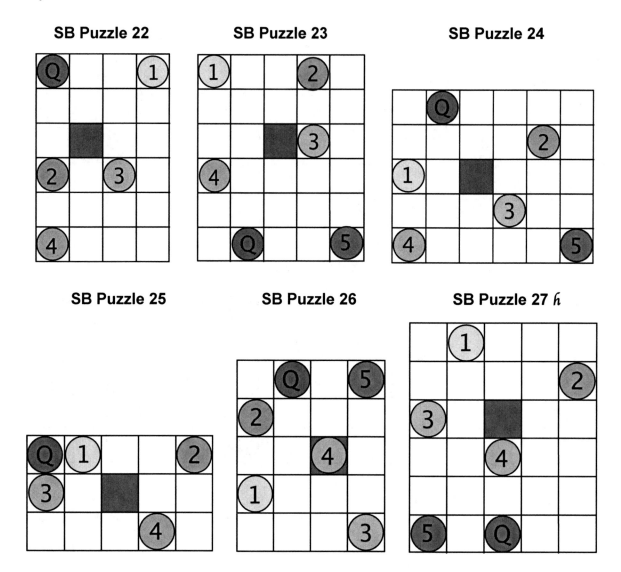

SB Puzzle 22 **SB Puzzle 23** **SB Puzzle 24**

SB Puzzle 25 **SB Puzzle 26** **SB Puzzle 27** *h*

You can also change the type of grid to create new challenges. The Queen Bee puzzles in Section 3.3 use a grid of regular hexagons instead of squares. Try creating your own sliding block puzzles.

3.3 Queen Bee Puzzles

A grid of squares is not the only possible playing field. A grid of regular hexagons, like a bee's honeycomb, can be used for a new sliding block puzzle. Instead of Spacepods and Helper-Bots, let's look at a set of puzzles on a honeycomb...

Queen Bee is trying to locate her throne, but she has been so busy (Busy as a bee!) that she is exhausted! She needs her worker bees to guide her to the throne so she can get her well-deserved rest and rejuvenation.

The Rules of Queen Bee

The objective in a Queen Bee puzzle is to maneuver the Queen Bee, (indicated by the letter Q) to land on the center, shaded hexagon (the Queen's throne). The Queen and the worker bees (indicated by numbers from 1-5) move according to these two rules:

- All pieces move along rows of adjacent hexagons, diagonally or vertically.

- A piece continues to move until its path is blocked by another piece. (As in earlier sliding block puzzles, the outer boundary does not stop a piece; only other pieces can act as brakes.)

Example A

How do you get Q onto the shaded hexagon?

Solution

The Queen Bee (Q) cannot move straight down because there is nothing to stop her (so she would continue past the shaded hexagon). However, if the 1-bee moves diagonally up-right it is stopped by the 3-bee. The Q can then move diagonally down and left until she is stopped by the 2-bee. Next, the Q moves diagonally down and to the right until she is stopped on the shaded, center hexagon (the Queen's throne) by the 1-bee.

Symbolically the solution is written: 1 ↗ Q ↙ ↘

Examples B and C

Write the solution for these puzzles in symbolic form.

Try to solve these puzzles before looking at the solutions shown at the bottom of the page.

Example B   ### Example C

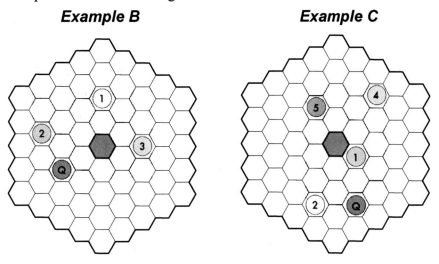

Solutions: **Example B**   **Example C**

2 ↗ ↘ Q ↗   Q↑ ↗ 2↑ 4↗ Q↑

Queen Bee Puzzles

Solve these puzzles. The first two or three moves are given below.

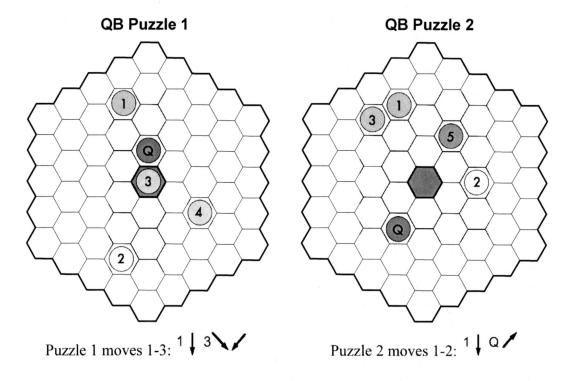

QB Puzzle 1

QB Puzzle 2

Puzzle 1 moves 1-3: 1 ↓ 3 ↘ ↙

Puzzle 2 moves 1-2: 1 ↓ Q ↗

Solve these Queen Bee puzzles. The first two moves are given below.

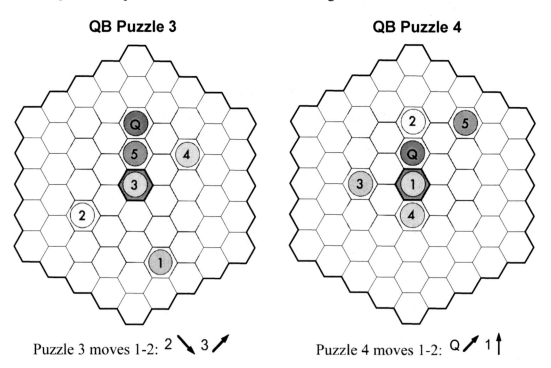

QB Puzzle 3

QB Puzzle 4

Puzzle 3 moves 1-2: 2 ↘ 3 ↗

Puzzle 4 moves 1-2: Q ↗ 1 ↑

Solve these Queen Bee puzzles. The first move is given below.

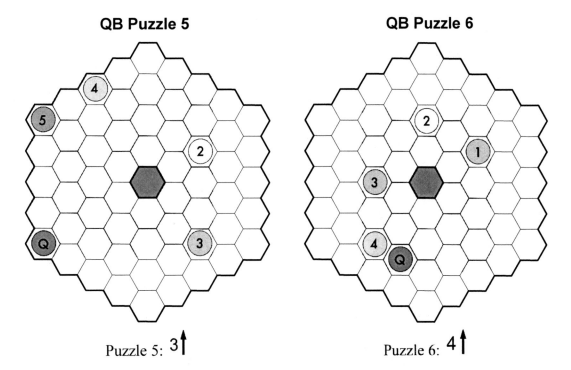

QB Puzzle 5   **QB Puzzle 6**

Puzzle 5: 3↑   Puzzle 6: 4↑

To solve the more complicated puzzles below, you will need six different colored or numbered pieces. A Queen Bee playing grid can be found in Appendix 2.

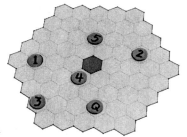

Once you have the necessary markers, place them on the grid according to the starting position of puzzles 7-14.

Now it is your turn. Solve these Queen Bee puzzles completely on your own.

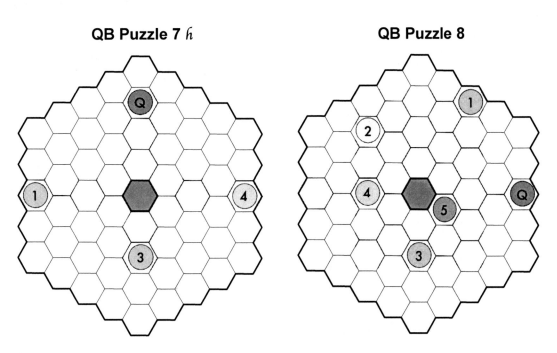

QB Puzzle 7 h **QB Puzzle 8**

QB Puzzle 9

QB Puzzle 10

QB Puzzle 11

QB Puzzle 12

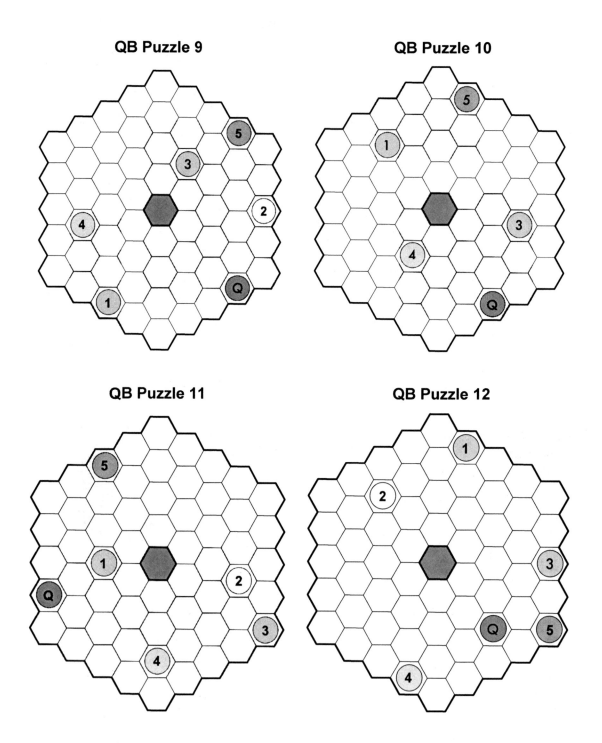

QB Puzzle 13   **QB Puzzle 14** *h*

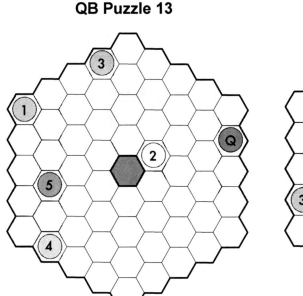

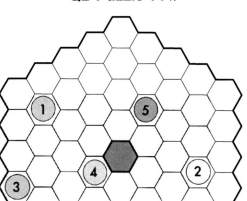

3.4 Mini Robot Puzzles

In 1999, Alex Randolph created a game called Ricochet Robots®, with moves similar to those used in Lunar Lockout®. Robots move about on a 16×16 grid and the objective is also similar: to get a particular robot to the like-numbered target. However, unlike Lunar Lockout, the grid for Ricochet Robots has perimeter walls, and bits of wall arranged within the grid, that stop a piece from continuing. Once any robot starts moving, it continues to move in that direction until a wall or another robot stops it. You can turn this puzzle into a game by having players race to see who can move the robot to the target in the fewest moves. Once someone finds a solution, the other players have a set time to find a shorter route.

Try your hand at the puzzles below.

MR Puzzle 1 *h*

The task is to get the 1-bot onto the 1-target.

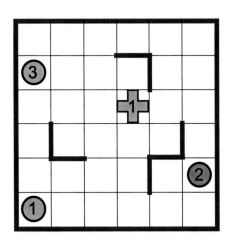

MR Puzzle 2

Move the 2-bot onto the 2-target

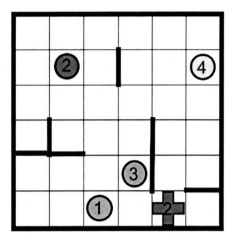

MR Puzzle 3

Move the 4-bot onto the 4-target

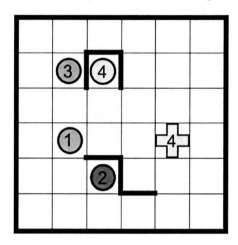

To solve the more complicated Mini Robot puzzles below, you will need four different colored pieces. They could be game tokens, buttons, multi-link cubes, dice, coins, or, whatever works on the large 6×6 playing grid. (See Appendix 2) Make one or more copies of the playing grid. If you wish to use one grid over again, you can place it in a plastic sheet protector and use an erasable pen to draw the walls for each game. You can also use broken toothpicks or chopsticks, pieces of fettuccini, or pieces of plastic drinking straws for the walls.

Once you have the necessary playing pieces and material for the walls, place them on the grid to match puzzles 4-13. Solve the Mini Robot puzzles completely on your own. If you are playing the puzzle as a game, the winner is the person who finds the solution with the fewest moves within a specified time.

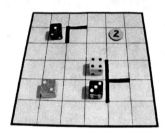

MR Puzzle 4

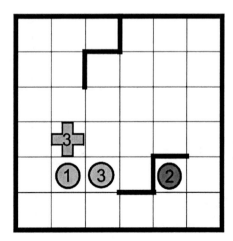

MR Puzzle 5

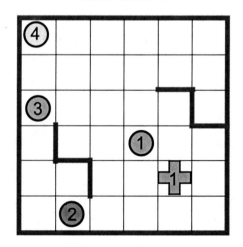

MR Puzzle 6 *h*

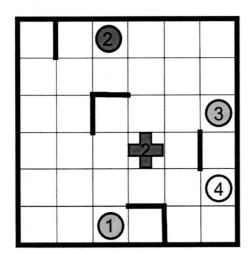

MR Puzzle 7

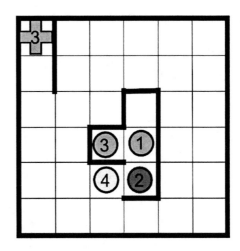

MR Puzzle 8

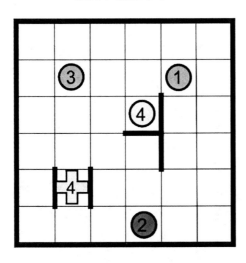

MR Puzzle 9 *h*

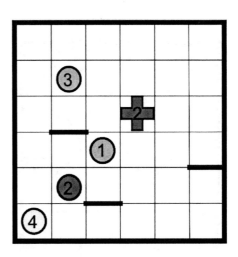

MR Puzzle 10

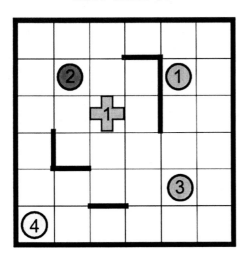

MR Puzzle 11

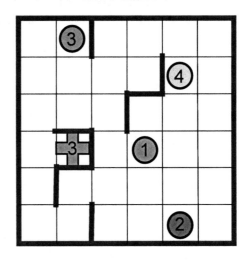

The Mini Robot puzzles below have a new type of barrier. When a robot hits a diagonal barrier, it changes its direction by 90° and continues to move until it is stopped by a vertical or horizontal barrier, or another robot.

Example

Move the 1-bot to the 1-target.

Solution

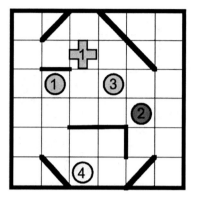

In the puzzle at right, after moving the 2-bot and the 4-bot out of the path, you can move the 3-bot up-left-down so that it is to the left of the 1-target, then you can move the 1-bot down-right-up-left.

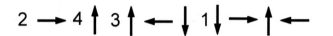

MR Puzzle 12

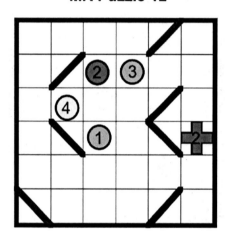

MR Puzzle 13

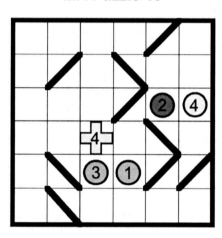

After solving these Mini Robot puzzles you might like to try playing the original Ricochet Robots game, currently available through Rio Grande Games®.

3.5 Mathematical Connections: Archimedean Tiling

The playing grids of Lunar Lockout and Queen Bee are tessellations of regular polygons. A tessellation, or tiling, is an arrangement of shapes that completely covers a surface, without gaps or overlaps. When the shapes are all the same regular polygon, the tessellation is called a **monohedral tessellation,** or **pure tiling**. (We will use the terms tessellation and tiling interchangeably.) The grid of squares in Lunar Lockout and the grid of regular hexagons in Queen Bee, are two of the three pure tessellations possible with regular polygons. Since the sum of the measures of all the angles about a vertex is 360°, and each angle of a square is 90°, then exactly four squares can meet at each vertex. Each angle of a regular hexagon is 120°, so three regular hexagons can meet at each vertex.

What other pure tilings are possible? Each angle of a regular, or equilateral, triangle is 60°, so exactly six regular triangles can meet at each vertex (Figure 1). Trying to put three regular pentagons about a point leaves a gap. If you place four regular pentagons about a point two would overlap (Figure 2). For any regular polygon with more than six sides, the measures of the angles are greater than 120°, thus no more than two polygons can meet at a vertex. For example, two regular octagons would leave a gap of 90° and three regular octagons would overlap by 55° (Figure 3). Therefore, the only regular polygons that create a pure tiling are equilateral triangles, squares, and regular hexagons.

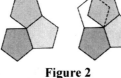
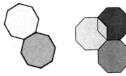

Figure 1 **Figure 2** **Figure 3**

Tessellations of regular polygons can use more than one type of polygon. Bathroom tiles are often arranged in a tessellation, like the example shown at right. In this tessellation a square and two regular octagons meet at each vertex without a gap or overlapping. Notice that the angles of a square each measure 90° and the angles of a regular octagon each measure 135°. Thus the sum of the angles at each vertex is 135° + 135° + 90° = 360°.

When every vertex of a regular polygon tessellation has the same combination of regular polygons in the same order, the tiling is called a **1-uniform tiling** or an **Archimedean tiling**. The three pure tilings above, and the octagon-square tessellation above right, are Archimedean tilings. The 1-uniform tilings are given numerical names according to the number of sides of the polygons that meet at each vertex. For example the octagon-square tiling above is a 4.8.8 Archimedean tiling, because one square and two octagons meet at each vertex. Here are two more 1-uniform tilings:

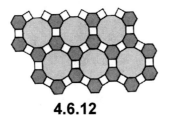
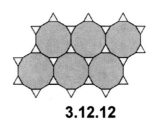

4.6.12 **3.12.12**

You have now seen six of the eleven 1-uniform tilings. The remaining five 1-uniform tilings use combinations of only squares, regular hexagons, or equilateral triangles.

Find the Remaining Five Archimedean Tilings

Can you find the remaining five Archimedean tilings? To do this investigation you will need a large collection of squares, equilateral triangles, and regular hexagons that have the same side lengths. You can use either a plastic template of squares, hexagons, and equilateral triangles, or use the polygons from a set of pattern blocks. If you have access to geometry software such as The Geometer's Sketchpad®, you can create equilateral triangle, square, and regular hexagon tools and use them to search for the Archimedean tilings. Patience and organization will also be needed. You will not need much geometry to do this investigation. You only need to know the measures of the angles of equilateral triangles (60°), squares (90°), and regular hexagons (120°).

When you think you have found the remaining five Archimedean tilings, check your results with the answers in Appendix 6.

Create Your Own Game Or Puzzle By Changing the Playing Field

Lunar Lockout has a 5×5 playing grid of squares while Ricochet Robots is played on a 16×16 square grid. Queen Bee is played on a grid of regular hexagons with five hexagons per side. You can create new games or puzzles by changing the size or type of grid for the playing field. For example, you can create different playing fields by using 1-uniform tilings for a sliding block puzzle. Try your hand at creating a game or puzzle using a different playing field.

Create Your Own Game Or Puzzle By Changing the Rules

Lunar Lockout and Queen Bee puzzles are played with no walls while Ricochet Robots has walls around the outer perimeter and within the playing grid. This simple change in the rules makes a big difference in the play. You can create new games or puzzles by changing the rules of an existing game. For example, if you use the 4.8.8 Archimedean tiling for a playing grid, what rules for moving the pieces would you need? You could create a rule where the pieces move only horizontally or vertically through the octagons and squares, or only diagonally through the octagons. Or perhaps one type of piece moves only horizontally and vertically, like a rook in chess, and another type of piece moves only diagonally, like a bishop. You get the idea. Try your hand at creating a game or puzzle by changing the rules of an existing game such as Lunar Lockout or Ricochet Robots.

The Similarity Between Games and Puzzles and Mathematics

Looking at a problem in a different way or seeing what happens when you change a rule is done quite often in mathematics. We sometimes look at simpler or analogous problems to gain insights into a problem we are attempting to solve. We ask, "What if the number is less than 1, or if the number is negative?" "What if the polygon is concave?" "If this works for two-dimensions will it work for three?" "What would happen if we take out the rule that says there is only one line parallel to a given line?" When you play games, solve puzzles, or create them, you are thinking like a mathematician.

Satisfaction lies in the effort, not in the attainment. Full effort is full victory.
—Mohandas K. Gandhi

Tour puzzles involve sequential reasoning with the common theme of *getting from point A to point B* by applying logical rules.

The History of Tour Puzzles

On an empty 8×8 chessboard, do you think it is possible to move a knight so that it visits each square exactly once? (A chess knight's move is the diagonal of a 2×3 rectangle.) This is the famous "Knight's Tour Puzzle" and it began the mathematical recreation of tours on square grids by knights, rooks, kings, and queens.

The first known occurrence of the Knight's Tour puzzle goes back to a 9th century Sanskrit poem by the Kashmiri poet Rudrata. It describes a knight's tour on half a chessboard.

The names of mathematicians who have contributed to the study of knight's tours reads like a Who's Who of Mathematics. The French mathematicians Abraham de Moivre[8] and Adrien Legendre[9], as well as the Swiss mathematician Leonhard Euler[10], were among the first to work on the knight's tour. Legendre was the first to create a tour that ends one knight's move from its starting point. This is called a **closed tour,** or re-entrant tour. The number of possible knight's tours on an 8×8 chessboard remains an unsolved problem. One knight's tour is shown at left. We'll return to knight's tour puzzles later in the chapter.

4.1   Rook's Tour Puzzles

The knight's move is one of the more complicated moves in chess, which contributed to the interest in knight's tours. Eventually the interest in tours spread to other chess pieces. A rook moves only horizontally or vertically, but not diagonally. It is clearly possible to move a rook over an empty board so it visits each of the 64 squares on its tour. But can you create a rook's tour given any two points on the board as starting and stopping points?

To answer that question let's look at some rook's tours on smaller boards. Below are ten 4×4 rook's tours. Numbers in the first tour show the sequence in which the rook visited the squares. The even squares are shaded. Do the same for the other tours and look for patterns.

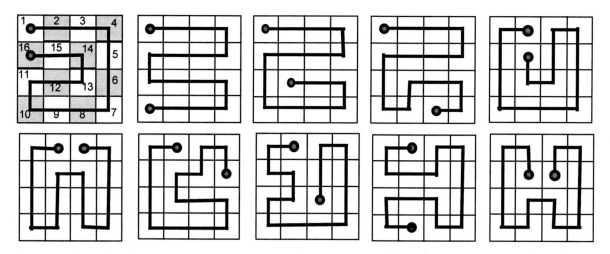

There are an even number of squares in the tour (16). You always start on an odd square (1) and end on an even square (16). What else do you notice about the pattern of odd and even squares? Can you start on any square and end on any square? Puzzle answers can be found in Appendix 6.

RT Puzzle 1 In which of the grids below can you create a tour starting at one dot and ending at the other dot? If you can, create the tour. If you cannot, explain why.

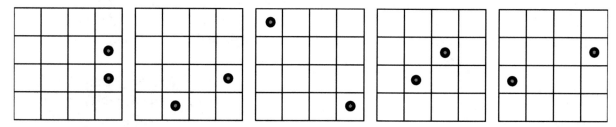

RT Puzzle 2 Create five more rook's tours that are different from the ten tours above.

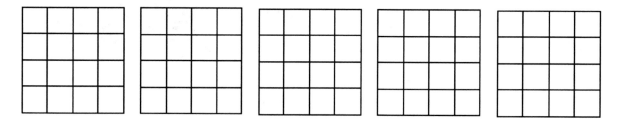

What about tours on boards with an odd number of squares? Can you create a rook's tour starting at one corner of a 7×7 chessboard and ending at the corner diagonally opposite? What about tours on boards with an even number of squares? Can you create a rook's tour starting at one of the corners of an 8×8 chessboard and ending at the corner diagonally opposite? Can you explain why or why not?

Rules of Rook's Tour Puzzles

Rook's tour puzzles are played on a square array or board and some of the squares contain numbers. For a 6×6 rook's tour puzzle, the objective is to fill the remaining empty squares with integers from 1 to 36 so when completed there is a continuous path of numbers from 1 through 36. The path may move horizontally or vertically from square to adjacent square, but not diagonally, just like a rook.

Rook's Tour Puzzles

Fill in the remaining empty squares in the rook's tour puzzles below. The empty circles mark the locations of the starting and ending squares. Puzzles with hints are marked with an *h*.

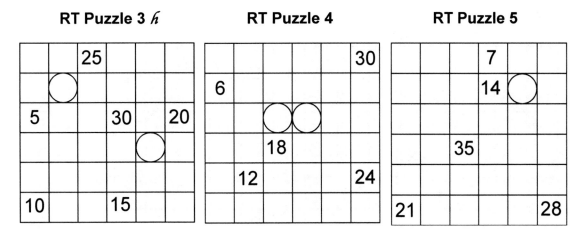

In the 7×7 rook's tour puzzles below, the starting and ending squares contain empty circles. Fill in the remaining empty squares with integers from 1 to 49.

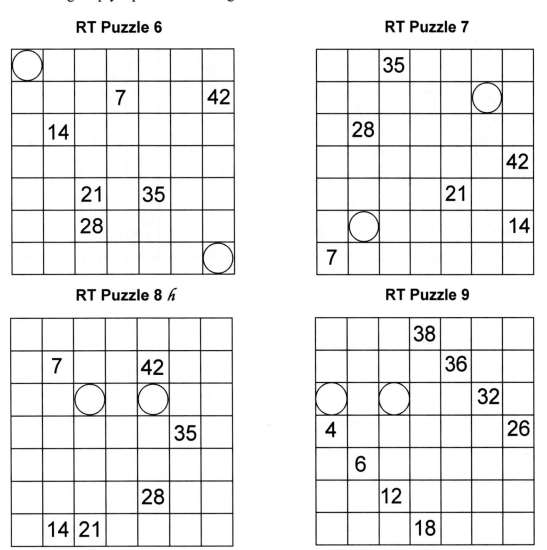

For puzzles 10-13, fill in the remaining empty squares with integers from 1 to 64.

RT Puzzle 10

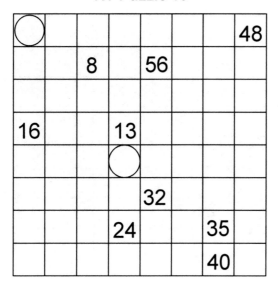

RT Puzzle 11

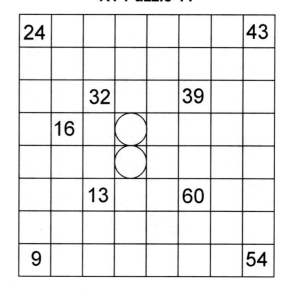

RT Puzzle 12

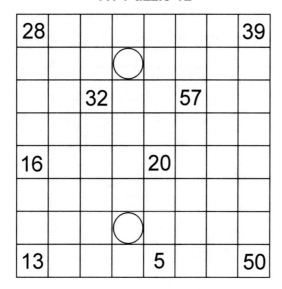

RT Puzzle 13

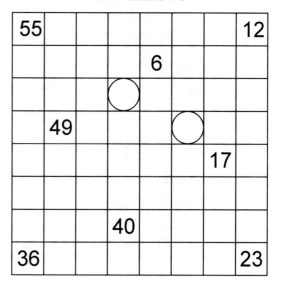

Rook's Tour Puzzles with Given Numbers on the Perimeter

Puzzles 14-17 have numbers given around the perimeter. The large empty set of squares in the center makes the puzzle seem difficult, if not impossible.

In the rook's tour puzzles below, fill in the missing numbers 1-49 for puzzle 14, and 1-64 for puzzle 15.

RT Puzzle 14 *h*

37	38	41	42	45	46	49
36						48
35						25
6						24
7						23
12						22
13	14	15	16	17	20	21

RT Puzzle 15

13	12	9	8	3	2	45	46
14							47
15							48
16							49
29							52
30							53
31							56
32	33	64	63	62	59	58	57

Fill in the missing numbers 1-81 in each puzzle below to complete a rook's tour.

RT Puzzle 16

47	46	43	42	33	32	31	24	23
48								22
49								21
52								20
53								19
62								18
63								17
68								16
69	70	71	72	73	74	3	2	1

RT Puzzle 17

3	2	9	10	11	12	13	14	15
4								16
5								23
78								24
77								25
68								30
67								31
64								34
63	62	61	58	57	38	37	36	35

Rook's Tour Puzzle Variations

For the rook's tour puzzles below, the given numbers produce different patterns. Fill in the missing numbers to generate a continuous path in each square.

RT Puzzle 18

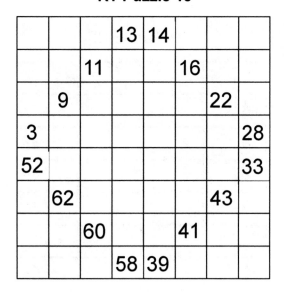

RT Puzzle 19

6			13	18			21
	8					27	
		10		29			
3							24
36							53
		47		64			
	45					62	
39							56

RT Puzzle 20

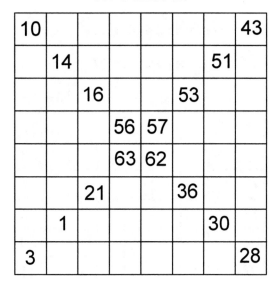

RT Puzzle 21

5		3		79		69		67
	7		81		71		65	
9								59
	15						61	
11								57
	13						55	
21								53
	25		29		37		49	
23		27		33		35		51

RT Puzzle 22

11		13		19		25		27
	9		17		23		29	
7								33
	3						35	
								49
	81						51	
79								53
	77		65		61		57	
75		73		63		59		55

RT Puzzle 23

35		39		45		55		57
33								61
	29				52			
27								65
	9				68			
7								81
5		3		17		73		79

More Rook's Tour Puzzle Variations

Fill in the missing numbers for each puzzle below to complete the rook's tour. Some puzzles have circles to indicate the locations of the first number (1) and/or the last number (81).

RT Puzzle 24 *h*

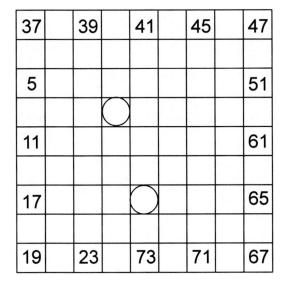

37		39		41		45		47
5								51
			◯					
11								61
17				◯				65
19		23		73		71		67

RT Puzzle 25

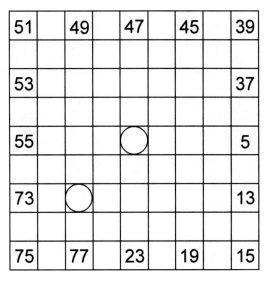

51		49		47		45		39
53								37
55				◯				5
73		◯						13
75		77		23		19		15

RT Puzzle 26

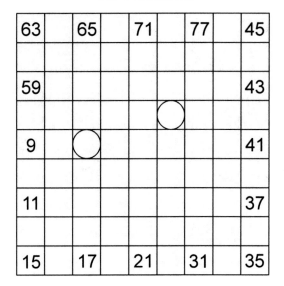

RT Puzzle 27

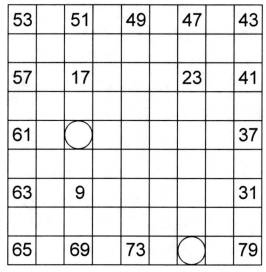

RT Puzzle 28

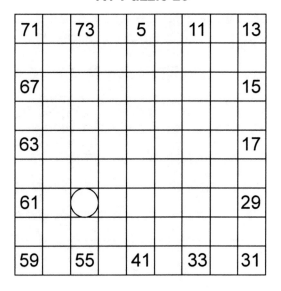

RT Puzzle 29

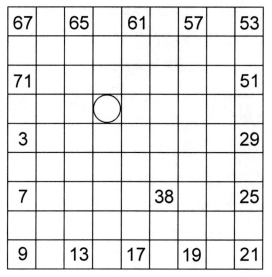

The next set of rook's tour puzzles has only 16 given numbers around the perimeter. Try your sequential reasoning skills on rook's tour puzzles 30-33.

RT Puzzle 30

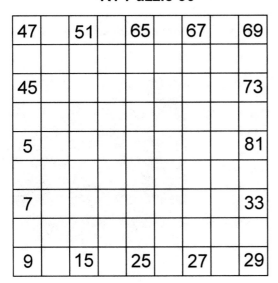

RT Puzzle 31

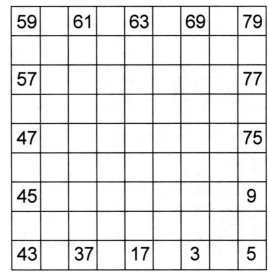

RT Puzzle 32

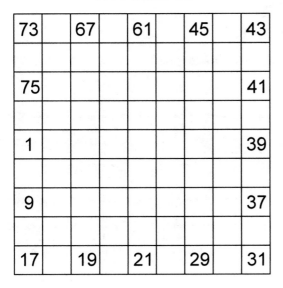

RT Puzzle 33

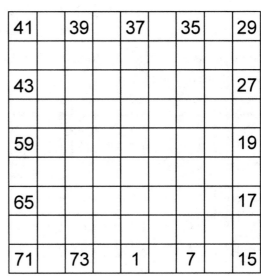

4.2 King's Tour Puzzles

It is clearly possible to move a king over an empty chessboard so it visits each of the 64 squares exactly once on its tour. A king moves one square horizontally, vertically, or diagonally, at a time. What is the least number of moves a chess king can make in order to complete a closed tour (finishing one move from its starting point) on an 8×8 chessboard? Yes, it's a trick question—all tours take the full 63 moves.

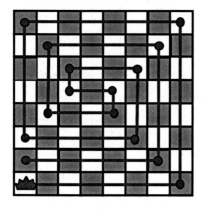

What about a queen's tour? A queen can move horizontally, vertically or diagonally and is not limited to one square. What is the least number of moves necessary for a closed queen's tour on an 8×8 chessboard? Can you do better than the 15 moves shown at left?

All the possible distinct king's tours on a 2×2 board are shown above. Twenty-one king's tours on a 3×3 board are shown below.

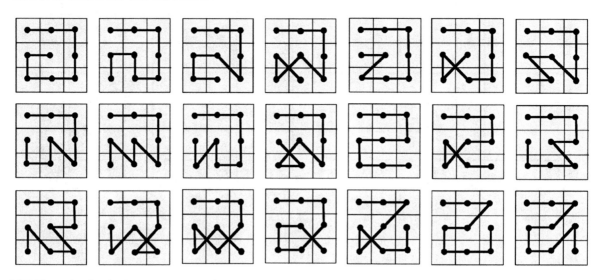

KT Puzzle 1 Find seven more king's tours on the 3×3 boards that are different from the 21 shown.

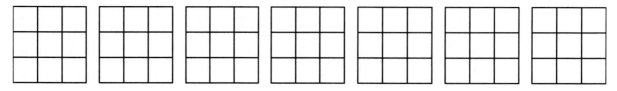

Rules of King's Tour Puzzles

The goal of a king's tour puzzle is to fill the grid with consecutive numbers that connect horizontally, vertically, or diagonally. The circles represent the locations of the smallest and the largest numbers on the grid (the starting and stopping points of the tour).

King's Tour Puzzles

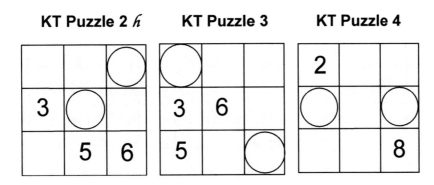

KT Puzzle 2 *h*   **KT Puzzle 3**   **KT Puzzle 4**

KT Puzzle 5   **KT Puzzle 6**   **KT Puzzle 7**

KT Puzzle 8   **KT Puzzle 9**   **KT Puzzle 10**

It can get a bit tricky as the grid gets larger. Solve these 6×6 king's tour puzzles.

KT Puzzle 11 *h*

		15	17		
13	14			21	20
26	9		23		
		24			3
29		34	33		
				◯	◯

KT Puzzle 12

29			7	8	
	30	26		4	
31		◯			
			◯	35	
	19	18	34	13	14
			17		

KT Puzzle 13

2		6	9		
	◯			10	
			16		13
25		20		32	
	26			◯	
		29			35

KT Puzzle 14

14		10			3
	15		8		
19			◯	7	
	20	◯			30
	22	34			
23			33		28

It can get even trickier if we remove some of the squares in the grid. In the puzzles below, you cannot move into the shaded squares.

KT Puzzle 15

	26			19	▓
◯			22	▓	
	24		▓	17	
	3	▓	◯		16
	▓		8	10	
▓	6			12	

KT Puzzle 16

▓	▓	▓			▓	▓	▓
▓		33				▓	▓
▓		26		30	▓	◯	
23			▓	17			
	24	20	▓		13		
▓	◯	▓			14	9	▓
▓	▓			4		▓	▓
▓	▓		5		▓	▓	▓

King's tour puzzles 17 and 18 are identical but have two different solutions. Find both. Again, you cannot move into the shaded squares and the circles indicate the positions of the first and last numbers.

KT Puzzle 17 *h*

KT Puzzle 18

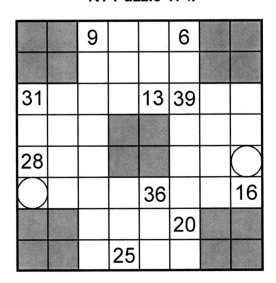

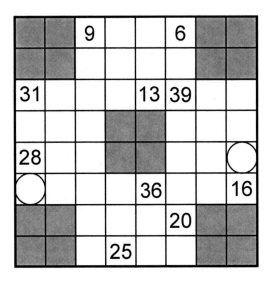

King's Tour on a Hexagonal grid

Let's change the tessellation grid from squares to regular hexagons. King's tour puzzles 14 and 15 are on hexagonal grids. The king can now move from a hexagon space into any one of the six adjacent hexagons. The circles indicate the positions of the first and last numbers.

KT Puzzle 19 *h*

KT Puzzle 20

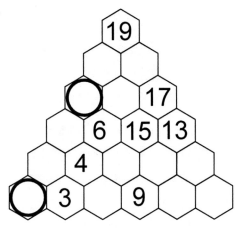

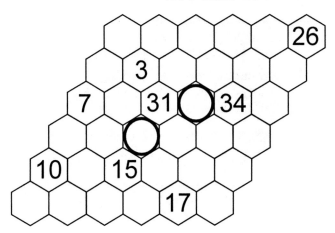

King's Tour on an Archimedean Tiling

Let's change the tessellation grid to the 1-uniform tilings[11] 4.8.8 and 3.4.6.4. The king can now move from any regular polygon region to any polygon region that shares a complete side. The circles indicate the positions of the first and last numbers.

KT Puzzle 21*h*   **KT Puzzle 22**

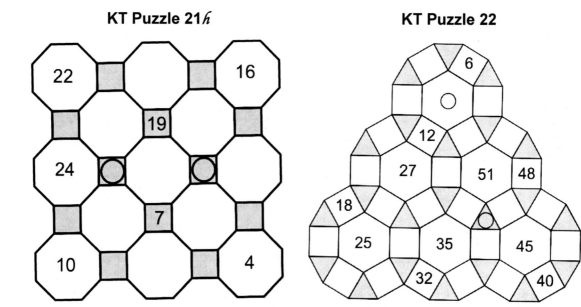

4.3   Knight's Tour Puzzles

At the beginning of the chapter we briefly introduced the most celebrated of tours, the knight's tour. The knight's tour puzzle asks: "Is it possible to move the chess knight so it visits each square of an empty 8×8 chessboard exactly once?" Indeed, not only is it possible but it is possible to start anywhere on the board and complete the tour ending one knight's move away from the starting position. This is called a **closed knight's tour**. Leonhard Euler was the first mathematician to give a comprehensive analysis of the knight's tour. The number of closed knight's tours on an 8×8 chessboard numbers in the trillions! The patterns generated by these tours are quite beautiful. One of the closed knight's tours created by Euler is shown at right.

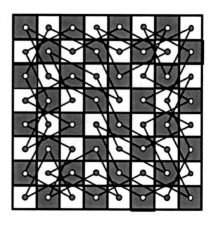

On what size boards can you create a knight's tour? Can you have a knight's tour on a 3×3 board? A quick check demonstrates why it is impossible.

There can be no knight's tour on a 4×4 board either. For a proof see Appendix 7.

The 3×4 grid is the smallest rectangular array on which a knight's tour is possible. There are only three possible tours on a 3×4 grid. One is shown below left.

KnT Puzzle 1 *h* Find the other two knight's tours on a 3×4 grid. To help you, a pair of start and finish points have been identified in each.

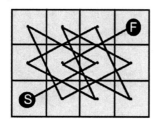   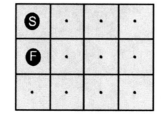   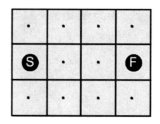

A knight's tour is also possible on a 4×5 rectangular array. One such open tour is shown below left.

KnT Puzzle 2 Complete the two knight's tours on the 4×5 grids that have been started for you below. Again, a pair of start and finish points have been identified for you.

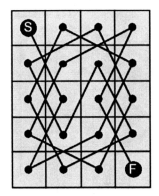 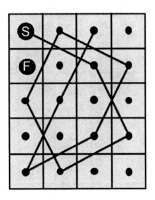 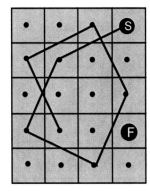

Rules of Knight's Tour Puzzles

The goal of a knight's tour puzzle is to fill the grid with consecutive numbers that are connected by the knight's L-move from one square to the next (a knight's tour). The circles represent the locations of the smallest and the largest numbers on the grid. Let's look at an example.

Example

Complete the 5×5 knight's tour puzzle at right.

Solution

The 1 cannot go in the center square because, from that position, there is no square for the 2 that would connect to the given 3. Therefore, the upper left square must contain the 1 and the center square must contain the 25 (Figure 1). The 2, 4, and 6, are forced to go in their squares between the 1, 3, 5, and 7, and there is only one square left for the 8 (Figure 2). There are only 3 positions available for the 9 but only one of them connects to a position for a 10 that connects to the 11 (Figure 3). The remaining numbers are forced, as shown (Figure 4).

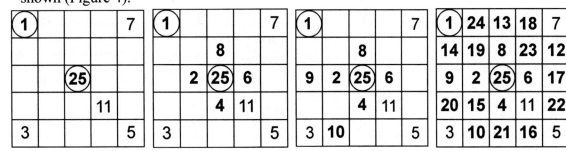

Figure 1   Figure 2   Figure 3   Figure 4

Knight's Tour Puzzles

Complete each of these 5x5 knight's tour puzzles. The circles represent the locations of the smallest (1) and the largest (25) numbers on the grid.

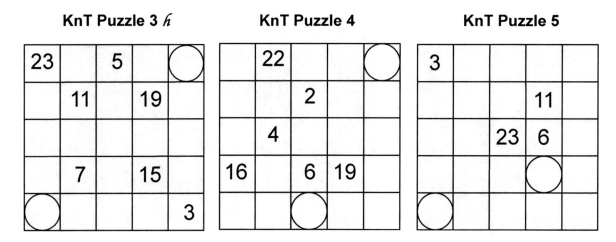

KnT Puzzle 3 *h*

23		5		◯
	11		19	
	7		15	
◯				3

KnT Puzzle 4

	22			◯
		2		
		4		
16		6	19	
	◯			

KnT Puzzle 5

3				
			11	
		23	6	
			◯	
◯				

Complete each of these 6x6 knight's tour puzzles. The circles represent the locations of the smallest (1) and the largest (36) numbers on the grid. These are closed knight's tours, since the starting and ending positions are one knight's move apart.

KnT Puzzle 6

32		30	21		23
				9	
26					
		◯			
			◯		
5		3	12		14

KnT Puzzle 7

	26			28	
22	◯				
		20			
◯					
				4	
10			8		

KnT Puzzle 8

					35
23	6				
	12				
	9		3		
30					
		14			

Complete each of these 7×7 open knight's tour puzzles. (There can be no closed tours on odd square grids such as 5×5, 7×7, or 9×9. For a proof, see Appendix 7.) The circles represent the locations of the smallest (1) and the largest (49) numbers on the grid.

KnT Puzzle 9

O		19		35		37
			41			
23		21		47		39
	17		25		33	
11		3		29		27
			9			
13		15		31		O

KnT Puzzle 10

O		21	36			19
	37					
45		35		29		O
34			11			30
		33		39		17
				41		
9			40	7		27

KnT Puzzle 11

17		33	46	15		25
7		34			3	
	48		44		38	
19		40	O		23	
9		29	36	11		O

KnT Puzzle 12

49			42			
		2	13	24		
		45			26	
38		32	O	46		34
	10				16	
		8	29	18		
			36			

Complete each of these 8×8 closed knight's tour puzzles. The circles represent the locations of the smallest (1) and the largest (64) numbers on the grid.

KnT Puzzle 13 *h*

57		49	40	51		13	4
			33				
		39		59			
	47				11		53
21						15	
			27				63
				O			
36	45			8		O	25

KnT Puzzle 14

	43		33		29		27
37				9			
	39				23		25
35		45		O			
					19	O	61
51		49				13	
			3				63
53		55		59		17	

KnT Puzzle 15   **KnT Puzzle 16**

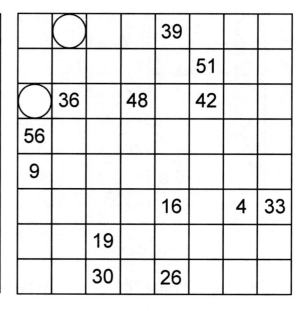

3		9			30		18
	23					14	
27		21			12		16
	7		◯			32	
	◯						
48		44			53		59
	46					55	
50		62			41		35

	◯			39			
					51		
◯	36		48		42		
56							
9							
				16		4	33
		19					
		30		26			

Knight's Tour Puzzles with Given Numbers on the Perimeter

Earlier in the chapter you solved rook's tour puzzles with the numbers given on the perimeter of the square grid. Does the knight's more complicated move make these puzzles more difficult? Try these knight's tour puzzles to find out.

KnT Puzzle 17 h   **KnT Puzzle 18**

11	8	13	16	51	42	37	40
14							43
9							38
18			◯				53
5							34
22				◯			57
27							62
24	21	26	3	32	61	56	59

3	48	57	8	5	12	59	10
56							13
47							22
52			◯				61
29							20
54				◯			15
45							24
42	27	44	37	40	25	16	35

KnT Puzzle 19

28	3	22	9	30	5	24	15
21							6
2							17
11		◯					32
◯							43
49							34
38							53
47	56	37	62	41	54	35	60

KnT Puzzle 20

◯	38	57	44	63	40	59	50
56		◯					41
37							52
46							61
29							14
20							5
9							24
18	27	8	31	12	25	6	33

Knight's Tour Puzzles on 9×9 and 10×10 grids

Complete each of these 9×9 open knight's tour puzzles. The circles represent the locations of the smallest (1) and the largest (81) numbers on the grid.

KnT Puzzle 21

75	58	45	32	77	60	47	34	79
44								48
57		21				23		35
30					13			62
73			◯				◯	
42			5					50
55		19				25		37
28								64
71	54	27	40	69	52	65	38	67

KnT Puzzle 22

13	76	15	20	11	74	25	22	9
16								24
77								69
18	◯							66
79								7
30								58
45				◯				35
50								64
47	40	49	32	53	38	63	34	5

Complete each of these 10×10 closed knight's tour puzzles. The circles represent the locations of the smallest (1) and the largest (100) numbers on the grid.

KnT Puzzle 23

86	91	88	69	84	71	80	67	64	61
89		98			77				66
92									63
5	2							73	44
96			◯	50	25				59
9				75	◯				46
94	23							52	55
13									42
16			27			48			39
11	14	17	30	21	34	19	38	41	36

KnT Puzzle 24

71	84	41	12	69	82	39	10	67	96
42									9
85						77			66
14		52			5				37
57			80		76				94
44				26	◯	30			7
87				55			2		64
16		27				◯			35
59									92
46	17	60	89	32	19	62	91	34	21

Creating Your Own Knight's Tour

The patterns created by knight's tours are quite stunning – especially those created by closed tours.

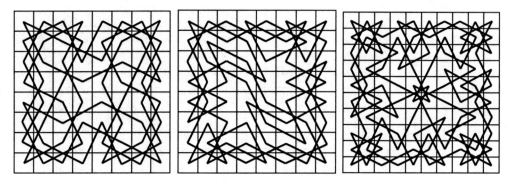

You can create your own designs in the next puzzles. Let's start with a 5×5 grid.

KnT Puzzle 25 *h* Create an open knight's tour on the 5×5 grid below. Begin in the center square and end in one of the corners.

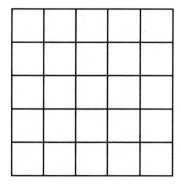

KnT Puzzle 26 You can use the open 5×5 knight's tour you just created above as the center of an open 9×9 knight's tour. Transfer your solution from puzzle 25 to the center 5×5 squares in the 9×9 grid below. Then, move the knight around the two-square-wide frame to complete the 9x9 knight's tour.

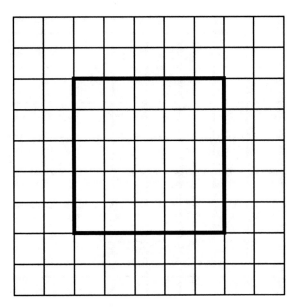

KnT Puzzle 27 *h* A knight's tour design often has rotational symmetry, or "almost" rotational symmetry. One quadrant of a closed 10×10 knight's tour has been started for you below. Use rotational symmetry to complete the tour. Each quadrant will be a 90° rotation of one of the adjacent quadrants.

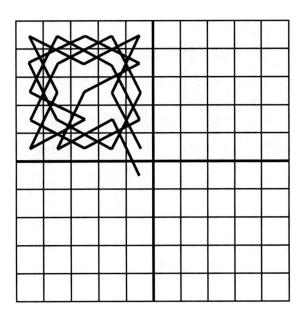

KnT Puzzle 28 The great puzzle master H.E. Dudeney created an 8×8 knight's tour by combining two 3×4 knight's tours and two 4×5 knight's tours. You completed these tours earlier in this chapter. Try your hand at reproducing Dudeney's 8×8 knight's tour in the topmost grid below. A hint is also shown below.

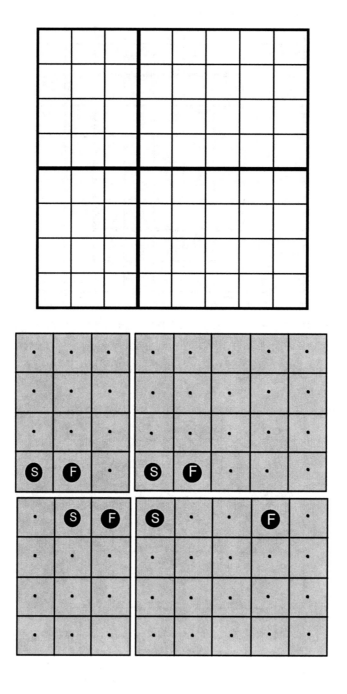

4.4. Mathematical Connections: Euler Paths

Labyrinths and Mazes

The earliest known tour puzzles are labyrinths. Labyrinths and mazes have been a part of human art and culture for thousands of years. They can be found all over the world from Latin America to Europe to Africa to India and Indonesia. The classic Labyrinth symbol is shown to the left.

Although there are exceptions, labyrinths, by definition, have only one path. The person traversing the labyrinth never has to decide which direction to take next. A person moving about in a maze[12], on the other hand, must make choices in the path. The hedge maze in Williamsburg, Virginia is shown below (Path Puzzle 1). Find the path from the outside entrance at the top to the center court.

Logic Mazes and Network Puzzles

Path Puzzle 1

Another more challenging type of maze is the logic maze. A logic maze has special rules for movement. These rules can include one-way paths, no right turns, no left turns, or even a path that must cross over or pick up particular objects, numbers, or colors in a preset order. Bookstores and the internet provide an unlimited supply of these puzzles. The robot programming puzzles, in Chapter 1 of this book, are examples of a type of logic maze.

"Hedge Maze" Williamsburg, VA

Network traveling puzzles are another popular maze-like puzzle that have been around for a long time. A network is a collection of points connected by line segments or curves called **edges**. The objective is to determine whether a network can be traveled or not. To travel a network, you must be able to trace or redraw the path without lifting your pencil or retracing an edge. However, points can be passed over more than once.

Path Puzzle 2 ℎ

Circle the networks that can be traveled and show the path.

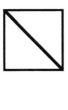   

The Seven Bridges of Königsberg

The most famous network traveling puzzle is the *Seven Bridges of Königsberg*. This puzzle became a tradition in the eighteenth century among students in the university town of Königsberg (now Kaliningrad, Russia). The river Pregal (now Pregolya) runs through the city and in the middle of the river are two islands. These two islands are connected to each other and the rest of the city by seven bridges. Townspeople challenged each other to see if anyone could walk over all seven bridges exactly once. Give it a try.

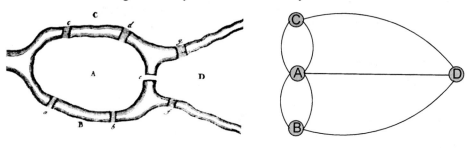

(From Euler's manuscript)

How did you do? No one in Königsberg was able to do it either. More importantly, no one was able to explain why nor prove it could not be done. Finally, in 1735, they wrote to Swiss mathematician Leonhard Euler and asked for his help, "Is it impossible or just difficult?" Euler studied the problem and reduced it to a network of vertices, which represented the land (islands and mainland), and edges connecting the land, which represented the seven bridges. He then demonstrated why it was impossible to travel over each edge, or bridge exactly once.

Here is a brief explanation. Let's look at what happens when you try to travel the network. You begin at one vertex, leave, and arrive at another. You then leave the second vertex, arrive at a third, and so on, until you came to a vertex from which all edges have already been used. This kept happening! What is the nature of these vertices? They all have an odd number of edges connected to them. The degree of a vertex is the number of edges that are connected to it. So, if the vertex has degree three, after you come-go-come, you are stuck. The vertex needs to be even so you can leave again. There are just too many of those pesky odd vertices! Wouldn't things be a lot easier if all the vertices were even? Or, if only two were odd, we could create a path. For a more detailed explanation of how to prove that this network cannot be traveled, see Appendix 7.

If you looked at the explanation in the Appendix, you may be ready to generalize this idea to any network. If all the vertices of a network are even can the network be traveled? Yes. In fact, you can start anywhere and end back at your starting point. Can you explain why? If a network has exactly two odd vertices, can it be traveled? Again, yes. Can you start anywhere? No. You must start at one of the odd vertices and you will end at the other odd vertex. Can you explain why? For answers to these questions see Appendix 7. You should now be able to return to the ten networks in Path Puzzle 2 and quickly determine which can or cannot be traveled.

If all the edges of a network, called a **graph** in Graph Theory, can be covered without retracing any edge, then the graph has an **Euler path**. If all edges of a graph can be covered without repetition and you can return to the starting point, then the graph has an **Euler circuit**.

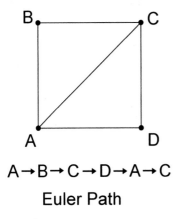

$A \rightarrow B \rightarrow C \rightarrow D \rightarrow A \rightarrow C$

Euler Path

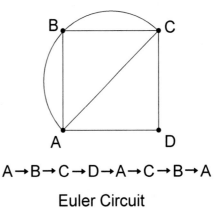

$A \rightarrow B \rightarrow C \rightarrow D \rightarrow A \rightarrow C \rightarrow B \rightarrow A$

Euler Circuit

Path Puzzle 3

Identify the following graphs as having an Euler path, an Euler circuit, or cannot be traveled.

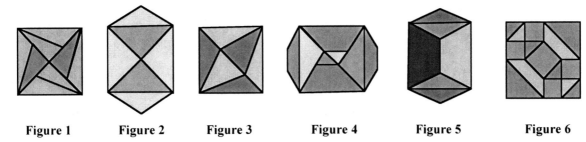

| Figure 1 | Figure 2 | Figure 3 | Figure 4 | Figure 5 | Figure 6 |

Of the graphs you've seen so far, some have had odd vertices. Have you come across any that have an odd number of odd vertices? Try creating a graph with an odd number of odd vertices. To learn more about the number of odd vertices in a graph, take a look at Appendix 7.

In Path Puzzle 4, below, add a bridge so that you can walk over all the bridges exactly once (an Euler path). In Path Puzzle 5, either remove or add a bridge so that you can walk over all the bridges exactly once and return to your starting point (an Euler circuit).

Path Puzzle 4   **Path Puzzle 5**

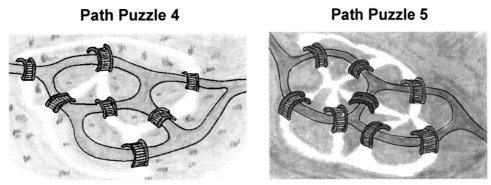

Mathematicians' explorations of recreational mathematics puzzles often end up having major applications. Euler's investigation of the *Seven Bridges of Königsberg* puzzle began a major branch of mathematics called Topology. A very important and vital branch of topology is Graph Theory, the study of the mathematical structures used to model relationships between objects.

There are a host of very famous problems studied in graph theory. The Four-Color Map problem is one of them, "Can any map in the plane be colored with four colors, so that no two regions sharing a common border have the same color?" Another famous problem is the Shortest Path problem. An example of this problem is finding the shortest way to get from one spot on a map to another.

Graph theory is used in many occupations, including anyone involved in scheduling. For instance, building contractors must organize their labor and materials as well as the time schedule in which the jobs need to be completed. Restaurant managers need to map out their meal planning, purchasing of fresh produce, prep time, and more. City managers, the street maintenance department, and parking meter managers need to organize the scheduling and routing of street cleaning, meter ticketing, and meter money collecting. Ecologists use graph theory (competition graphs) to study communities of species that feed on common prey. In electrical engineering, graph theory is used in communication networks and coding theory. Graph theory helps with all of this.

In recreational mathematics, graph theory (Hamiltonian circuits) is used to find knight's tours on chessboards of different sizes and dimensions. And what are the humble beginnings of all this? Leonhard Euler's 1736 published paper on the *Seven Bridges of Königsberg* puzzle.

Never be afraid to sit awhile and think.
–Lorraine Hansberry

5.1   Introduction to Magic Squares

MS Puzzle 1 Place the numbers 1 through 9 in the nine squares of the grid at right. Use each number exactly once and arrange them so the sum of the numbers in each row, column, and both main diagonals is the same. This puzzle is called a magic square.

Most math historians believe the magic square originated in China around 2200 BCE, where it was associated with the Legend of Lo-Shu. According to the legend, there was a huge flood on the river Lo and in order to calm the river god's anger, the peasants of the river valley left sacrifices. However, after each sacrifice a turtle appeared and walked around the offerings but did not take them. The people interpreted this rejection of the offerings to mean that the river god did not accept the amount of the sacrifice. After this happened a number of times, a child noticed markings on the turtle's shell. The peasants realized the sum of the markings in each row, column, and both main diagonals was 15 and thus 15 should be the number of offerings. The puzzle was solved! Over the centuries this magic square appears as good luck charms called Lo-Shu. The 3×3 magic square is found in cultures all over the world including the ancient Babylonians, the ancient Greeks, and the ancient Mayans. In Islamic cultures the magic square symbolized the power of Allah.

What is a Magic Square?

A **magic square** is a square array of distinct integers such that the numbers in any row, column, or main diagonal have the same sum (called the magic sum or magic constant). If the n^2 numbers in an n by n magic square are the positive integers 1 through n^2, then the magic square is a **normal magic square**. The 3×3 magic square above, when completed using the numbers 1 through 9, is a normal magic square. To calculate the magic sum for any normal $n \times n$ magic square, see Appendix 7.

3×3 Magic Square Sculpture

Artist: Brian O'Doherty/Patrick Ireland

The smallest magic square (1×1) is of little interest since there is only one square with one number in it. Can there be a 2×2 magic square? This would be an arrangement of four consecutive positive integers 1, 2, 3, and 4, so the sum is the same in each row, column, and both main diagonals. Once a number is placed in one of the four squares, it becomes impossible to place any other number to create a magic square.

1	?
?	?

5.2   3x3 Magic Squares

If you were able to solve the puzzle from the previous page, your solution may have looked like the one shown at right.

4	9	2
3	5	7
8	1	6

Are their other solutions? Well, if we reflect it horizontally or vertically it is still the same magic square but with a different orientation.

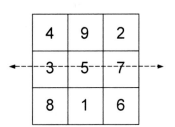
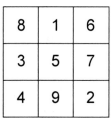
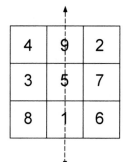
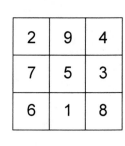

Reflected top to bottom   **Reflected right to left**

If we rotate the magic square 90° or 180° is it still the same magic square?

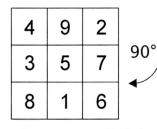
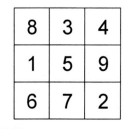
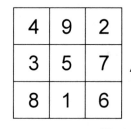
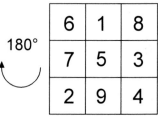

Rotated 90°   **Rotated 180°**

If we reflect the original magic square across a main diagonal, is it still the same magic square? Try it. Complete each grid below by reflecting the remaining digits across a main diagonal.

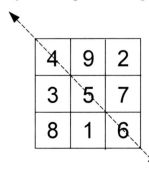
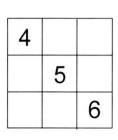
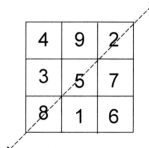
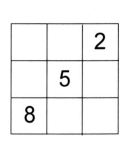

Reflected across the 4-5-6 diagonal   **Reflected across the 2-5-8 diagonal**

You've seen seven different reflections and rotations of the same 3×3 magic square. There is one more. Can you find it? See Appendix 7 for all eight arrangements.

4	9	2
3	5	7
8	1	6

Is there a different 3×3 magic square that is not just a rotation or reflection of the original? If we cannot find one, can we prove that one does not exist? Go to Appendix 7 for the proof.

In the exercises below, take the basic normal 3×3 magic square shown at right and perform the given arithmetic operation on each number.

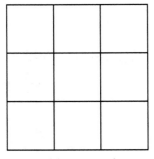

Add 5 to each

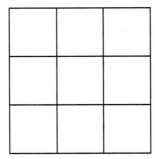

Subtract 4 from each

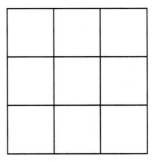

Multiply each by 2

Check that these squares are also magic squares. Magic squares that do not use just the first nine positive integers, such as those above, are called **simple** 3×3 magic squares. This definition extends to any $n \times n$ magic square that does not use just the first n^2 positive integers.

An incomplete magic square, like the grids below, is a magic square puzzle in which your task is to figure out the missing numbers. Complete the 3×3 simple magic square puzzles below. Place the given numbers so that the sum of the numbers is the same in each row, column, and on both main diagonals.

MS Puzzle 2 *h*

12	7	
5		13
		6

Use 8, 9, 10, 11

MS Puzzle 3

	14	
18		2
	6	16

Use 4, 8, 10, 12

MS Puzzle 4

11		15
3		7

Use 1, 5, 9, 13, 17

MS Puzzle 5

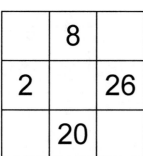

	8	
2		26
	20	

Use 5,11,14,17,23

MS Puzzle 6

	11	
7		-1
	-5	

Use -3,1,3,5,9

MS Puzzle 7

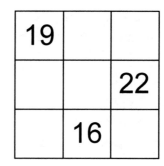

19		
		22
	16	

Use -2,1,4,7,10,13

Solve these puzzles using the given clues.

MS Puzzle 8 h

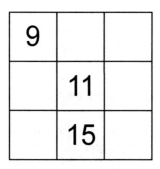

9		
	11	
	15	

The magic sum is 33

MS Puzzle 9

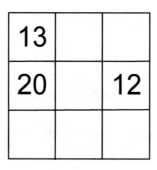

13		
20		12

The numbers are consecutive

MS Puzzle 10

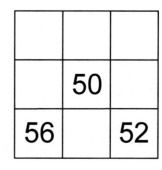

	50	
56		52

All consecutive even

5.3   4x4 Magic Squares

The magic square shown at right is a normal 4×4 magic square. Unlike the normal 3×3 magic square, which has only one solution, there are 880 normal 4×4 magic squares. This does not even count the reflections and rotations of each of the solutions! This 4×4 magic square is a favorite of many mathematicians. It appeared in Renaissance artist Albrecht Durer's woodcut titled, *Melencolia I.* A quick check reveals the magic sum for a normal 4×4 magic square is 34. To determine the magic sum for any *n×n* normal magic square, see Appendix 7. This magic square is even more magical than most; not only does every row, column, and

16	3	2	13
5	10	11	8
9	6	7	12
4	15	14	1

both main diagonals add to the same magic sum of 34, but the magic sum also appears in more than two-dozen symmetric patterns. Each set of four squares, shown in the patterns below, has numbers that add up to the magic sum of 34.

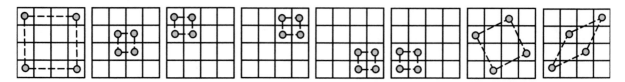

© Michael Serra 2011

MS Puzzle 11 Eight of the more than 24 symmetric patterns are shown in the previous diagrams. Find at least eight more patterns that sum to 34.

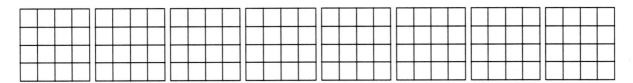

Complete each puzzle below. Puzzles 12–20 are all normal 4×4 squares, so they all have the same magic sum of 34.

MS Puzzle 12 *h*

	8	12	
3			15
2	11		
	5	9	4

MS Puzzle 13

7	2		
		3	6
1	8		15
	11	5	

MS Puzzle 14

13		2	16
8			
	6	7	
1			4

MS Puzzle 15

10		8	
5			14
	6	13	
	9	2	

MS Puzzle 16

	14		1
9			12
5		10	
	2	3	13

MS Puzzle 17

2	14	11	
1	13	8	
			9

MS Puzzle 18

	14		
5			
9		6	
	2	3	13

MS Puzzle 19

8		5	
	3		2
12	6		
	15		14

MS Puzzle 20

	2		
13		4	
	7		6
	11	5	

Puzzles 21-26 are simple magic squares. Solve them using the given integers.

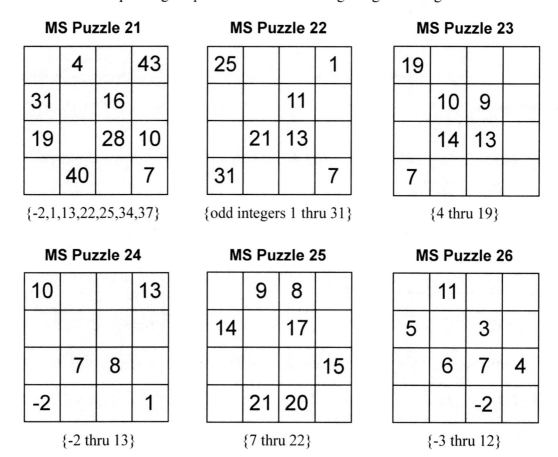

MS Puzzle 21

	4		43
31		16	
19		28	10
	40		7

{-2,1,13,22,25,34,37}

MS Puzzle 22

25			1
		11	
	21	13	
31			7

{odd integers 1 thru 31}

MS Puzzle 23

19			
	10	9	
	14	13	
7			

{4 thru 19}

MS Puzzle 24

10			13
	7	8	
-2			1

{-2 thru 13}

MS Puzzle 25

	9	8	
14		17	
			15
	21	20	

{7 thru 22}

MS Puzzle 26

	11		
5		3	
	6	7	4
		-2	

{-3 thru 12}

Solve these puzzles using the given clues.

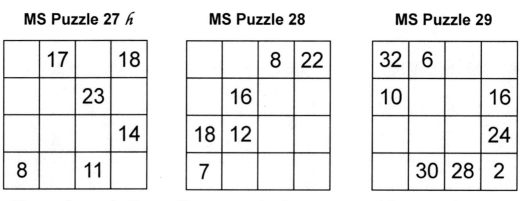

MS Puzzle 27 ℏ

	17		18
		23	
			14
8		11	

The magic sum is 62.

MS Puzzle 28

		8	22
	16		
18	12		
7			

Use consecutive integers.

MS Puzzle 29

32	6		
10			16
			24
	30	28	2

All consecutive even.

5.4   5x5 Magic Squares

24	19	1	3	18
6	10	17	12	20
5	15	13	11	21
22	14	9	16	4
8	7	25	23	2

There are 275,305,224 normal 5×5 magic squares (again, not counting rotations and reflections). Here is an interesting example: the magic square at left is called a **bordered magic square**. Ignore or remove the outer border of squares of this 5×5 magic square and you get a 3×3 grid of numbers. Is there anything special about this 3×3 grid? You guessed it—it is a simple 3×3 magic square!

Notice that each number in the center 3×3 grid is eight more than the corresponding number in a normal 3×3. So the center 3×3 magic square has a magic sum of 39. The magic sum for a normal 5×5 is 65. Therefore, each pair of opposite numbers in the ring must add to 26. Are there other arrangements of numbers around the perimeter that give another 5×5 bordered magic square? Rotating the ring by 90°, 180°, or 270° produces three others. But there are still more which we will see in the next puzzle.

MS Puzzle 30 Complete the 5×5 bordered magic square at right.

1	22			
	10	17	12	24
	15	13	11	
21	14	9	16	
			7	

1	19	7	25	13
22	15	3	16	9
18	6	24	12	5
14	2	20	8	21
10	23	11	4	17

As you may recall, Albrecht Durer's 4×4 magic square contained more than two dozen symmetric patterns of connecting numbers whose magic sum is 34.

The magic square at left has a magic sum of 65. You will also find a number of symmetric patterns of connecting numbers whose sum are 65. Four of these patterns are shown in the diagrams below.

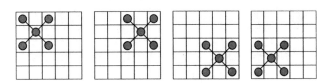

MS Puzzle 31 Find at least three more symmetric patterns that sum to 65.

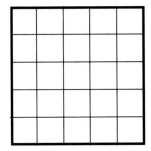 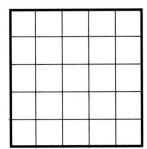 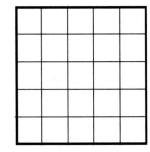

Complete each 5×5 normal magic square puzzle below.

MS Puzzle 32

	24	1		
23	5		14	16
4		13		22
10	12			3
11		25	2	

MS Puzzle 33

	11	18		16
8		4	12	
				2
	6	23	1	10
14	9		24	

MS Puzzle 34

		4		14
11	3		19	9
		5	7	6
1			15	
	2	13		

MS Puzzle 35

	21		7	
	6			1
16		10		12
	8	11	22	
18	17	4		24

MS Puzzle 36

15				
		18		20
	23	21		12
24	14		16	10
6	8	22		4

MS Puzzle 37

	11	18		16
8		4	12	
				2
	6	23	1	10
14	9		24	

MS Puzzle 38

23			2	
10	18			22
	5		21	9
4			8	
	24	7		3

MS Puzzle 39

23				15
		25	8	
10	18	1		22
		7	20	
17			21	9

MS Puzzle 40

		13	2	
	15			1
6	7	5		
9	19		3	11
14		4		

Solve these 5×5 simple magic square puzzles using the given clues.

MS Puzzle 41 *h*

8	16		12	25
	22			1
20		11		
21				13
2	15	23		19

The magic sum is 65.

MS Puzzle 42 *h*

	29	16		25
31	23	40		
	17		21	38
		28	20	
18	35			26

Use consecutive integers.

MS Puzzle 43

		14		6
34		26		
46	12			30
	24	50		32
20		2	28	

All consecutive even.

5.5 6×6 and 7×7 Magic Squares

Solve the following 6×6 and 7×7 magic square puzzles.

MS Puzzle 44

6		3		35	1
7	11		28	8	
19	14	16			24
			21	17	
25	29		9		
	5	33	4	2	31

MS Puzzle 45

22		31	6		20	
40		10	9	44		15
7	1	30	49		32	35
		25				34
23	38			3	26	37
36	18	28	45	19		16
	29	5	17	41		27

5.6 8×8 Magic Squares

There are 275,305,224 normal 5×5 magic squares. There are an *estimated* 1.7745×10^{19} normal 6×6 magic squares. The number of $n \times n$ normal magic squares for $n > 5$, such as the 8×8 magic squares shown below, is still unknown. Solve the following 8×8 normal magic square puzzles.

MS Puzzle 46

43	47	2	26	1		37	59
54	18	63	17	14		58	
40	36		44	50	21	9	25
					32	38	51
	23	52	15		46	11	62
28	34		49		64	13	8
	19	5	41		33	55	29
31		57	56	7	3		

MS Puzzle 47

	17	52	36	19	48	59	4
43	33		47	38	57		16
49		24		11		10	28
1	60	46		64	12	35	
37		30		45		51	62
22	32		23	6	13	56	58
41	18	9	40			26	
	61	44	15	14	27		55

Solve the following odd-even magic square puzzles using odd numbers in unshaded squares and even numbers in shaded squares.

MS Puzzle 48 *h*

8			32	40	17	9	
58	15	23			47	55	2
	14	22	35	27	46	54	
5	52	44		37		12	61
4		45	28	36	21		60
62	11	19	38		43	51	6
63	10		39	31		50	7
	56	48	25	33	24		

MS Puzzle 49

43	47		26	1	45	37	59
54		63	17			58	20
	36	35		50	21	9	25
10		42		53	32		51
24	23		15	27		11	62
28	34		49	60		13	8
	19	5	41		33	55	29
31	61	57		7	3	39	

The great statesman and scientist Benjamin Franklin created an amazing 8×8 square with many magic sum and half-sum patterns. It is called a **semi-magic square** because the two main diagonals do not add to the magic sum of 260. But not only does each row and column have a magic sum of 260 but each half-row has a sum of 130, or half the magic sum. So, each 4×4 corner is also a semi-magic square. Although the diagonals do not add to 260, the "bent-diagonals" (one is shown below left) do add to the magic sum. One of the many symmetric magic sums is shown below, right.

52	61	4	13	20	29	36	45
14	3	62	51	46	35	30	19
53	60	5	12	21	28	37	44
11	6	59	54	43	38	27	22
55	58	7	10	23	26	39	42
9	8	57	56	41	40	25	24
50	63	2	15	18	31	34	47
16	1	64	49	48	33	32	17

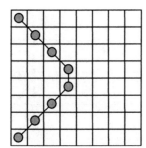

Bent-diagonal with magic sum

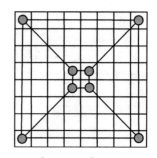

A symmetric magic sum pattern

MS Puzzle 50 Find three more symmetric magic sums in Ben Franklin's 8×8 semi-magic square.

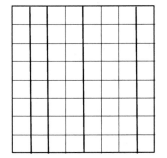 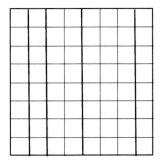 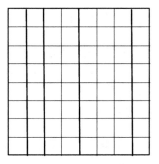

In Chapter 4 we introduced rook's tour, king's tour, and knight's tour puzzles. The numbers in the rook's tour puzzles represented the order of the squares that the rook passed over. This is shown in the solution to Rook's Tour Puzzle 3 below left. The given numbers are larger and in bold.

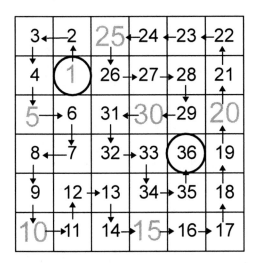 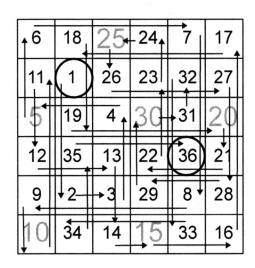

If we allow the numbers in the tour puzzle to represent the position at each stop of the rook rather than the squares passed over, this would be a different puzzle. There would be many possible paths for the numbers given in Rook's Tour Puzzle 3. Above right is a solution to Rook's Tour Puzzle 3 if the numbers in the puzzle represent the location of each stop in the 36 moves of the rook's tour.

In the *Journal of Recreational Mathematics*, computer programmer Stanley Rabinowitz published an 8×8 rook's tour with unrestricted rook's movement that is also a normal 8×8 magic square. The classic *Mathematical Recreations and Essays* by W.W. Ball and H.S.M. Coxeter, contains an 8×8 magic square that is also a king's tour.

Complete the 8×8 rook's tour normal magic square below, left (where each number represents the position at each step of the rook's tour rather than the squares passed over) and the 8×8 king's tour magic square below, right. Again, the squares containing circles indicate the locations of 1 and 64.

MS Puzzle 51: Rook's Tour

	44	52	28				4
30			6		54		
	42	50	26				
32		16		57	17	56	1
		49	25		48	9	
34			39	58			63
	22	14	38	59	19	11	
			37		20	12	61

MS Puzzle 52: King's Tour

		21	20		12	60	
35				14	59		62
	39		18		10		
33		24		16	9		○
		41					○
31	26		47	50		7	
	43		46				3
29		44	45			5	

One spectacular 8×8 semi-magic square[13], which some believe was created by Leonhard Euler, has all the properties of Ben Franklin's semi-magic square and more. Like Franklin's, this semi-magic square has the magic sum of 260 and the 4×4 corners have the magic sum of 130. But Euler arranged the numbers of the magic square so that moving from one number to the next completes a knight's tour. That is, it is possible to start at 1 position and move to 2, 3, and so on, all the way to 64 by making the L-shaped move of the chess knight. You never land on the same square more than once and never miss a square! Euler's semi-magic square is started for you in the next puzzle.

MS Puzzle 53 *h*: Euler's Semi-Magic Square

This semi-magic square is also called a knight's tour semi-magic square. Use the following clues to help you complete Euler's 8×8 semi-magic square. The magic sum is 260. The half sums are 130. The moves are those of a chess knight.

1		31		33		63	
	51		3		19		
		49		15			
			45		61	36	13
		25				21	
28		8	41	24			
43	6	55			10		
			58		38		

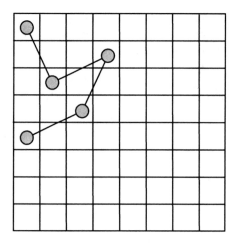

Once you have solved Euler's semi-magic square puzzle above, draw the knight's path from 1 to 2, to 3, all the way to 64, in the grid above right. The first four moves are shown.

There was a flurry of activity on knight's tour semi-magic squares in the nineteenth century. In 1848, the Englishman, William Beverley, created his first knight's tour semi-magic square. Little is known of Beverley, but it is believed he was a set designer, not a mathematician. Complete Beverley's semi-magic square below left, and draw the knight's tour on the blank grid on the right.

MS Puzzle 54: Beverley's Semi-Magic Square

	2		32		34		64
30		46		62		14	
1	48						18
	29		45	20	61	36	
5		25		9	40		60
28	53		41	24		12	37
43		55			10		
		42	7	58	23		

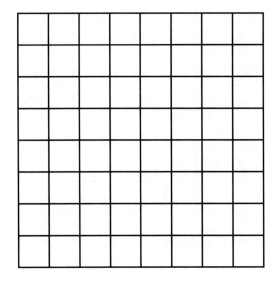

The Hungarian, Carl Wenzelides, created chess problems and knight's tours to entertain himself (he was an invalid). In 1849, Wenzelides created his first knight's tour semi-magic square which was a breakthrough because it was a **closed tour**. A closed tour is a tour that ends at 64, one knight's move from the starting 1. Complete Wenzelides' semi-magic square below and then draw the complete tour on the blank grid.

MS Puzzle 55: Wenzelides Semi-Magic Square

	11		63		37		35
23		51		25		15	
		64			13		
	22		52		28		16
48	7					54	29
59		45		53		17	
	47		57		19		55
3		5		31		43	

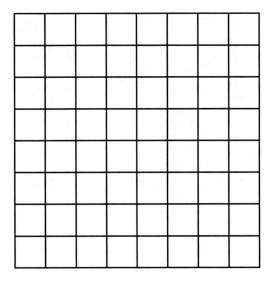

In 1862, the Russian, C.F. Jaenisch, created the first of his knight's tour semi-magic squares. Many of his knight's tour semi-magic squares were also **closed tours**.

Complete Jaenisch's semi-magic square below left. The circles are the locations for 1 and 64. Draw the complete tour on the blank grid.

MS Puzzle 56: Jaenisch's Semi-Magic Square

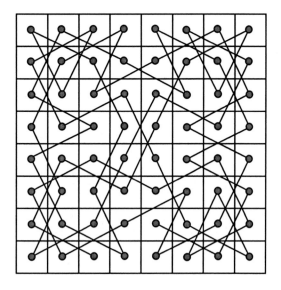
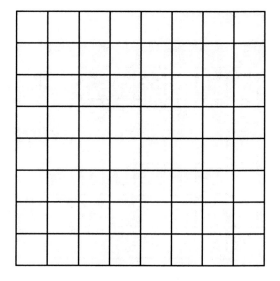

It has been known for a long time that there can be no knight's tour magic squares with an odd number of squares on a side. It was also suspected there exists no 8×8 knight's tour magic square. In 2003, after 61 days of computer computations, the exhaustive search for an 8×8 knight's tour magic square was completed. None exist—we have to settle for a semi-magic one. So far 140 distinct semi-magic knight's tours on an 8×8 grid have been found. Below are two examples.

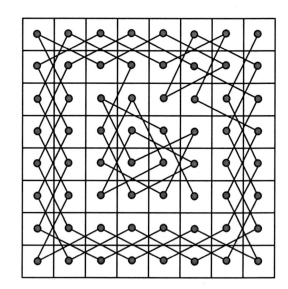

5.7 12×12 Magic Squares

Krishnaraj Wadiar, the nineteenth century Rajah of Mysore, India, was a knight's tour magic square enthusiast. He created a number of 8×8 closed knight's tour semi-magic squares but was also the first to create a closed knight's tour semi-magic square on a 12×12 board. In this 12×12 square every row and column (though not the diagonals) adds to the same magic sum, and the knight completes the tour of the 144 squares one knight's move from 1. Complete the Rajah of Mysore's closed knight's tour semi-magic square. The circles are the locations for 1 and 144.

MS Puzzle 57: The Rajah of Mysore's Semi-Magic Square

	126	53	20	93			22	107	110	35	
54		92	125	52			123	34	37		111
127	90	17		121	96	23	50		106	39	36
18	55									112	105
	130	57				45			116	41	
		88			25	100			29		
		13			98	27			102		
	59	132			47				43	114	
83	12								◯	73	2
62	133	84		66	7	78	139		3	70	143
11		135	64	137			68	141	72	◯	74
	63	10	81	8			77	4	75	142	

The year 2003 was a big one for knight's tour magic square enthusiasts. Awani Kumar of Lucknow, India succeeded in creating the first 12×12 knight's tour magic square. It is magic, not just semi-magic because the main diagonals also sum to the magic sum. The tour, however, is an open tour since 1 and 144 are not one knight's move away. In the grid at right, the first 35 knight's moves are shown beginning with the white circle and the last 35 knight's moves are shown ending with the white square.

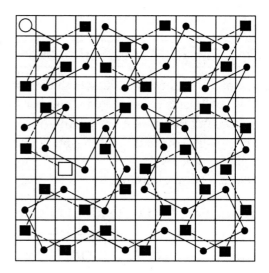

Complete Awani Kumar's 12×12 open knight's tour magic square in the blank 12×12 grid below.

MS Puzzle 58: Awani Kumar's 12x12 Knight's Tour Magic Square

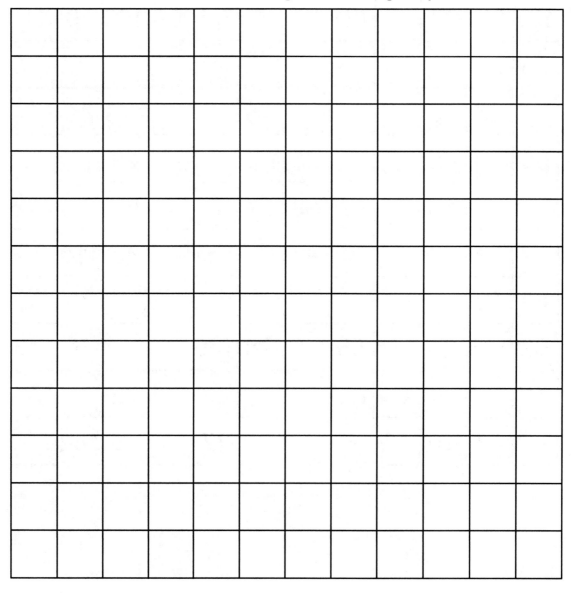

Chapter 6   Sequential Reasoning and Algebra

Only those who do nothing...make no mistakes.
—Joseph Conrad

An Introduction to Sequential Reasoning and Algebra

The first time I experienced algebra I was hooked: it was like playing games and solving puzzles. You play the game of algebra like the game of Clue® —you follow the rules of the game and use your reasoning skills to solve the mystery. The goal in algebra is, quite often, to find the unknown. Not only did I find algebra a delightfully organized way of thinking, but it was fun and exciting to solve puzzles and mysteries. How great is that!

One of the important uses of algebra is to solve complex problems that cannot be solved easily with arithmetic. To do this you need the primary skill of solving equations, and to solve equations you need sequential reasoning. It is, again, like being a detective and using logical clues to find that mysterious x. You are given some clues about the unknown, x, and you use the rules of algebra to determine what x represents. You need to get to the last statement that says x = something; you move one step at a time and reason sequentially.

With algebra, you can translate a pattern or relationship into a rule or equation. Once you have found a rule, you can use it to solve problems that might be difficult to solve directly. In this chapter you will find rules for a variety of relationships. These include, how the number of chirps made by a cricket depends on the temperature, the relationship between altitude and temperature, the relationship between altitude and the boiling point of water, and a rule for determining the cost of a speeding ticket.

The puzzles in this chapter try to capture the fun of puzzles while helping you learn and practice some algebra skills. In the first section, 6.1, Algebraic Magic Square Puzzles, you will need to be able to solve equations in one or two variables. In section 6.2, Squaring the Square Puzzles, you will need to be able to express lengths in terms of other lengths, make algebraic substitutions, and solve equations in one variable. Section 6.3, Number Chase Puzzles, calls on a wider range of algebra and math skills. In addition to solving equations in one, two, or three variables, you will need to recall order of operations, special products, and factoring. You will also need to be familiar with function notation and to find a linear function given a table of values. You will need to recall some basic geometry, such as perimeter and area formulas for rectangles, triangles, and trapezoids. If you need to review the basic properties of algebra, see Appendix 3.

6.1 Algebraic Magic Square Puzzles

2	9	4
7	5	3
6	1	8

In chapter 5, you solved magic square puzzles. If you recall, a magic square is a square array of distinct integers such that the numbers in any row, column, or main diagonal have the same sum, called the magic sum. If the n^2 numbers in an $n \times n$ magic square are the positive

48	9	6	39
15	30	33	24
27	18	21	36
12	45	42	3

integers 1 through n^2, then the magic square is a **normal** magic square. The 3×3 magic square at left uses the numbers 1 through 9 and, thus, is a normal 3×3 magic square. If the n^2 numbers in an $n \times n$ magic square are not the positive integers 1 through n^2, then the magic square is a **simple** magic square. The 4×4 magic square above uses the multiples of 3 from 3 through 48, so it is a simple 4×4 magic square.

An algebraic magic square is a magic square puzzle where letters have replaced some of the numbers. Let's look at an example of how you would solve an algebraic magic square.

Example

Solve the 4×4 simple magic square for x and y.

Solution

All the rows, columns, and both main diagonals have the same sum, called the magic sum. So we begin by adding the terms in a few rows. For example:

48	x/2	x/3	y
x–3	30	y–6	24
x+9	x	y–x	2x
x–6	y+6	y+3	x/6

Row 2: $x - 3 + 30 + y - 6 + 24$, which simplifies to $x + y + 45$.
Row 3: $x + 9 + x + y - x + 2x$, which simplifies to $3x + y + 9$.
Since the row sums are equal we set $x + y + 45 = 3x + y + 9$ and solve for x.
Subtract y from both sides, then subtract x from both sides, then subtract 9 from both sides. This leaves: $36 = 2x$ or $x = 18$. If $x = 18$ then the magic sum (from the first column) is $48 + 15 + 27 + 12 = 102$. Thus, from row 2: $x + y + 45 = 102$. Therefore $y = 39$.

Solve for x and y in the 3×3 algebraic magic square puzzles below.

AMS Puzzle 1 *h*

x+2	x	2x+3
3x–2	11	x–4
x–2	2x+1	2x–1

$x =$ _____

AMS Puzzle 2

3x–2	x–4	x
x–12	x+4	3x+2
2x–1	2x+3	1

$x =$ _____

AMS Puzzle 3

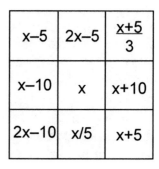

$x =$ _____

AMS Puzzle 4

x–y	y	24
x+6	2y–3	3
y–3	x	2y

$x =$ _____ $y =$ _____

AMS Puzzle 5

3y–x	x	y
x–6	2x	4x
15	2y	y–x

$x =$ _____ $y =$ _____

AMS Puzzle 6

x+y	8	-x
-4	x–6	x–2
x	y	y+10

$x =$ _____ $y =$ _____

Solve for x, y, and z in the 4×4 algebraic magic square puzzles below.

AMS Puzzle 7

1	x	2x–1	x+2
14	x+3	x/2	5
x+4	13	x–2	x–5
x–1	2	x+1	2x

$x =$ _____

AMS Puzzle 8

x+4	x/12	x	14
x–2	16	x+2	x/6
10	x–4	x/4	x+8
x/3	30	x/2	18

$x =$ _____

AMS Puzzle 9

45	x/4	x/2	x–6
x+12	x/3	3x/4	15
x/6	x+6	21	x–3
x/12	x+3	x	24

$x =$ _____

AMS Puzzle 10

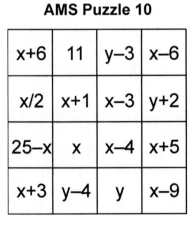

x+6	11	y–3	x–6
x/2	x+1	x–3	y+2
25–x	x	x–4	x+5
x+3	y–4	y	x–9

$x =$ ___, $y =$ ___

AMS Puzzle 11

x	18	2x	x+y
3x	y	2x+2	y–3
3x–1	y+1	17	x+1
y–2	2x+1	y–1	2y–2

$x =$ ___, $y =$ ___

AMS Puzzle 12

x/5	y+2	y	16
y/6	3x–2	y–x	y–2
3x+2	y/3	y–6	x
3x	y/4	y/2	2x

$x =$ ___, $y =$ ___

AMS Puzzle 13 $\hbar$

2–y	45	-7z	z
x+8	x	x–4	2x+3
-3y	2x–1	2x–5	yz
3x+2	y	y+4	41

$x =$___, $y =$___, $z =$ ___

AMS Puzzle 14

43	y–6	z	5y–1
x+3	4z	y+6	4y+3
y+3	4y	6z+1	x
y	2x–1	40	z–6

$x =$___, $y =$___, $z =$ ___

AMS Puzzle 15

2–z	2x+1	7z	2–x
z–2	4z+1	x+2	x–2
x	y	z	3y
23	-y	-z	2x–1

$x =$___, $y =$___, $z =$ ___

Solve for *w, x, y,* and *z* in the 5×5 algebraic magic square puzzles below.

AMS Puzzle 16

17	2x–1	16–x	x–2	11
2x	x–7	x/2	x	30–x
x/12	x–5	13	x+7	2x+1
x–4	x+2	2x–4	x+9	x/6
15	x+4	22	x/4	9

$x =$___

AMS Puzzle 17

10	y/8	25	x–1	18
y/4	17	2y+6	11–y	2x–3
x+1	x+y	13–y	2x–1	x–y
2y	2y–1	y–1	19	y
2x	x	x/2	y+1	14

$x =$___, $y =$___

AMS Puzzle 18

20	18–x	50	22	2x+4
x/4	2x+2	y+20	y/4	2y–6
y+2	40	26–x	4x–2	y/3
2x	30	x–2	38	x
3x	y	y/2	y–6	y+4

$x =$___, $y =$___

AMS Puzzle 19

2y	8	4	21	6x
9	3y–2	26–x	x	11
6	y	x+2	3y+1	25
12	2y+1	3y–1	6x–1	1
3y+x	16	13	2	x+y

$x =$___, $y =$___

AMS Puzzle 20 $\hbar$

15				y+2
	x		y–2	y/2
		y+3x	x+3	4+y
	20–y	y+6x	2y–9	x+10
y	2y–3	5x	y–6x	y–x

$x =$___, $y =$___

AMS Puzzle 21

2x–1	3x	4x+1	x/3	y+2
x+4	2x	z–2	z	x/2
x–2	x	13	z–1	z+1
z+2	x–1	y	2y	z–5
z–4	4x	y–x	y+1	2y+1

$x =$___, $y =$___, $z =$ ___

AMS Puzzle 22

y+1	2y+1	y−1	4y+1	z−2
z−y	z	z−1	z+1	y/2
2x−1	4y	14	y	x/5
2x	x	x−1	y−2	4y−2
x−2	y−5	2x+1	2y	4y−1

$x =$ ___, $y =$ ___, $z =$ ___

AMS Puzzle 23

13			14	2z−1
	20		y/4	y
		y/3	y+2	z−4
19	y−6	z−1	2z	z
2x−3	x	z−2	x−3	x+2

$x =$ ___, $y =$ ___, $z =$ ___

AMS Puzzle 24

22	2z	2z−1	y	2w+2
y+1	x+11	3z−1	x−1	w−2
x	y+3	y−3	43−w	2w−2
3y−1	2w−1	x+1	w	z−1
x−4	z	3y	w+z	20

$w =$ ___, $x =$ ___, $y =$ ___, $z =$ ___

6.2   Squaring the Square Puzzles

The phrase "squaring the square" is probably a play on the mathematical expression "squaring the circle."[14] The problem of squaring the square asks: Can you dissect a square into smaller non-congruent squares?

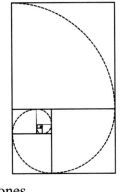

Any rectangle with rational sides can be dissected into congruent squares.[15] What if only two squares are congruent and all other squares are non-congruent? Yes, it is also possible to assemble squares into a rectangle in which at most two squares are congruent. The rectangle shown on the right is an approximation to the **Golden Rectangle**.[16] It begins with two congruent squares and then non-congruent squares are added. The steps in the construction are shown below. Notice that these rectangles are composed of non-congruent squares, except for the initial pair of congruent ones.

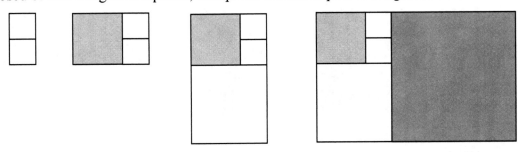

W.T. Tutte[17], A.H. Stone, R.L. Brooks, and C.A.B. Smith were four students of Trinity College in Cambridge, England from the years 1936–1938. They called themselves "important members of the Trinity Mathematical Society." They came across a puzzle by H.E. Dudeney that suggested it was impossible to dissect a square into non-congruent smaller squares. They studied this problem together and published their results in a paper titled, *The Dissection of Rectangles into Squares.* Included in their research was Stone's discovery of the dissection of a rectangle with sides 176 by 177 into 11 unequal squares (see SS Puzzle 4). The puzzles in this section are called "squared square puzzles" (even though most are non-congruent squares in rectangles) in honor of the name used by the original four mathematical researchers.

SS Puzzle 1 *h* In 1946, British mathematician T.H. Willcocks created the dissection shown at right. This is an order nine rectangle because it is composed of nine non-congruent squares. Order nine is the smallest order possible. The smallest square Y has an edge of one unit. The square X has an edge of four units. Find the dimensions of all the squares and the dimensions of the rectangle.

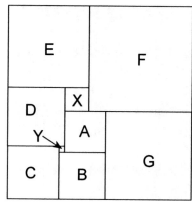

Squared Square Puzzle 2 is a 61×69 rectangle dissected into nine squares. Find the dimensions of all nine squares.

Squared Square Puzzle 3 is a 47×65 rectangle dissected into ten squares. Square Y has an edge of five units. Find the dimensions of the other nine squares.

SS Puzzle 2

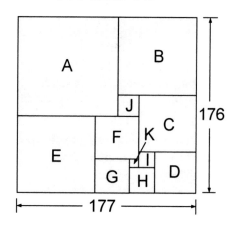

SS Puzzle 3

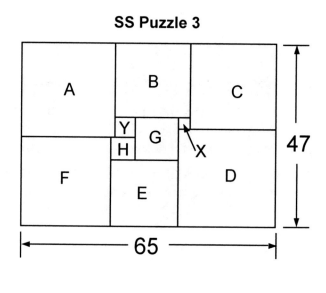

Squared Square Puzzle 4 is a 176×177 rectangle dissected into 11 squares. Find the dimensions of all 11 squares.

Squared Square Puzzle 5 is a rectangle dissected into 13 squares. Square A has an edge of 39, square D has an edge of 33 units, and square H has an edge of 20 units. Find the dimensions of the other ten squares and the dimensions of the entire rectangle.

SS Puzzle 4 *h*

SS Puzzle 5

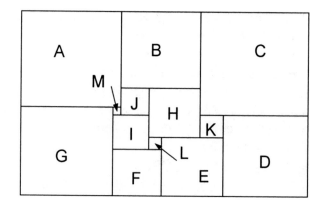

Squared Square Puzzle 6 is a 94×111 rectangle dissected into 13 squares. Find the dimensions of all 13 squares.

Squared squares and squared rectangles are called compound if they contain a smaller squared square or rectangle. If they do not, they are called simple squared squares or rectangles.

In Squared Square Puzzle 7, you finally have a square (175×175) dissected into 24 squares. T. H. Willcocks found this squared square in 1946. It is the smallest order (24 squares) **compound squared square**. Find the remaining 11 squares, A through K.

SS Puzzle 6

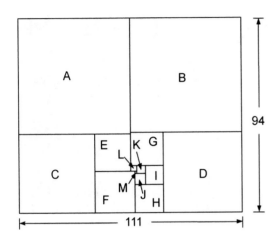

SS Puzzle 7

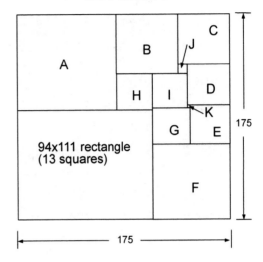

SS Puzzle 8 *h*

In 1978, Dutch mathematician A. Duijvestijn, found the figure shown in Squared Square Puzzle 8 after running a computer program through the night. It is 21 squares arranged into a square, with a measurement of 112 units on each edge. This is the squared square with the fewest number of squares known (order 21).

Square G has an edge of 42 units and square T has an edge of four units. Find the dimensions of the remaining 19 squares.

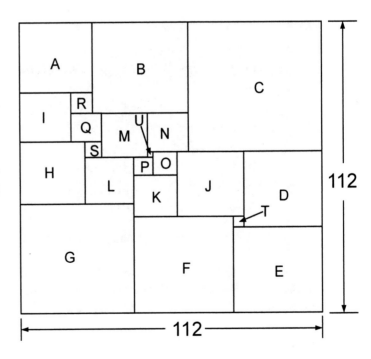

6.3   Number Chase Puzzles

In Number Chase puzzles the task is to solve the algebra problems and then use those values to complete the puzzle. Let's look at a few examples.

Example A

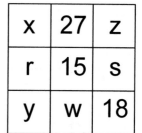

Solve the three equations below for A, B, and C. Then place their values into the 3×3 square at right. Find values for the remaining squares to complete a simple magic square. (Simple doesn't mean easy—see Chapter 5 for the difference between simple and normal magic squares.)

$$A + 5 = 23 \qquad 3B - 11 = 70 \qquad 5(C + 3) - C = 3C + 30$$

Solution

Step 1: Solve the first equation: $A + 5 = 23$
Subtract 5 from both sides: $A = 18$

Step 2: Solve the second equation: $3B - 11 = 70$
Add 11 to both sides: $3B = 81$
Divide both sides by 3: $B = 27$

Step 3: Solve the third equation: $5(C + 3) - C = 3C + 30$
Subtract $3C$ from both sides: $5(C + 3) - 4C = 30$
Clear the parentheses (using the distributive property): $5C + 15 - 4C = 30$
Combine like terms: $C + 15 = 30$
Subtract 15 from both sides: $C = 15$

Step 4: Place $A = 18$, $B = 27$, and $C = 15$ into the square.

Step 5: In a magic square, every row, column, and main diagonal has the same sum. Set column 2 equal to row 3:
$w + 27 + 15 = w + y + 18$. Solving for y, you get $y = 24$.

Step 6: Set the bottom-left to top-right diagonal equal to row 1:
$24 + 15 + z = x + 27 + z$. Solving for x, you get $x = 12$.

Step 7: This completes the other diagonal, so the magic sum is $12 + 15 + 18 = 45$.
Solving for w, z, r, and s, you get $w = 3$, $z = 6$, $r = 9$, and $s = 21$.

x	27	z
r	15	s
y	w	18

12	27	6
9	15	21
24	3	18

Example B

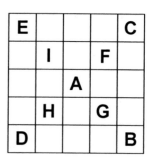

Calculate the values of the nine expressions below, then place them in the grid at right. Fill in the remaining squares to complete a rook's tour: a path that can be traveled by a rook (moving only horizontally or vertically) from 1 to 25.

$A = 6^2 - 5^2$ $B = 11^2 - 10^2$
$C = 8^2 - 7^2$ $D = 4^2 - 3^2$
$E = (8^2 - 7^2) - (6.5^2 - 5.5^2)$ $F = 9^2 - 8^2$
$G = 3^2 + 2(3)(2) + 2^2$ $H = 7^2 - 2(7)(4) + 4^2$
$I = 6^2 - 2(6)(5) + 5^2$

Solution

You could do each of these calculations the long way, but there are some neat shortcuts that might ring an algebraic "bell." Each of these expressions can be written as a **special product**. One special product is the difference of squares, which, when stated algebraically, says:

$$x^2 - y^2 = (x + y)(x - y)$$

Applying this rule to expression A gives $A = 6^2 - 5^2 = (6 + 5)(6 - 5) = (11)(1) = 11$. Since the squared numbers differ by one, the second factor is 1 and the answer is just the sum of the numbers. This shortcut works for all expressions A–F above.

Another type of special product is the perfect square trinomial:

$$a^2 + 2ab + b^2 = (a + b)^2, \text{ or } a^2 - 2ab + b^2 = (a - b)^2$$

So in expression G, $G = 3^2 + 2(3)(2) + 2^2 = (3 + 2)^2 = 25$.

And $H = 7^2 - 2(7)(4) + 4^2 = (7 - 4)^2 = 9$.

With these shortcuts in mind, here are the steps for solving the puzzle:

Step 1: Find the values A–I and place them in the grid, as shown at right.

3				15
	1		17	
		11		
	9		25	
7				21

$A = 11$ $B = 21$ $C = 15$
$D = 7$ $E = 3$ $F = 17$
$G = 25$ $H = 9$ $I = 1$

Step 2: There is only one option for a rook's path between 3 and 7, so the first column is 3, 4, 5, 6, 7.

Step 3: The numbers 2, 8, and 10 in the second column are forced, so the second column is 2, 1, 10, 9, and 8.

Step 4: You need to get from 11 up to 15. If you try going to the right and up you block the path from 17 to 21. So the route from 11 to 15 must be up, then right.

Step 5: The rest is forced. The completed rook's tour is shown at right.

3	2	13	14	15
4	1	12	17	16
5	10	11	18	19
6	9	24	25	20
7	8	23	22	21

Example C

Solve each pair of equations below and place the solutions in the grid at right. Fill in the remaining squares to complete a knight's tour: a path that can be traveled by a knight (moving in an L) from 1 to 25.

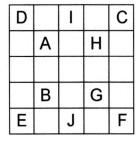

1. $A + B = 34$
   $B - A = 4$

2. $2C + 3D = 19$
   $2D - C = 1$

3. $4E + 3 = F$
   $5E + F = 12$

4. $G - H = 12$
   $G - 2H = 1$

5. $2I - 3J = 3$
   $2J - I = 5$

Solution

For the first pair of equations, add to get $2B = 38$ or $B = 19$, substitue to get $A = 15$. In the second pair of equations, solve for C to get $C = 2D - 1$ and substitute $2D - 1$ for C to find D. In the third pair, substitute $4E + 3$ for F into the second equaton and solve for E. In the fourth set, subtract to get $H = 11$. In the last set of equations, solve for I ($I = 2J - 5$) then substitute into the other equation and solve for J. Solving the five pairs of equations gives us $(A, B) = (15, 19)$, $(C, D) = (5, 3)$, $(E, F) = (1, 7)$, $(G, H) = (23, 11)$, and $(I, J) = (21, 13)$. This forces $w = 2$, $x = 4$, $y = 6$, and $z = 8$. The only possible sequence of knight's moves from 8 to 11 is 8 to u to v to 11, so $u = 9$ and $v = 10$. The remaining positions are forced: $20 = m$, $22 = n$, $24 = p$, $25 = q$, $12 = r$, $14 = s$, $16 = t$, $17 = j$, and $18 = k$.

3	v	21	t	5
m	15	x	11	n
u	w	q	y	j
s	19	z	23	r
1	p	13	k	7

3	10	21	16	5
20	15	4	11	22
9	2	25	6	17
14	19	8	23	12
1	24	13	18	7

Try your hand at these Number Chase puzzles.

NC Puzzle 1: Solving Equations in One Variable

Solve these equations for A–E, then place the values into the 3×3 square at right. Find values for the remaining squares to complete a simple magic square.

1. $3A + 17 = 2(5 - A) - 18$

2. $2(3B - 4) + 3(3B - 4) = 5(4 + 2B) + 15$

3. $(3/4)(C - 7) - (1/4)(C - 7) = 2(C - 7)$

4. $2D - (1/2)(D - 4) = (1/2)(D - 4) + 3$

5. $7(E - 2) + 5(2 - E) = (1/3)(E + 13)$

E	C	
A		B
	D	

NC Puzzle 2: Solving Equations in One Variable

Solve these equations for A–J, then place the values into the 4×4 square below. Find values for the remaining squares to complete a simple magic square.

1. $3A - 7(3 - A) = 4(2A - 1) - 3$

2. $6(2 - 3B) + 3(3B - 2) = 1 - (31 + 7B)$

3. $5(2 - C) + 15 = C + 1$

4. $1/(D - 7) + ½ = 1 - 1/(D - 7)$

5. $2E - 7 - 3(7 - 2E) = 4(E + 6)$

6. $(2/3)(2F - 5) + (1/3)(2F - 5) = 19$

7. $4(G - 7) + 6(G - 7) = 2(4G - 25)$

8. $(1/4)(H - 3) + (1/2)(H - 3) = (3/4)(3H - 35)$

9. $1/(J - 9) + 9/10 = 1$

A		F	J
		G	
B	E		
C	D		H

NC Puzzle 3: Solving Equations in Two Variables

Solve each pair of equations and place the solutions in the grid below. Fill in the remaining squares to complete a 5×5 normal magic square. (A **normal** 5×5 magic square uses the numbers 1–25 and the magic sum is 65.)

1. $A + B = 37$
$\quad B - A = 9$

2. $2C + 3D = 62$
$\quad 2D - C = 4$

3. $4E + 7 = F$
$\quad 5E + F = 25$

4. $9G - H = 1$
$\quad 5G - H = -3$

5. $2J - 3K = 20$
$\quad 2K - J = -7$

6. $2L - M = 16$
$\quad M - L = -16$

7. $N - 6P = 3$
$\quad N + P = 24$

		J		H
A	K	P		
B	L			G
	M	N		F
C		D	E	

NC Puzzle 4: Solving Equations in Two Variables

Solve each pair of equations, then place the solutions in the grid at right. Fill in the remaining squares to complete a 6×6 rook's tour: a path that can be traveled moving only horizontally or vertically, from 1 to 36.

1. $A + B = 47$
$\quad B - A = 5$

2. $2C + 3D = 161$
$\quad 2D - C = 42$

3. $E - F = 4$
$\quad 2F - E = 10$

4. $9G - H = 2$
$\quad 5G - H = -2$

A			E		
		D			
B				F	H
				G	
C					

NC Puzzle 5: Order of Operations and Special Products

Use special products and the order of operations to calculate the 15 expressions below, then place them in the grid. Fill in the remaining squares to complete a rook's tour: a path (moving only horizontally or vertically) from 1 to 49. The circles indicate the start and end of the path.

$A = 4^2 - 3^2$

$B = 17 - 7 \div 14 \cdot 4 - 9 \div 3$

$C = 16^2 - 2(16)(12) + 12^2$

$D = 7 - 6 \cdot 4 + 5 \cdot 3 + 20$

$E = 7.5^2 - 2(7.5)(4.5) + 4.5^2$

$F = (4^2 - 3^2) - 2^2 \cdot 1^2$

$G = 3^2 + 2(3)(2) + 2^2 - 9 \div 3$

$H = 5^2 + 2(5)(2) + 2^2 - 16 \div 8$

$J = (2.5)[1^2 + 2(1)(3) + 3^2]$

$K = 16^2 - 15^2$

$L = 15^2 - 14^2$

$M = (4\frac{1}{4} + 1\frac{3}{4})^2 + 2$

$N = (4\frac{1}{3})^2 + 2(4\frac{1}{3})(1\frac{2}{3}) + (1\frac{2}{3})^2$

$P = (18^2 - 16^2) \div 2$

$Q = 2.7^2 + 2(2.7)(2.3) + 2.3^2$

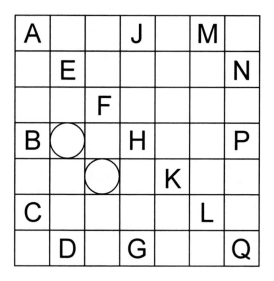

NC Puzzle 6: Properties of Exponents

Calculate the nine expressions below, then place them in the grid. Fill in the remaining squares to complete a king's tour: a path moving horizontally, vertically, or diagonally, from 1 to 25. The circles indicate the start and end of the path.

$A = 2^4 + 5^0$

$B = 5^2 - 2^2$

$C = 7^2 - 6^2 + 3^2$

$D = (13^2 - 5^2)/(4^2 - 2^2)$

$E = (17^2 - 8^2)/(3^2 + 6)$

$F = (3^7 \cdot 2^4 \cdot 4^2)/(3^6 \cdot 4^4)$

$G = (4^6 \cdot 9^3 \cdot 2^2)/(12^6)$

$H = (100^2 \cdot 2^8 \cdot 9^2)/(12^4 \cdot 10^3)$

$K = (16^2)/(4^2 \cdot 2^3) + 5$

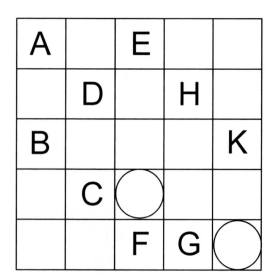

NC Puzzle 7 h : Area and Perimeter

Solve these problems to find the values $A-L$, then place them in the grid below. Fill in the remaining squares using the knight's L-move from 1 to 25 to complete a knight's tour.

1. A rectangle has an area of 56 m^2 and a perimeter of 36 m. Find the length, A, and the width, B. (The width is less than the length.)

2. A rectangle has a length that is 15 cm greater than the width. The perimeter is 62 cm. Find the length, C, and the width, D.

3. The perimeter of a right triangle is 36 cm. The shortest leg is 9 cm. The area of the triangle is 54 cm^2. Find the length of the hypotenuse, E, and the length of the third side, F.

4. The perimeter of a triangle is 57 m. The three sides are consecutive integers. Find the length of the shortest side, G, and the length of the longest side, H.

5. Three sides of a quadrilateral are consecutive odd numbers and the fourth side is 6 cm. The perimeter is 21 cm. The length of the shortest side is I, and J is the length of the longest side.

6. The perimeter of an isosceles trapezoid is 26 m. The height is 4 m and the area is 32 m^2. The three smallest sides are the same length. The larger base has length K, and $L = 2K$.

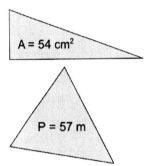

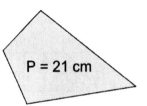

I	H		A	
	E			L
	B		D	
	K		C	G
			F	J

NC Puzzle 8 *h*: Linear Functions

Solve the exercises below to find *A–N,* and *P*, and place the values in the grid. Fill in the remaining squares to complete the king's tour: a path moving horizontally, vertically, or diagonally, from 1 to 36. The circles indicate the start and end of the path.

1. If $f(x) = 13 - x$, then $f(4) = A$.

2. If $f(x) = 3x - 12$, then $f(6) = B$.

3. If $f(x) = 27 - 5x$, then $f(5) = C$.

4. If $f(x) = (1/2)x + 1$, then $f(18) = D$.

5. If $f(x) = (3/4)x - 2$, then $f(20) = E$.

6. If $f(x) = 118 - 6x$, then $f(17) = F$.

7. If $f(x) = 25 - (1/2)x$, and $f(G) = 14$, find G.

8. If $f(x) = 100 - 2x$, and $f(H) = 50$, find H.

9. If $f(x) = (3/4)x + 21$, and $f(I) = 36$, find I.

10. If $f(x) = 3x + 58$, and $f(J) = 100$, find J.

11. $f(x)$ is a linear function, find K if $f(11) = K$.

x	0	1	2	3	4	......	11	...
$f(x)$	4	6	8	10	12	......	K	...

12. $f(x)$ is a linear function, find L if $f(24) = L$.

x	0	1	2	3	4	...	24	...
$f(x)$	125	121	117	113	109	...	L	...

13. If $f(x)$ is a linear function, find M if $f(M) = 347$.

x	0	1	2	3	4	...	M	...
$f(x)$	17	28	39	50	61	...	347	...

14. If $f(x)$ is a linear function, find N if $f(N) = -138$.

x	0	1	2	3	4	...	N	...
$f(x)$	2	-2	-6	-10	-14	...	-138	...

15. If $f(x)$ is a linear function, find P if $f(18) = P$.

x	0	1	2	3	4	...	18	...
$f(x)$	-94	-87	-80	-73	-66	...	P	...

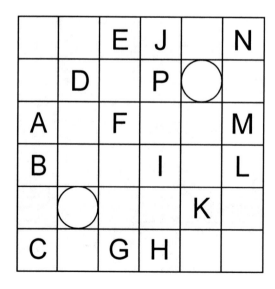

NC Puzzle 9 *h*: Linear Functions

Solve these problems to find the values *A–J*, then place them in the grid at right. Fill in the remaining squares using the knight's L-move from 1 to 25 to complete a knight's tour.

F			A	
B		E		J
H	G			
D	C		I	

1. One rule of thumb for estimating the surface area of your body is to multiply the surface area of the palm of your hand by 100. If the surface area of Michael's body is 1100 square inches, let *C* equal the approximate number of square inches on his palm. If the surface area of Angie's body is 600 square inches, let *D* equal the approximate number of square inches on her palm.

2. Handicap bowling leagues award extra points to a player's game score if the player has a low average (below 200). To calculate a handicap for a low-average player in one league, you take 80% of the difference between 200 and the player's average. Let *A* equal the handicap for a player with a low average of 190. In another bowling league the formula is handicap = 0.75(200 − player's average). Let *B* equal the handicap for a person in this league, with an average of 184.

3. A well-known rule for estimating how many miles you are from a thunderstorm is to count the seconds between the lightning and thunder and divide them by five. Let *E* equal the distance, in miles, you are from a thunderstorm if you count 10 seconds between the thunder and lightning. Let *F* equal the distance, in miles, you are from a thunderstorm if you count 5 seconds between the lightning and thunder.

4. For every 550 feet in elevation, the boiling point of water falls by one degree Fahrenheit. Suppose you are standing at an elevation of 12,100 feet. Let *G* equal the number of degrees that the boiling temperature has dropped, at that elevation, from the sea-level temperature of 212°F. If you are standing at an elevation of 9,350 feet, then let *H* equal the number of degrees that the boiling temperature has dropped from the same sea level temperature.

5. If a weight is hung from one end of a spring, the length of the spring is a function of the weight. The equation for a particular spring is $L(w) = 0.4w + 15$, where w is the weight in grams and $L(w)$ is the length of the spring in cm. Let *I* equal the length of the spring when a weight of 10 grams is hung from it. Let *J* equal the weight in grams that causes the spring to stretch to 23 cm.

NC Puzzle 10 *h*: Linear Functions

Solve the problems to find the values *A–N* and *P,* then place them in the grid at right. Fill in the remaining squares to complete a normal magic square.

	M	A	B	D
	I		L	
G			F	
H		N		J
	K	E	C	P

1. A general rule says a hospital should have four beds for every thousand people in its community. If a community has 5,500 people, let *A* equal the number of beds the hospital should have. If a community has 4,000 people, let *B* equal the number of beds that hospital should have.

2. An architectural rule states a well-planned office building should be able to accommodate one person for every 225 square feet of floor space. If an office has 5,175 square feet of floor space, let *C* equal the number of employees the building should be able to accommodate. If an office has 3,375 square feet of floor space, let *D* equal the number of employees that the building should be able to accommodate.

3. The speed of an ant varies with the temperature and according to the formula $S(t) = (1/6)(t - 4)$, where $S(t)$ is the speed of the ant in centimeters per second, and *t* is temperature in degrees Celsius. Let *E* equal the speed of an ant at 28°C, or as an equation, $E = S(28)$. Let *F* equal the temperature in degrees Celsius when an ant is moving with a speed of 0.5 cm/sec, in other words, find *F* when $(1/6)(F - 4) = 0.5$.

4. Male crickets chirp at different rates depending on their species and the temperature of their environment. The higher the temperature, the faster the rate at which the male crickets will chirp. The relationship between temperature and the rate of chirping is known as *Dolbear's Law*. For example, the temperature, in degrees Fahrenheit, can be calculated for a common species, the Snowy Tree cricket, by adding 40 to the number of chirps produced in 14 seconds. If the temperature is 65°F, then let *G* equal the number of chirps produced in 14 seconds by the Snowy Tree cricket. If the temperature is 76°F, then let *H* equal the number of chirps produced in 7 seconds by the Snowy Tree cricket.

5. Smallville gives speeding tickets according to the following formula: amount of ticket = $50 + $15 for each mph over the speed limit. If Isabella got a ticket for $365, let *I* equal the number of miles per hour that she went over the speed limit. If Jose got a ticket for $410, let *J* equal the number of miles per hour that he went over the speed limit.

6. Fahrenheit and Celsius are related by the linear function $F = (9/5)C + 32$. If it is a cool 50° F, then let K equal the temperature in degrees Celsius. If it is a very cold -10° C then let L equal the temperature in degrees Fahrenheit.

7. There is a linear relationship between an airplane's altitude in meters and the air temperature outside the plane. The temperature drops 6° C for every 1000 meters. If we assume the average temperature at sea level is approximately 15° C then let M equal the air temperature outside a plane at an elevation of 2000 meters. If the temperature outside the plane is -21°C, let N equal the elevation measured in kilometers.

8. Maxine has a workout routine that includes jogging to the gym, which burns 315 calories, and working out on the elliptical trainer, which burns calories at the rate of 5 calories/minute. If she wishes to burn at least 400 calories, let P equal the minimum number of minutes Maxine needs to work out on the elliptical trainer.

NC Puzzle 11: Solving Equations in Three Variables

Solve for the three variables in each set of equations and then place the values in the grid below. Fill in the remaining squares to complete a knight's tour: a path that can be traveled by a knight (moving in an L-shape) visiting each square, from 1 to 49.

1. $A + B + C = 82$
$2A + B = 58$
$B + C = 58$

2. $D - E + F = 6$
$2D - E = 23$
$E + F = 2D - 8$

3. $G + 2H + 3I = 29$
$2H - G = 1$
$G - H + I = 7$

4. $4J + L + 1 = K$
$2L - K - 11 = J$
$K - L = 5$

5. $P - N + 11 = M$
$2M - P = 10$
$2N - P = M - 7$

6. $V - 6U = 10$
$U + V - Q = 1$
$Q + V + 1 = 18U$
$Z = Q - 1$

7. $W + Y = 88$
$Y - X = 1$
$2X - Y = W + 2$

		M	Z		P	L
N	Q					H
	B					
		D	J	Y		V
G	C	X				F
K		I		A	E	U
			W			

NC Puzzle 12 h: Distance = Rate × Time

Solve for *A–L*. Then place the values in the grid at right. Fill in the remaining squares to complete a knight's tour: a path that can be traveled by a knight (moving in an L-shape) visiting each square, from 1 to 36. The squares containing circles indicate the location of the 1 and 36.

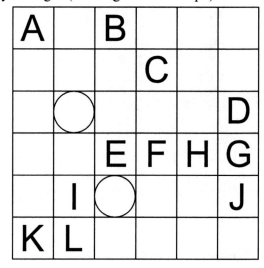

1. Matt and Easton begin biking towards each other at noon. Matt's average speed is 3.75 mph and Easton's speed is 1.25 mph faster. They meet at 4 pm. Let *A* equal the distance apart at noon. Let *B* equal Easton's speed.

2. Diane leaves the stable on horseback at 9 am. John leaves the stable at 10:25 am. on his dirt bike in an effort to catch Diane. At 11:15 he finally catches up to her, 22.5 miles from the stable. Let *C* equal John's speed on the dirt bike and *D* equal Diane's speed on horseback.

3. Zack leaves Angie and begins walking due west. One hour later, Angie begins walking due east. Angie walks one mile per hour slower than Zack. When Zack has walked for four hours and Angie for three hours, they are 25 miles apart. Zack has walked seven miles more than Angie. Let *E* equal the number of miles Zack walked and let *F* equal the number of miles Angie walked. Let *G* equal the rate at which they were walking away from each other, once they both started walking.

4. Amber works at a nature preserve in South Africa and recorded a race between her elephant and giraffe. From the same starting point, and with both running in the same direction for 15 minutes, the giraffe covered 2.5 more miles than the elephant. When they ran in opposite directions from the same starting point, for 15 minutes, they ended up 13.5 miles apart. Let *H* equal the speed of the elephant and *I* equal the speed of the giraffe. Let *J* equal their distance apart if it was possible for them to run in the same direction for 3 hours.

5. The Greatyear Blimp took 51 minutes to travel from point A to point B with a tail wind, and 63 minutes to travel from point B back to point A with the same wind, now a headwind. The airspeed of the blimp is 17 miles per hour faster than the speed of the wind. Let *K* equal the speed of the wind in miles per hour and let *L* equal the speed of the blimp in miles per hour, without any wind.

Chapter 7   Sequential Reasoning and Geometry

When people say, "It can't be done," or "You don't have what it takes,"
it makes the task all the more interesting.
–Lynn Hill

While algebra is a language using symbols to generalize the logical rules of arithmetic, geometry is more about using visual thinking in combination with logical reasoning. To a great extent, both rely on sequential reasoning.

Here is an example of the reasoning used in geometry.

Example

Given: A, B, and C are collinear.
$\triangle ABE$ is isosceles with AB = BE.
$\triangle BCD$ is equilateral.
$m\angle BAE = 63°$
Find the measure x of $\angle DBE$.

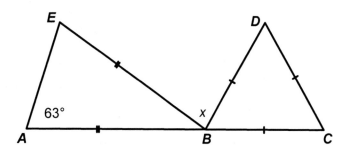

Solution

Since $\triangle BCD$ is equilateral, each angle measures 60°. Therefore $m\angle DBC = 60°$. Since $\triangle ABE$ is isosceles, the two base angles $\angle BAE$ and $\angle BEA$, are congruent. Therefore $m\angle BEA = 63°$. The measures of the three angles of a triangle add to 180°, so 63° + 63° + $m\angle ABE = 180°$. Hence, $m\angle ABE = 54°$. Because A, B, and C are collinear, $m\angle ABE + m\angle EBD + m\angle DBC = 180°$. Therefore, 54° + x + 60° = 180°. Hence, x = 66°.

If you need to review the basic properties of geometry before continuing, see Appendix 4.

7.1   Angle Chase Puzzles

Angle Chase puzzles are diagrams with some given and some unknown angle measures, labeled with letters. You will use geometric relationships, given in the figure, and your sequential reasoning skills to find the unknown angle measures. In most cases you will need to determine some of the unlabeled angle measures in order to find the labeled angle measures.

There is no need for a protractor. In fact, using a protractor will almost guarantee that your answers will be incorrect because the diagrams are purposely not drawn to scale. These puzzles are all about reasoning, not measurement.

The following Angle Chase puzzles can be worked individually but are best worked with a partner. If you have a partner, take turns finding the measures of the labeled angles. Take turns with one person finding an angle's measure and the other explaining how it was done. Then switch roles.

AC Puzzle 1.1 *h*: Vertical Angles, Linear Pair, and Parallel Lines

Given: $l_1 \parallel l_2 \parallel l_3 \parallel l_4$.

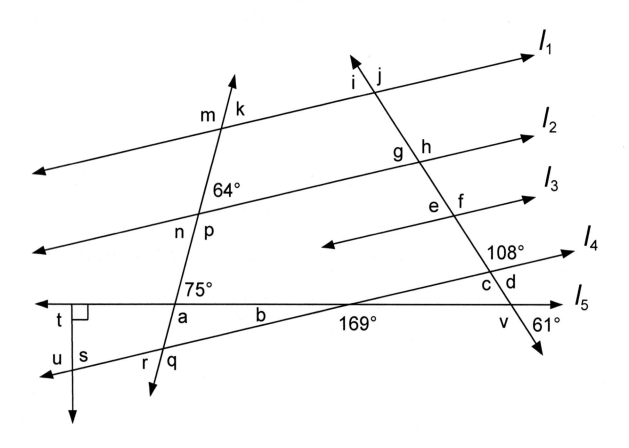

a	b	c	d	e	f	g	h	i	j

k	m	n	p	q	r	s	t	u	v

AC Puzzle 1.2: Vertical Angles, Linear Pair, and Parallel Lines

Given: l_1 // l_2 // l_3 // l_4.

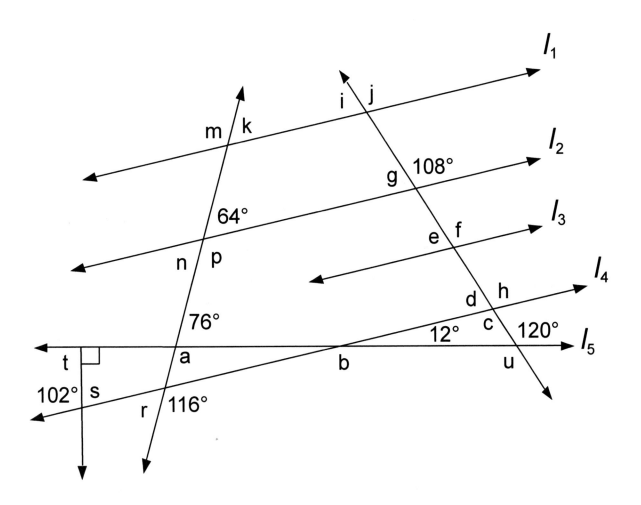

a	b	c	d	e	f	g	h	i

j	k	m	n	p	r	s	t	u

AC Puzzle 2.1: Parallel Lines, Triangle Sum, and Isosceles Triangles

Given: $l_1 \, /\!/ \, l_2$, $l_3 \, /\!/ \, l_4$.

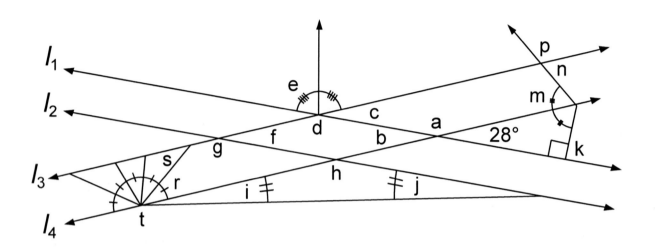

a	b	c	d	e	f	g	h	i

j	k	m	n	p	r	s	t

AC Puzzle 2.2: Parallel Lines, Triangle Sum, and Isosceles Triangles

Given: $l_1 \,/\!/\, l_2$, $l_3 \,/\!/\, l_4$.

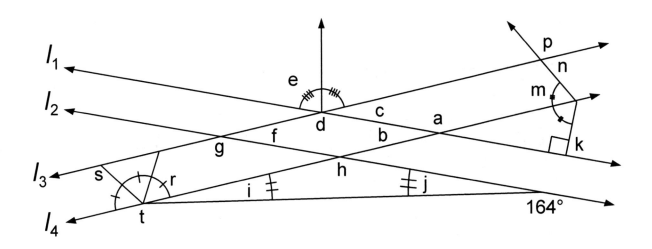

a	b	c	d	e	f	g	h	i

j	k	m	n	p	r	s	t

AC Puzzle 3.1 *h*: Parallel Lines, Triangle Sum, and Isosceles Triangles

Given: $l_1 \mathbin{/\mkern-3mu/} l_2,\ l_3 \mathbin{/\mkern-3mu/} l_4.$

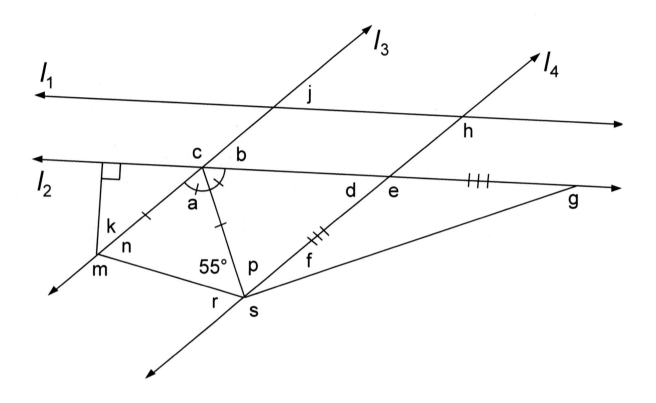

a	b	c	d	e	f	g	h

j	k	m	n	p	r	s	

AC Puzzle 3.2: Parallel Lines, Triangle Sum, and Isosceles Triangles

Given: $l_1 \parallel l_2$, $l_3 \parallel l_4$.

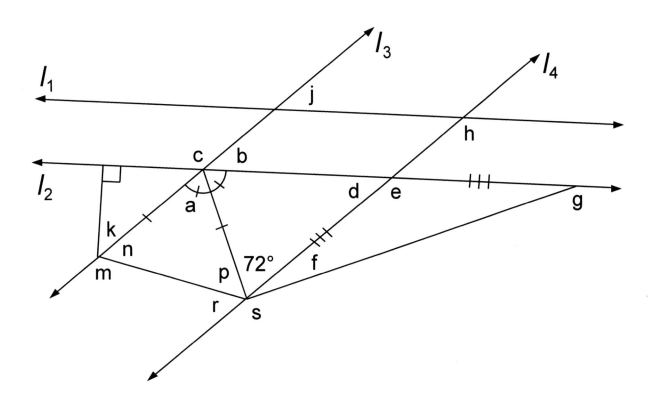

a	b	c	d	e	f	g	h

j	k	m	n	p	r	s

AC Puzzle 4.1: Parallel Lines, Triangle Sum, and Isosceles Triangles

Given: $l_1 \parallel l_2$, $l_3 \parallel l_4$.

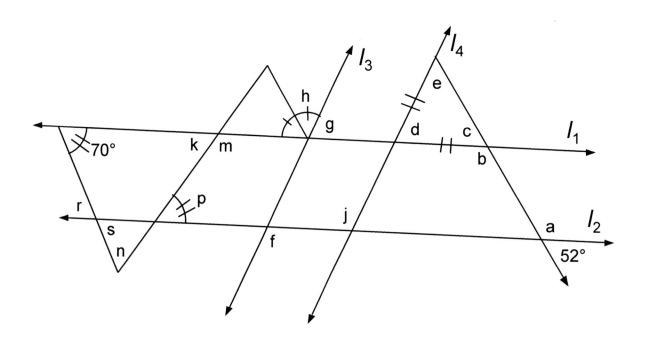

a	b	c	d	e	f	g	h

j	k	m	n	p	r	s

AC Puzzle 4.2: Parallel Lines, Triangle Sum, and Isosceles Triangles

Given: $l_1 \ // \ l_2, \ l_3 \ // \ l_4.$

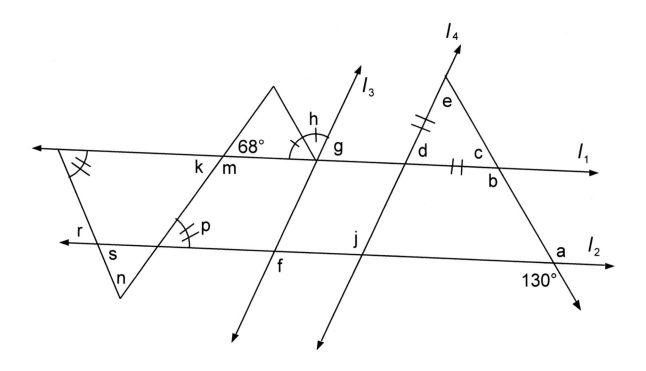

a	b	c	d	e	f	g	h

j	k	m	n	p	r	s

AC Puzzle 5.1: Parallel Lines, Polygon Sum, and Isosceles Triangles

Given: $l_1 \parallel l_2 \parallel l_3$.

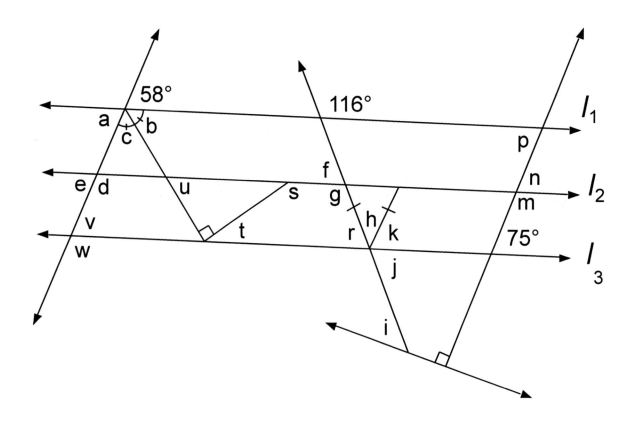

a	b	c	d	e	f	g	h	i	j

k	m	n	p	r	s	t	u	v	w

AC Puzzle 5.2: Parallel Lines, Polygon Sum, and Isosceles Triangles

Given: l_1 // l_2 // l_3.

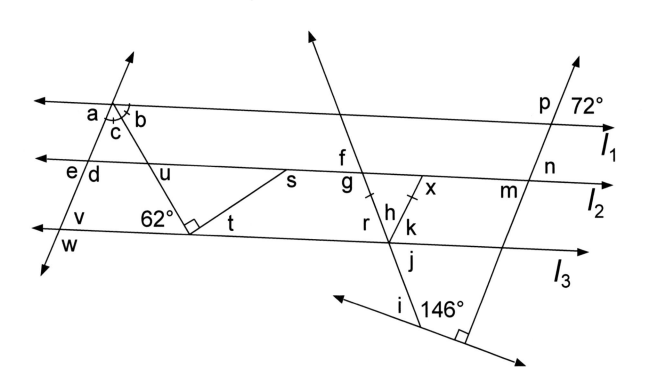

a	b	c	d	e	f	g
h	**i**	**j**	**k**	**m**	**n**	**p**
r	**s**	**t**	**u**	**v**	**w**	**x**

AC Puzzle 6.1: Parallel Lines, Polygon Sum, and Isosceles Triangles
Given: $l_1 \parallel l_2$, $l_3 \parallel l_4$.

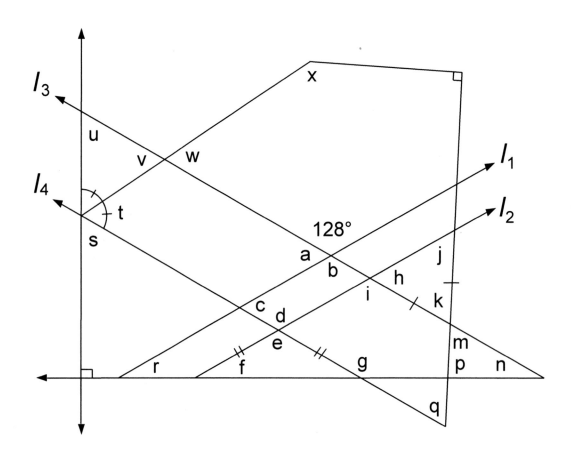

a	b	c	d	e	f	g	h

i	j	k	m	n	p	q	r

s	t	u	v	w	x

AC Puzzle 6.2: Parallel Lines, Polygon Sum, and Isosceles Triangles

Given: $l_1 \,//\, l_2$, $l_3 \,//\, l_4$.

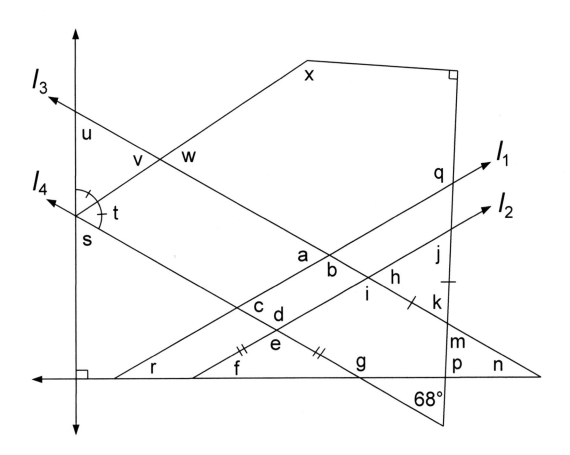

a	b	c	d	e	f	g	h

i	j	k	m	n	p	q	r

s	t	u	v	w	x

AC Puzzle 7.1: Parallel Lines, Polygon Sum, and Isosceles Triangles

Given: $l_1 \parallel l_2$.

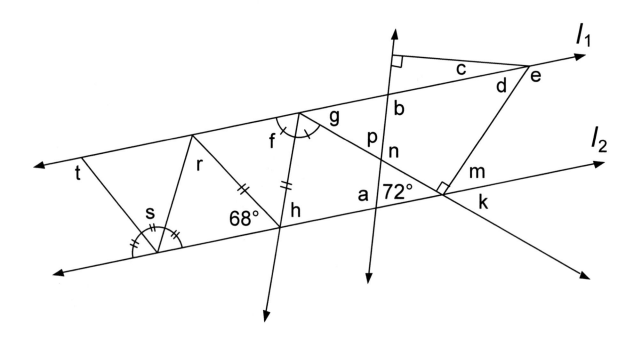

a	b	c	d	e	f	g	h

k	m	n	p	r	s	t

AC Puzzle 7.2: Parallel Lines, Polygon Sum, and Isosceles Triangles

Given: $l_1 // l_2$.

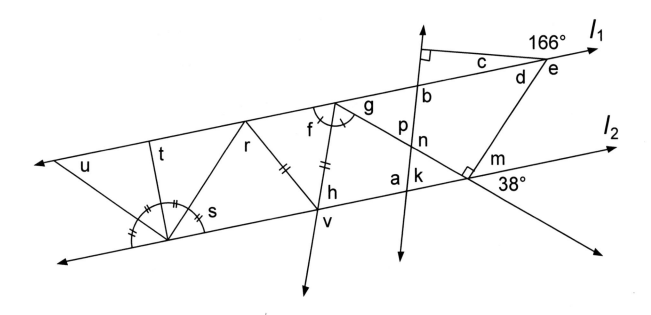

a	b	c	d	e	f	g	h

k	m	n	p	r	s	t	u

AC Puzzle 8.1: Parallel Lines, Polygon Sum, and Isosceles Triangles
Given: $l_1 \; // \; l_2$.

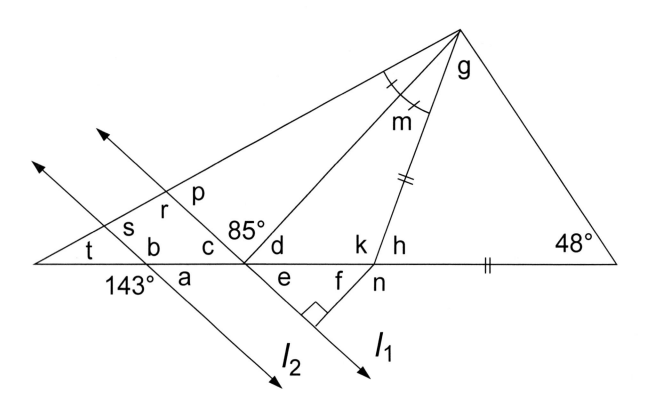

a	b	c	d	e	f	g	h

k	m	n	p	r	s	t

AC Puzzle 8.2: Parallel Lines, Polygon Sum, and Isosceles Triangles

Given: l_1 // l_2.

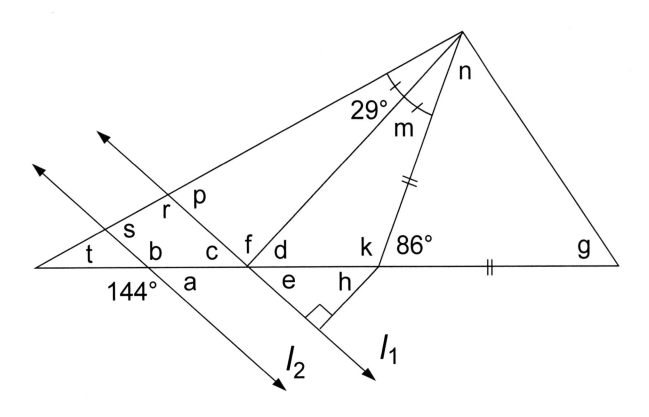

a	b	c	d	e	f	g	h

k	m	n	p	r	s	t

AC Puzzle 9.1 *h*: Polygon Sum and Isosceles Triangles

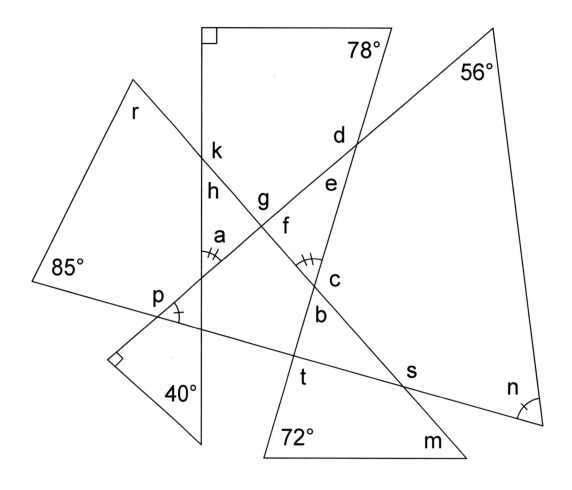

a	b	c	d	e	f	g	h

k	m	n	p	r	s	t

AC Puzzle 9.2: Polygon Sum and Isosceles Triangles

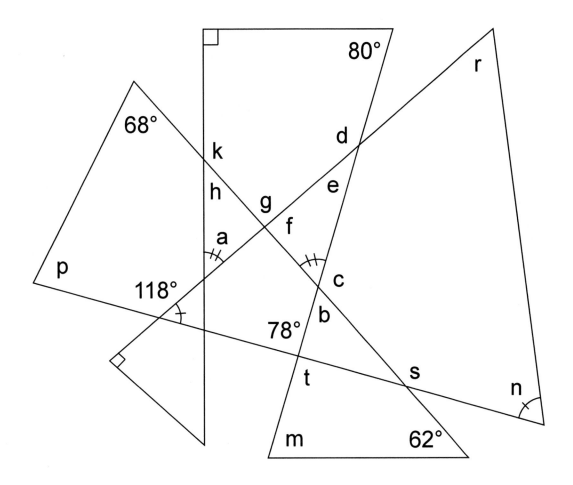

a	b	c	d	e	f	g	h

k	m	n	p	r	s	t

AC Puzzle 10.1: Polygon Sum and Isosceles Triangles

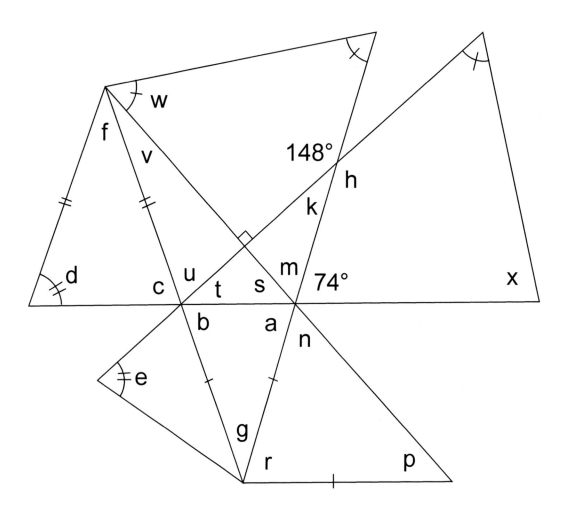

a	b	c	d	e	f	g

h	k	m	n	p	r	s

t	u	v	w	x

AC Puzzle 10.2: Polygon Sum and Isosceles Triangles

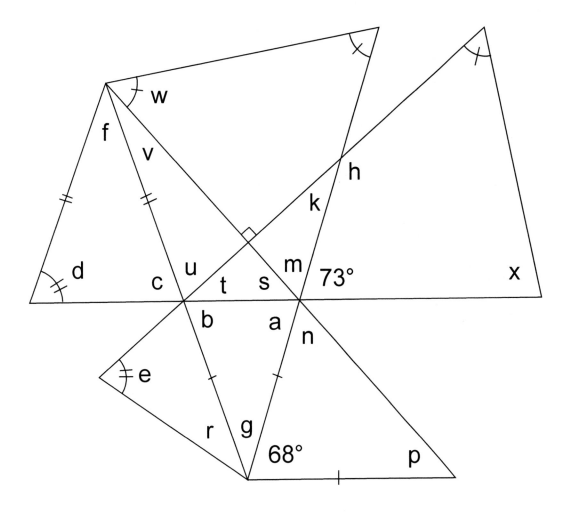

a	b	c	d	e	f	g

h	k	m	n	p	r	s

t	u	v	w	x

AC Puzzle 11.1: Polygon Sum and Isosceles Triangles
Given: $l_1 \,/\!/\, l_2$.

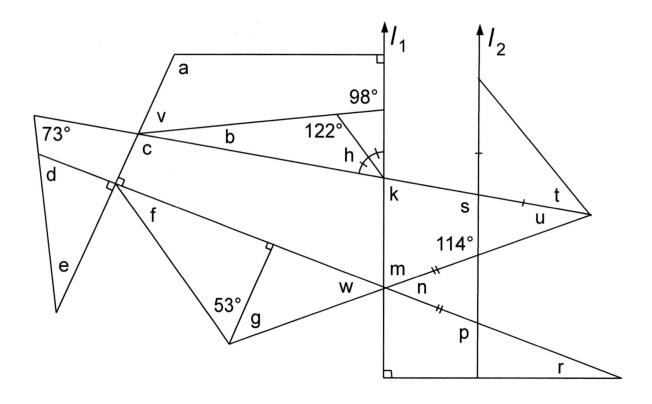

a	b	c	d	e	f	g	h	k

m	n	p	r	s	t	u	v	w

AC Puzzle 11.2: Polygon Sum and Isosceles Triangles

Given: l_1 // l_2.

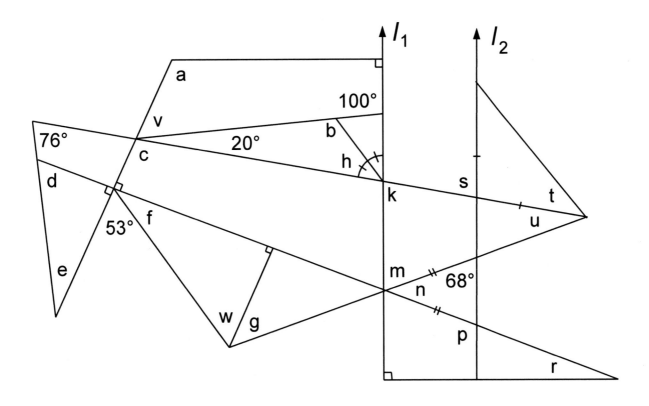

a	b	c	d	e	f	g	h	k

m	n	p	r	s	t	u	v	w

AC Puzzle 12.1: Parallel Lines and Polygon Sum
Given: $l_1 // l_2$.

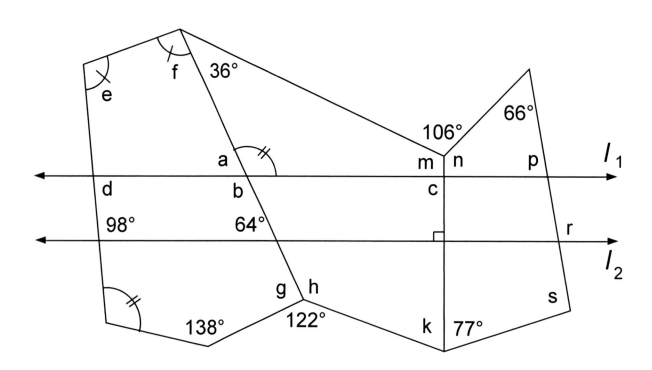

a	b	c	d	e	f	g

h	k	m	n	p	r	s

AC Puzzle 12.2: Parallel Lines and Polygon Sum
Given: $l_1 \parallel l_2$.

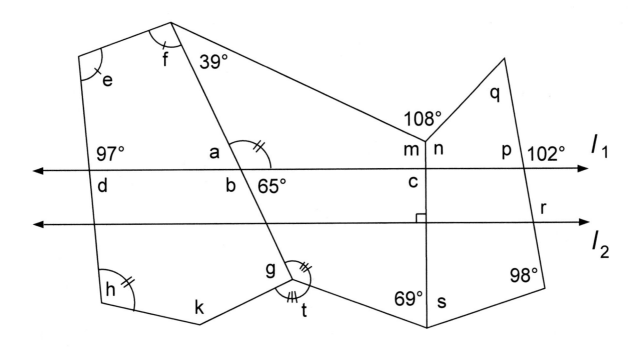

a	b	c	d	e	f	g	h
k	**m**	**n**	**p**	**q**	**r**	**s**	**t**

AC Puzzle 13.1 *h*: Isosceles Triangles and Equiangular Polygons

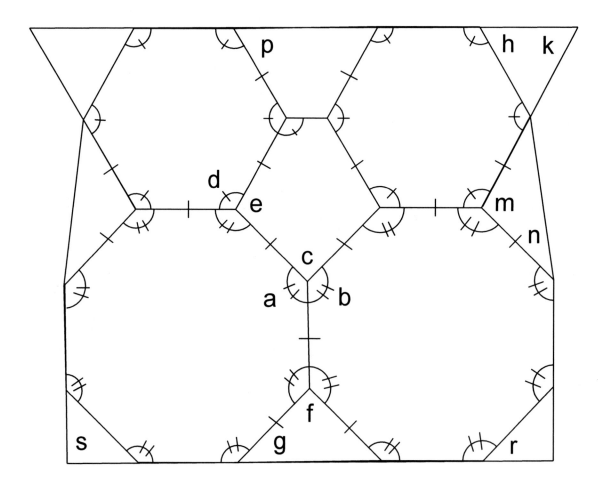

a	b	c	d	e	f	g

h	k	m	n	p	r	s

AC Puzzle 13.2: Isosceles Triangles and Equiangular Polygons

Given: There are ten congruent obtuse isosceles triangles.

There are ten congruent acute isosceles triangles.

There are ten congruent equilateral triangles.

There are ten congruent regular pentagons.

There is one regular decagon.

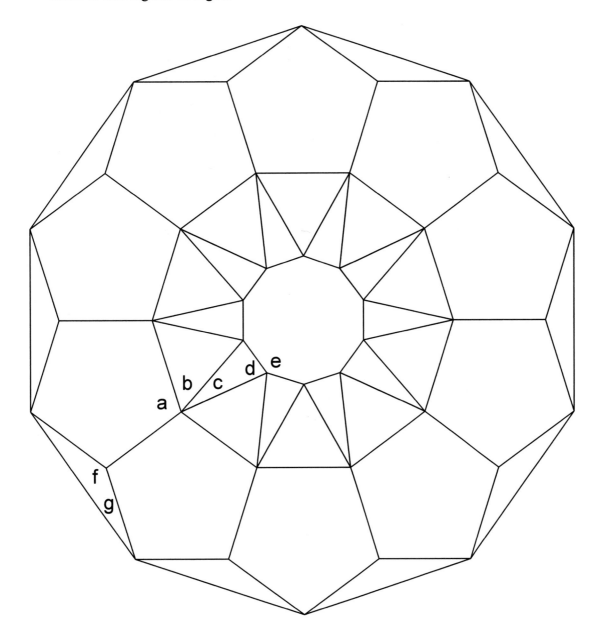

a	b	c	d	e	f	g

AC Puzzle 14.1: Parallel Lines and Polygon Sum
Given: l_1 // l_2.

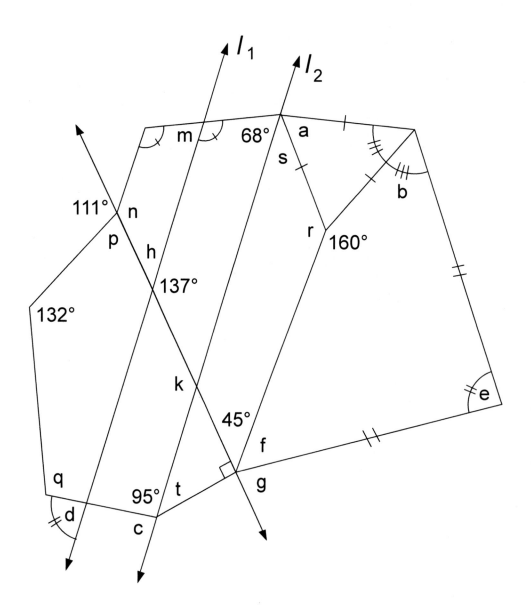

a	b	c	d	e	f	g	h
k	**m**	**n**	**p**	**q**	**r**	**s**	**t**

AC Puzzle 14.2: Parallel Lines and Polygon Sum

Given: $l_1 // l_2$.

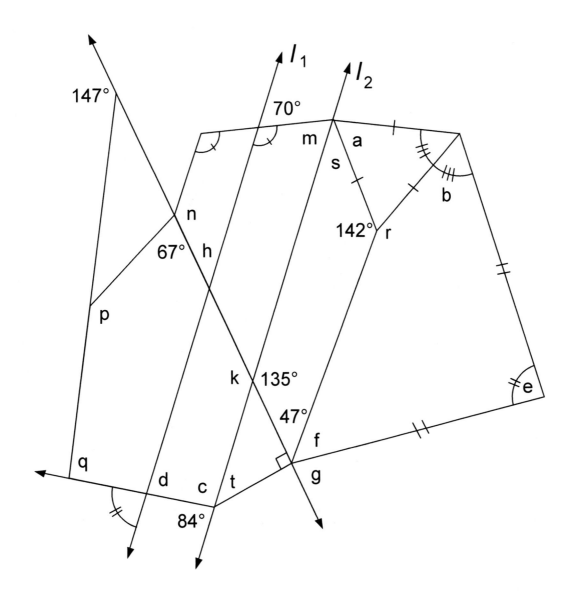

a	b	c	d	e	f	g	h

k	m	n	p	q	r	s	t

AC Puzzle 15.1 *h*: Circle Properties

Given: T_1 and T_2 are tangents.

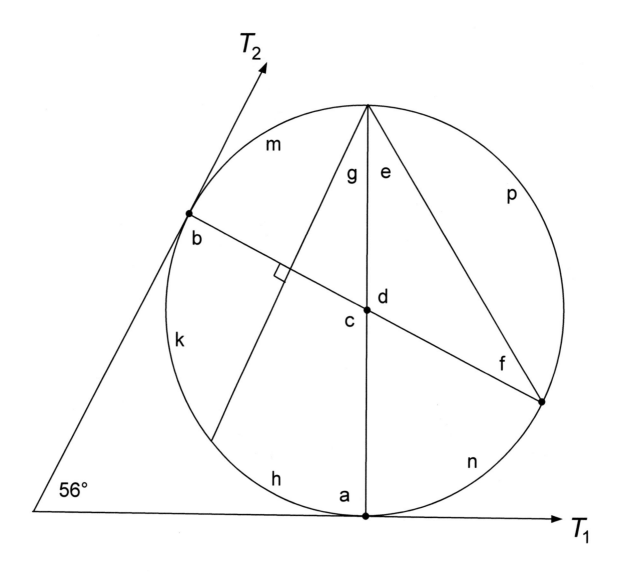

a	b	c	d	e	f
g	**h**	**k**	**m**	**n**	**p**

AC Puzzle 15.2: Circle Properties

Given: T_1 and T_2 are tangents.

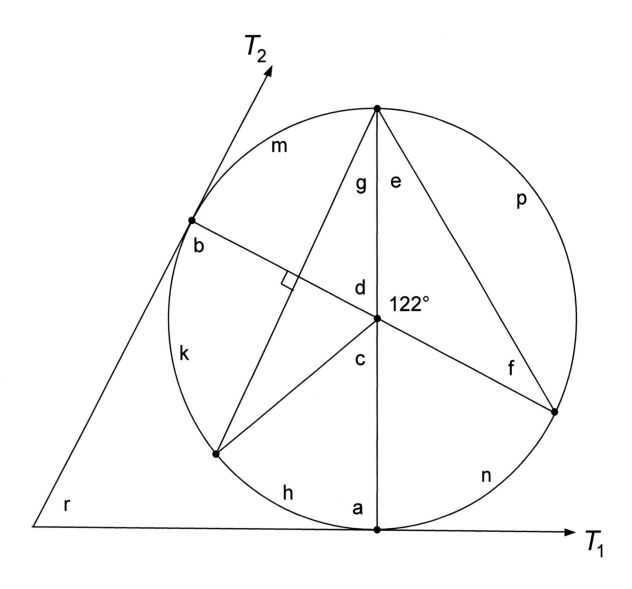

a	b	c	d	e	f	g

h	k	m	n	p	r

AC Puzzle 16.1: Circle Properties

Given: T_1 and T_2 are tangents.

AD and *BE* are diameters.

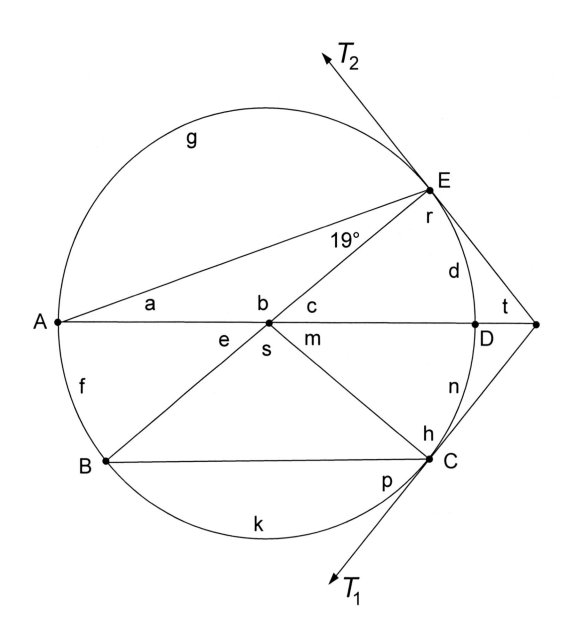

a	b	c	d	e	f	g	h

k	m	n	p	r	s	t

AC Puzzle 16.2: Circle Properties

Given: T_1 and T_2 are tangents.

AD and BE are diameters.

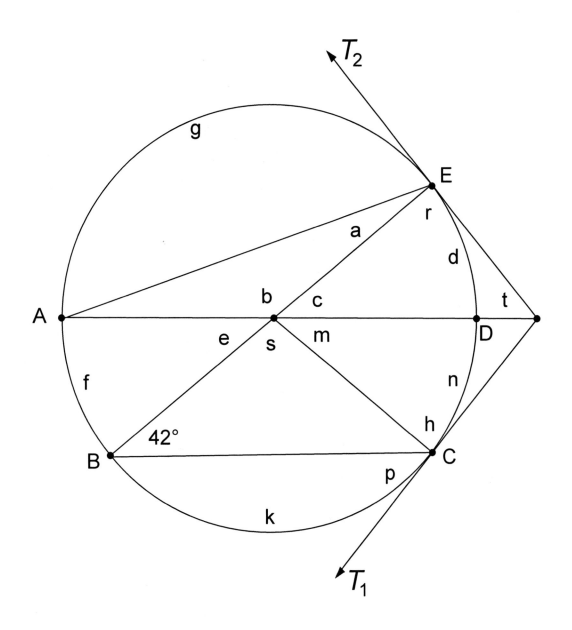

a	b	c	d	e	f	g	h

k	m	n	p	r	s	t	

AC Puzzle 17.1: Circle Properties

Given: T_1 and T_2 are tangents.

BD and AC are diameters.

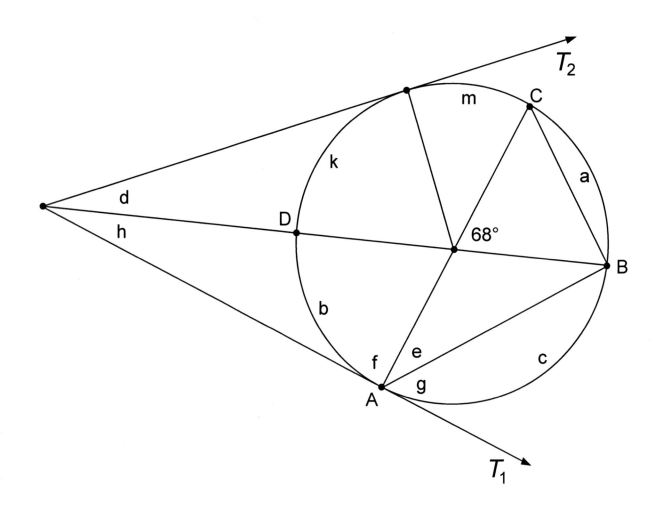

a	b	c	d	e	f	g	h	k	m

AC Puzzle 17.2: Circle Properties

Given: T_1 and T_2 are tangents.

BD and AC are diameters.

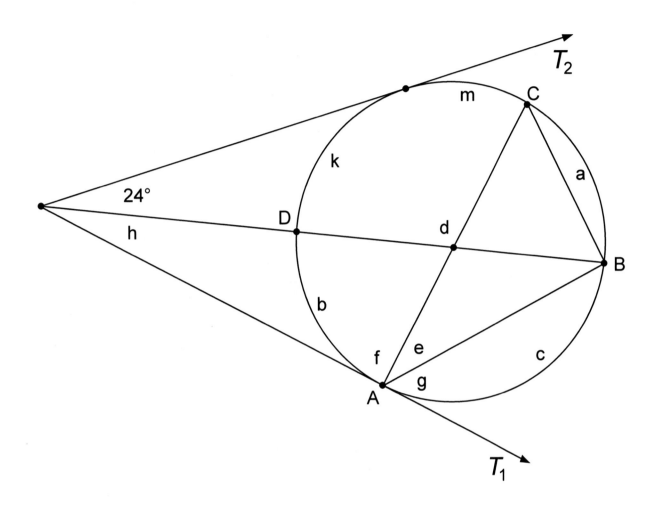

a	b	c	d	e	f	g	h	k	m

AC Puzzle 18.1 *h*: Circle Properties

Given: T_1 and T_2 are tangents.

AB is a diameter.

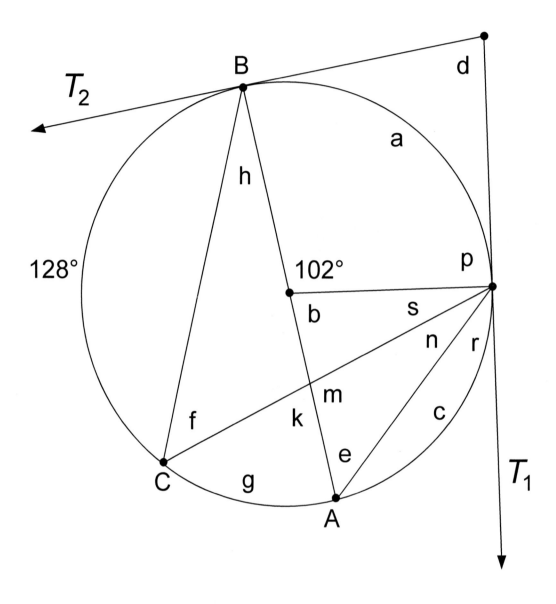

a	b	c	d	e	f	g
h	**k**	**m**	**n**	**p**	**r**	**s**

AC Puzzle 18.2: Circle Properties

Given: T_1 and T_2 are tangents.

AB is a diameter.

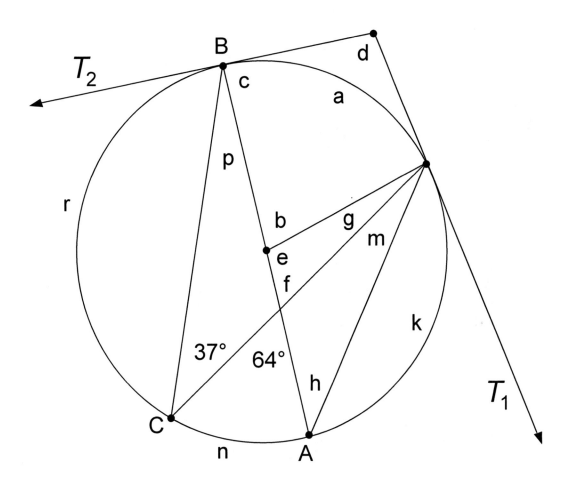

a	b	c	d	e	f	g

h	k	m	n	p	r

AC Puzzle 19.1: Circle Properties

Given: T_1, T_2, and T_3 are tangents.

AB and CD are diameters.

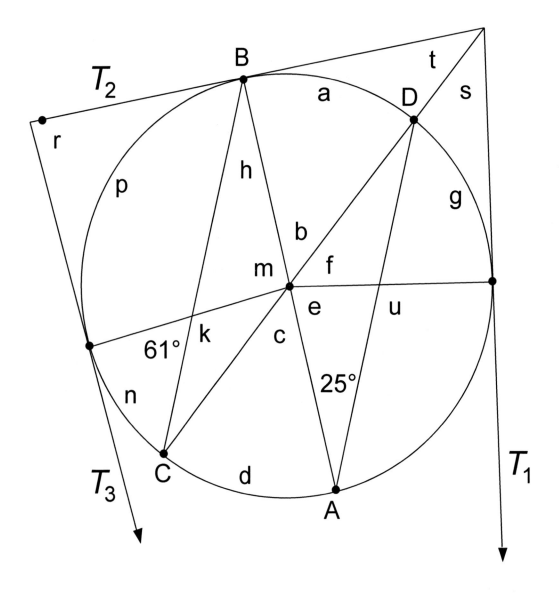

a	b	c	d	e	f	g	h

k	m	n	p	r	s	t	u

AC Puzzle 19.2: Circle Properties

Given: T_1, T_2, and T_3 are tangents.

AB and *CD* are diameters.

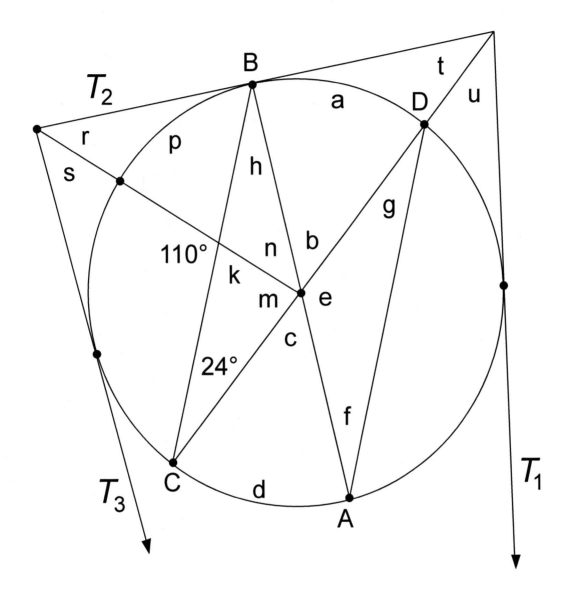

a	b	c	d	e	f	g	h

k	m	n	p	r	s	t	u

AC Puzzle 20.1 *h*: Circle Properties

Given: $l_1 \parallel l_2, l_3 \parallel l_4$.

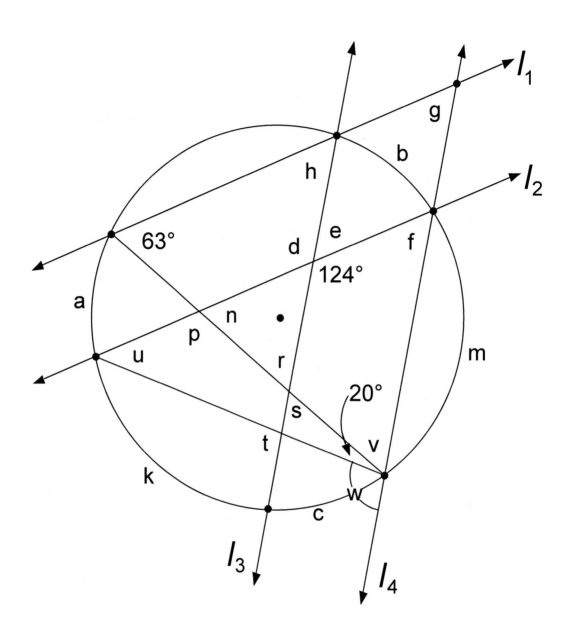

a	b	c	d	e	f	g	h	k

m	n	p	r	s	t	u	v	w

AC Puzzle 20.2: Circle Properties

Given: l_1 // l_2, l_3 // l_4.

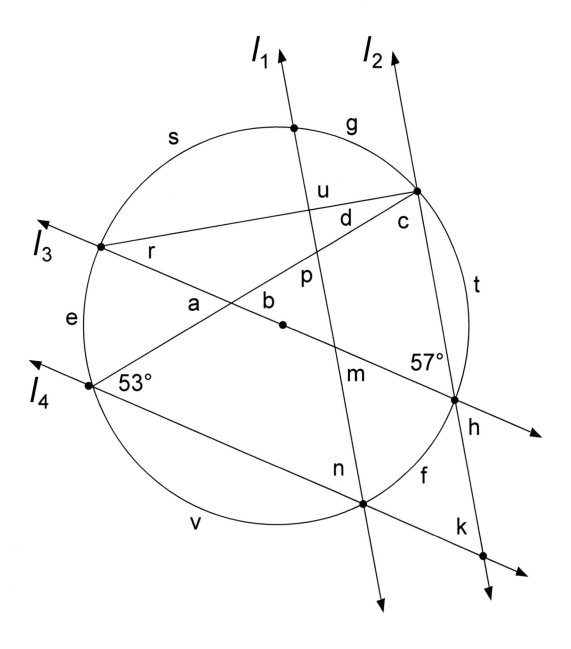

a	b	c	d	e	f	g	h	k

m	n	p	r	s	t	u	v

AC Puzzle 21.1: Circle Properties

Given: l_1 and l_2 are tangents.

AB is a diameter.

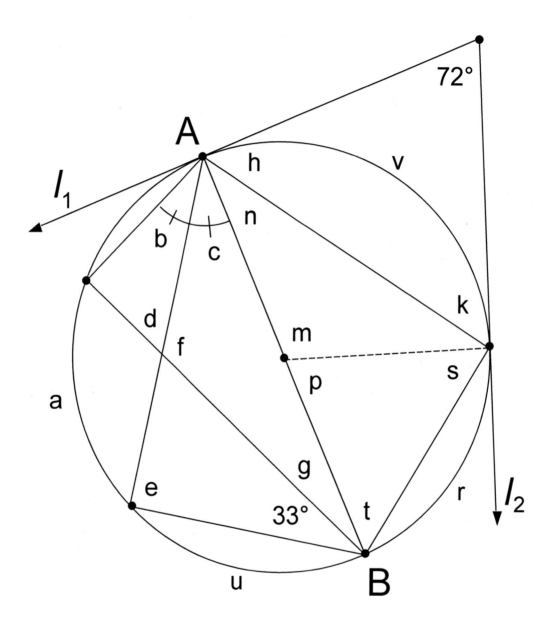

a	b	c	d	e	f	g	h	k

m	n	p	r	s	t	u	v	

AC Puzzle 21.2: Circle Properties

Given: l_1 and l_2 are tangents.

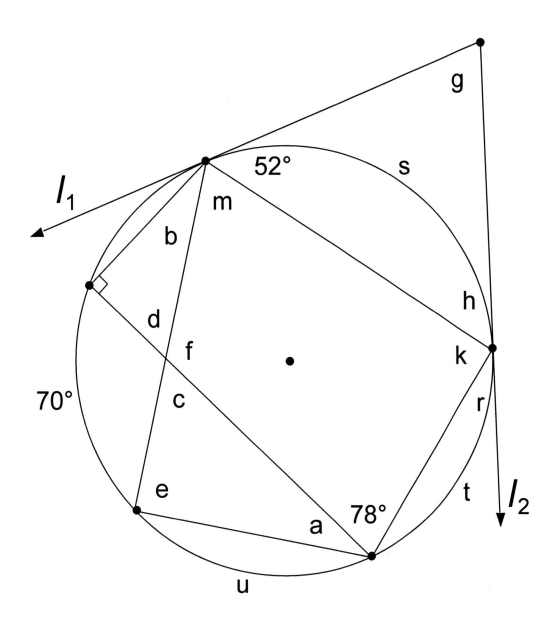

a	b	c	d	e	f	g
h	**k**	**m**	**r**	**s**	**t**	**u**

AC Puzzle 22.1: Circle Properties

Given: l_1, l_2 and l_3 are tangents.

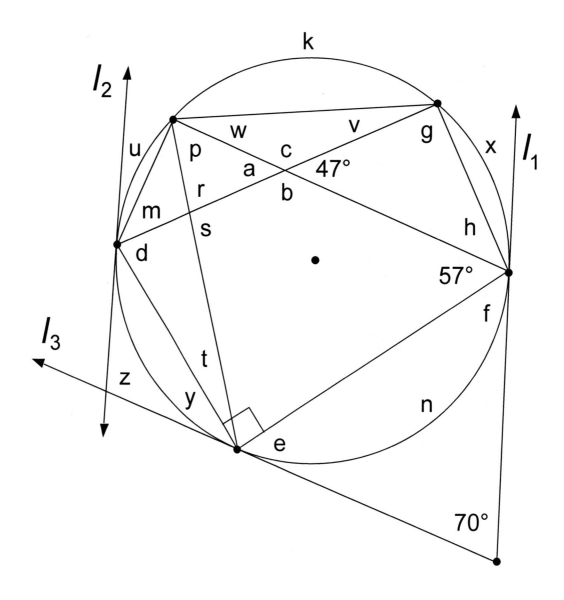

a	b	c	d	e	f	g

h	k	m	n	p	r	s

t	u	v	w	x	y	z

AC Puzzle 22.2: Circle Properties

Given: l_1, l_2 and l_3 are tangents.

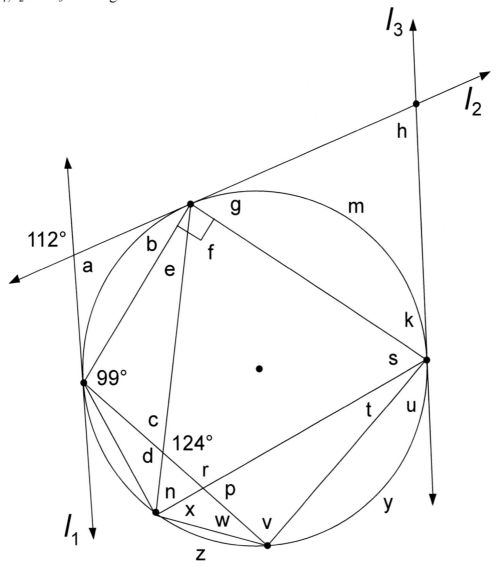

a	b	c	d	e	f	g

h	k	m	n	p	r	s

t	u	v	w	x	y	z

Appendices

Appendix 1: Racetracks

Beginner's Racetrack

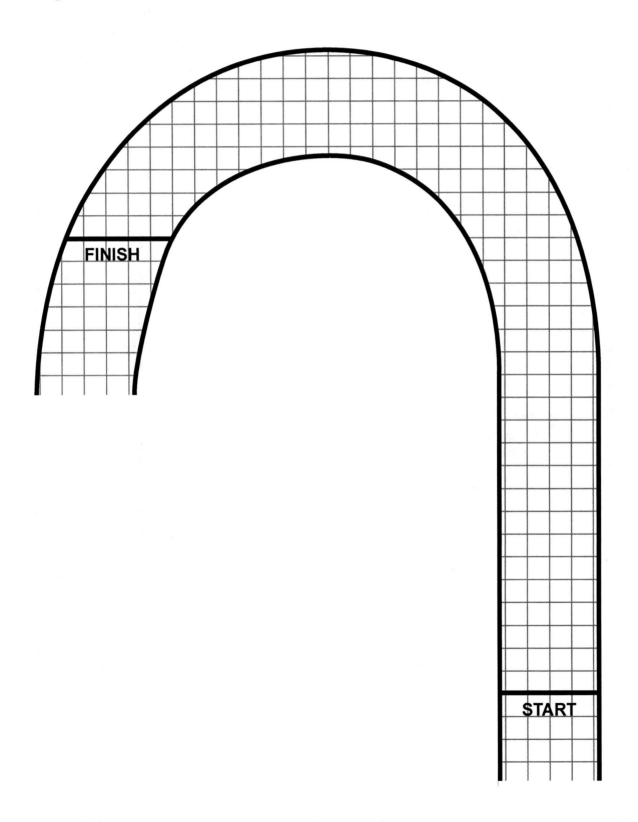

Racetrack 1

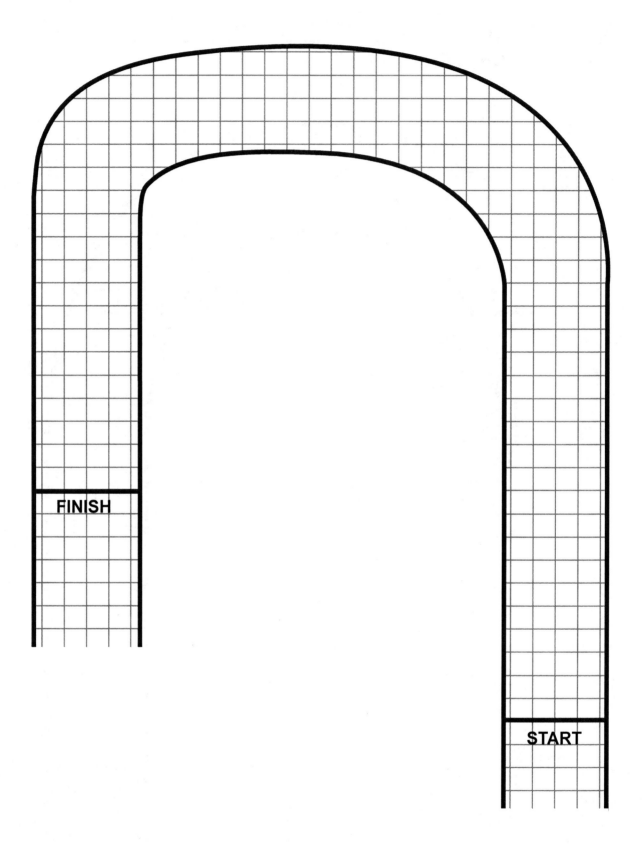

Racetrack 2

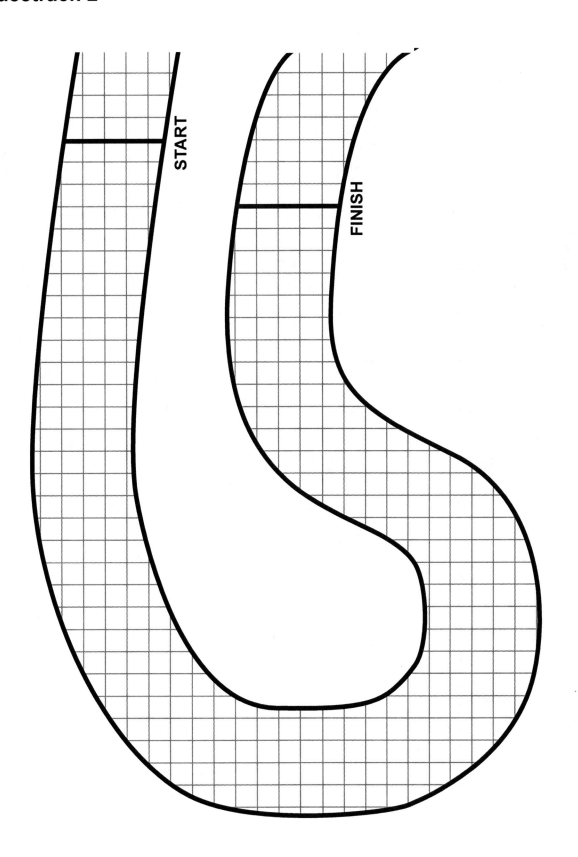

Racetrack 3

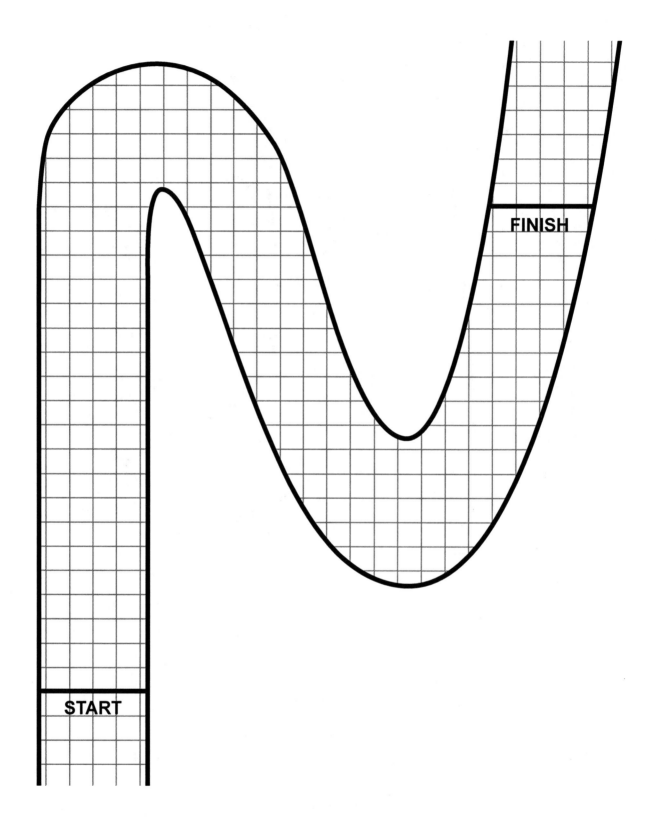

Racetrack 4

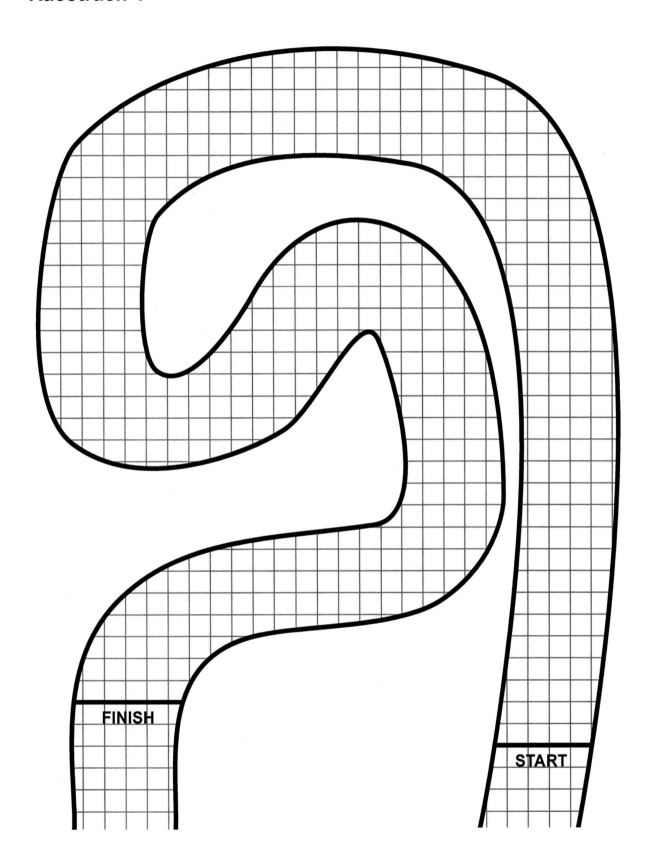

Racetrack 5

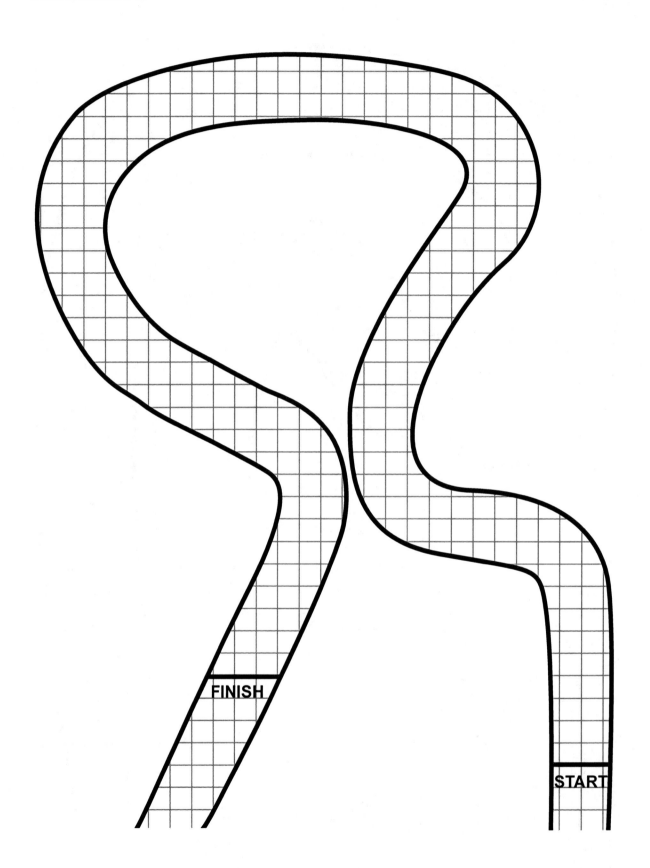

FINISH

START

Racetrack 6

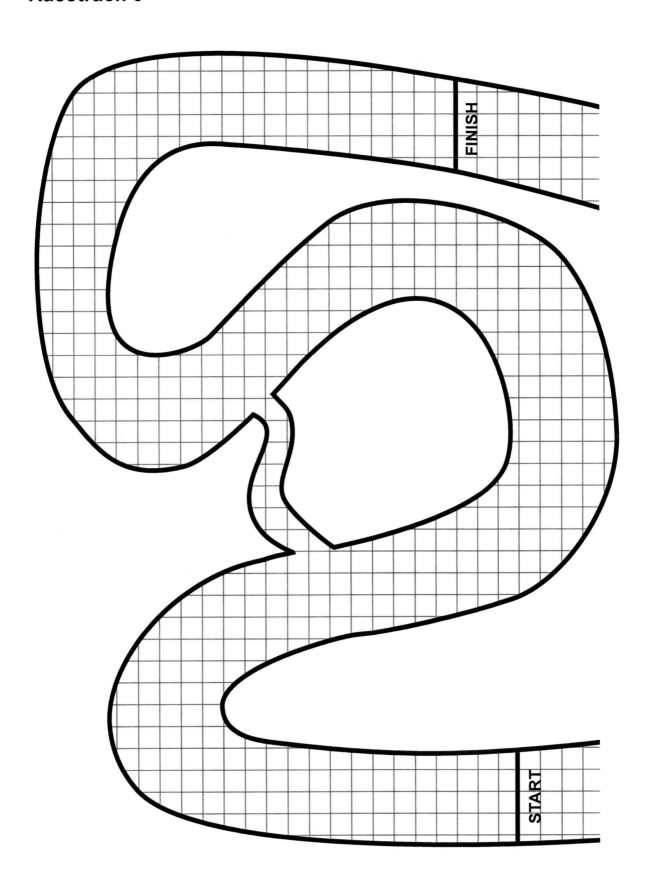

FINISH

START

Racetrack 7

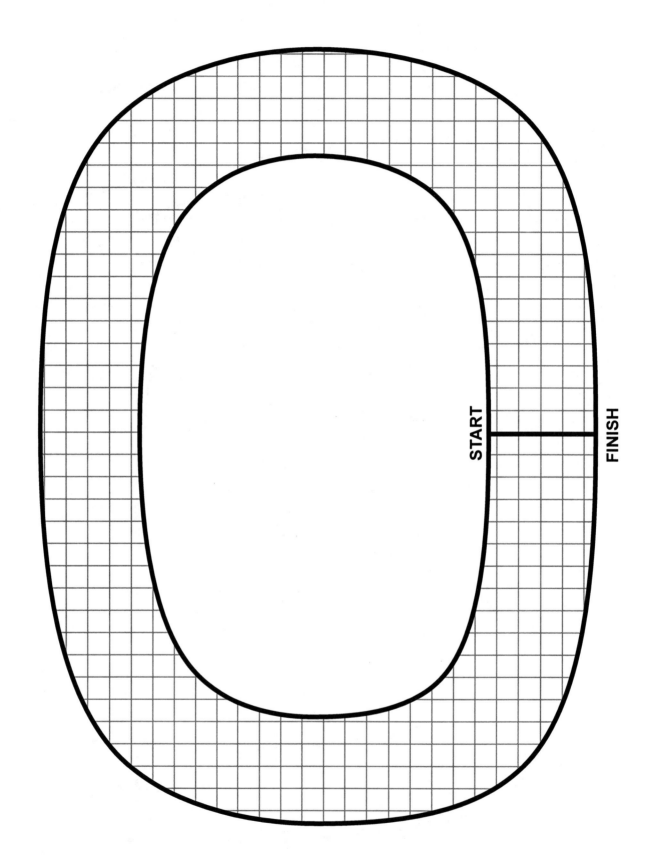

Racetrack 8

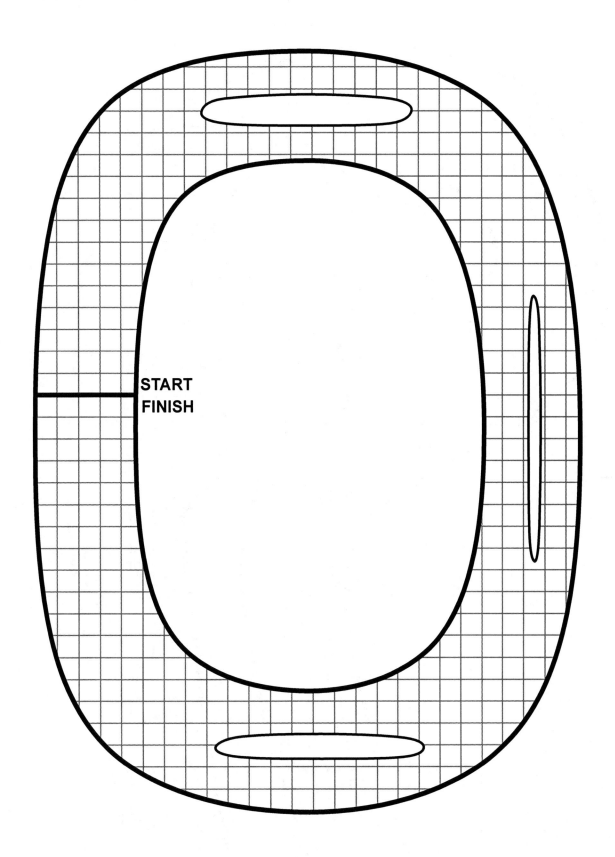

START
FINISH

Racetrack 9

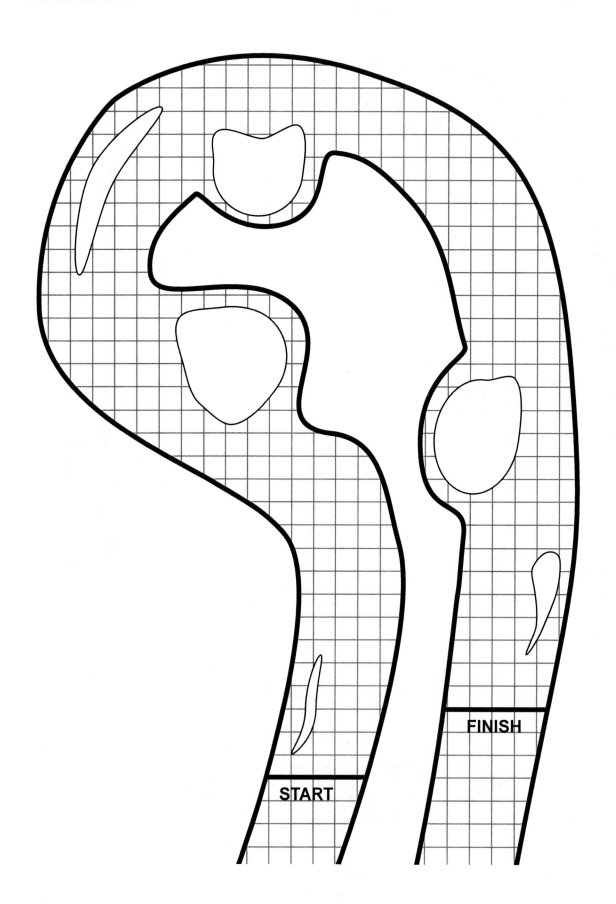

Racetrack 10

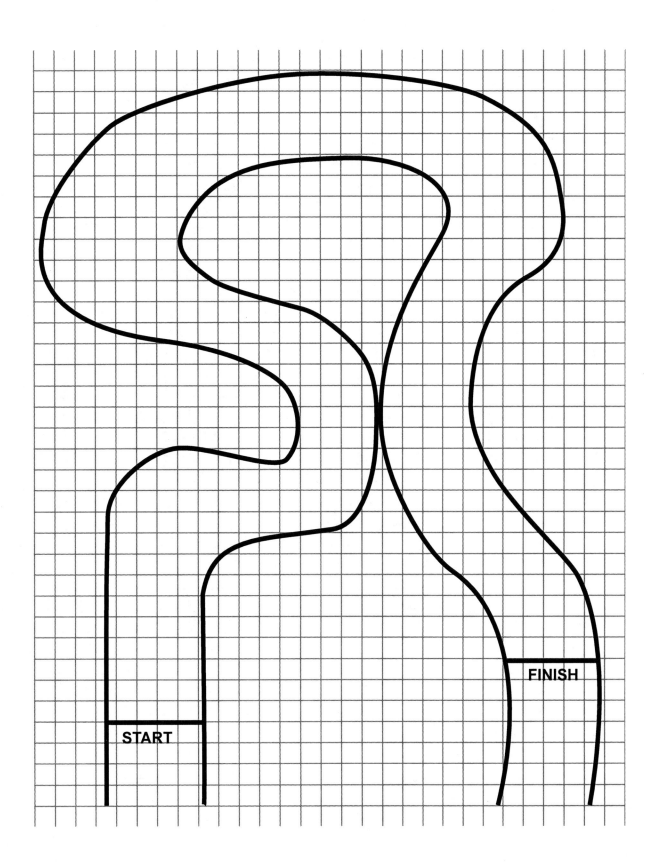

START

FINISH

Racetrack 11

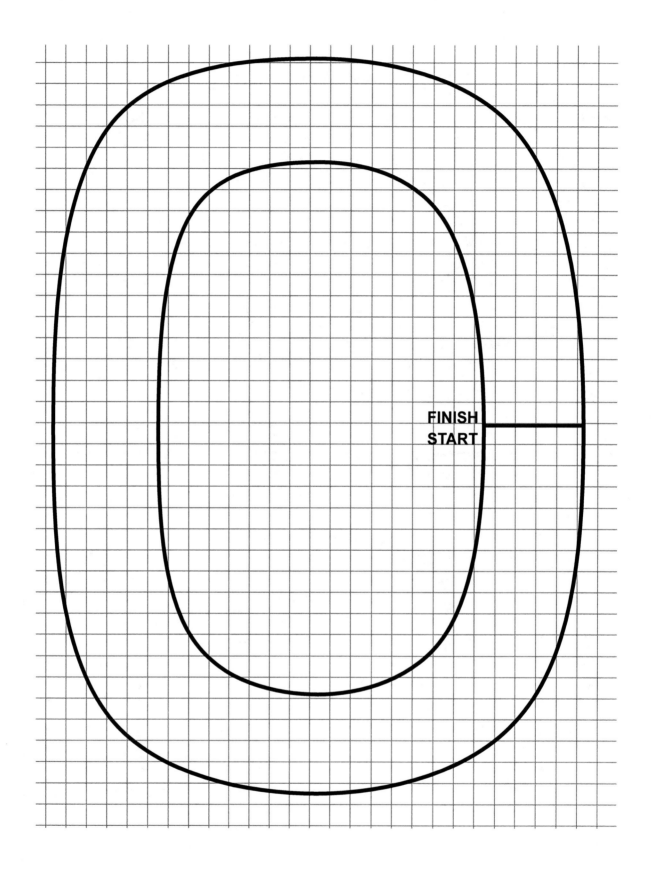

FINISH
START

Racetrack 12

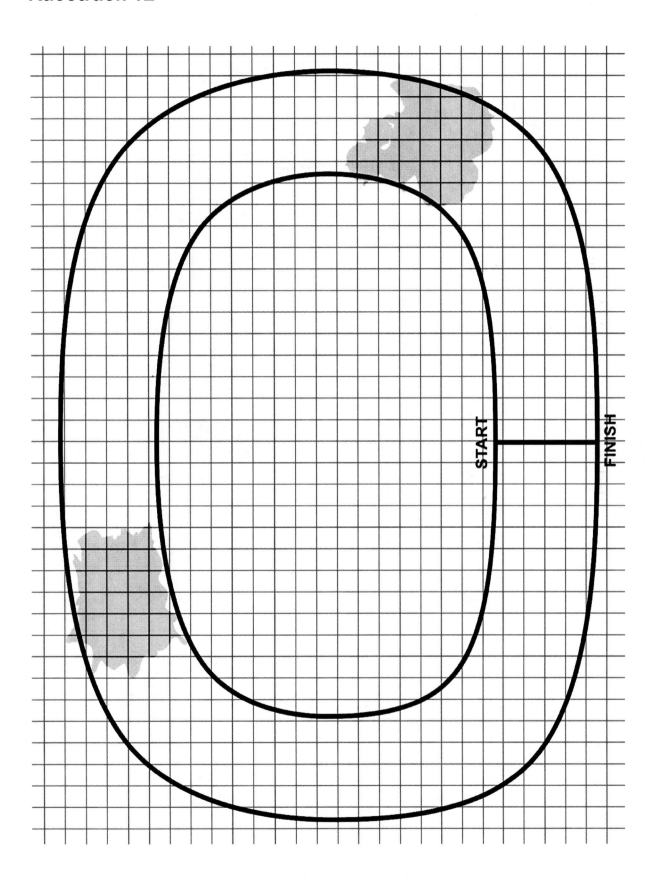

START

FINISH

Racetrack 13

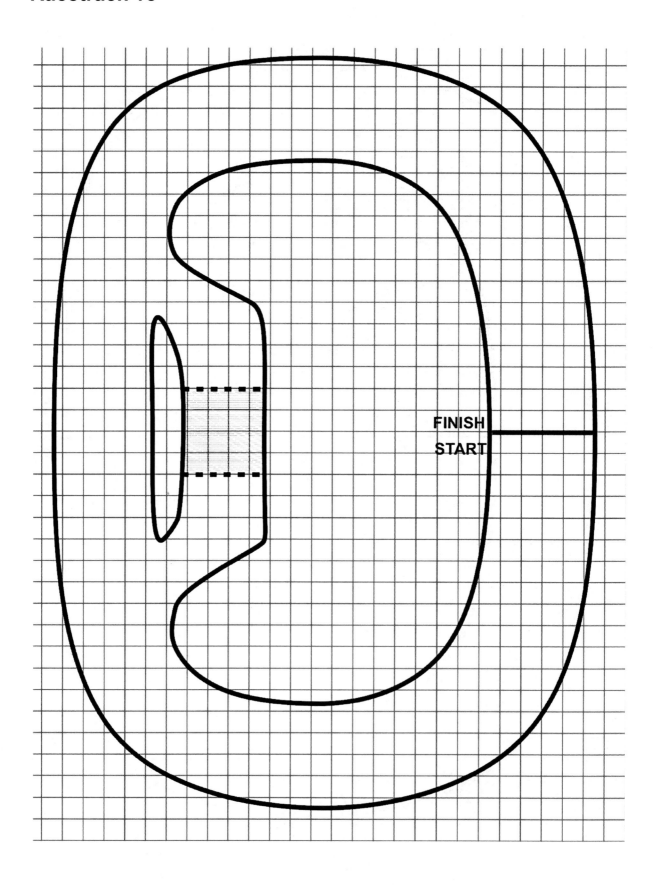

FINISH
START

Racetrack 14

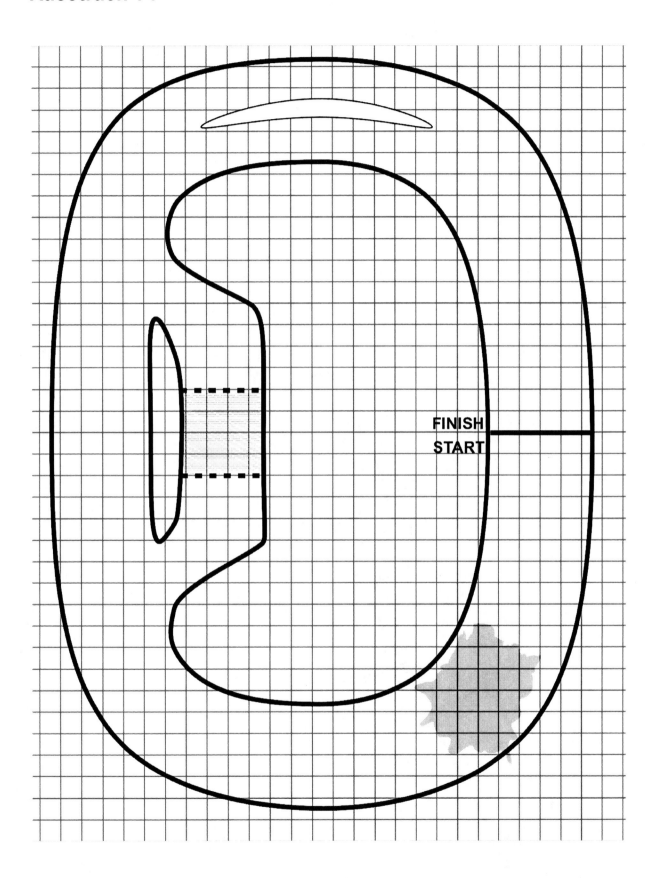

Coin Slide Playing Board

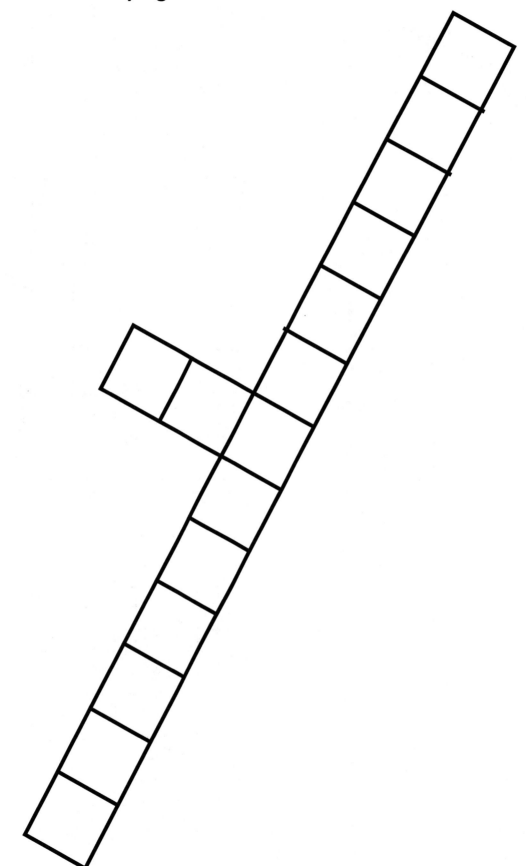

Coin Jump Playing Board

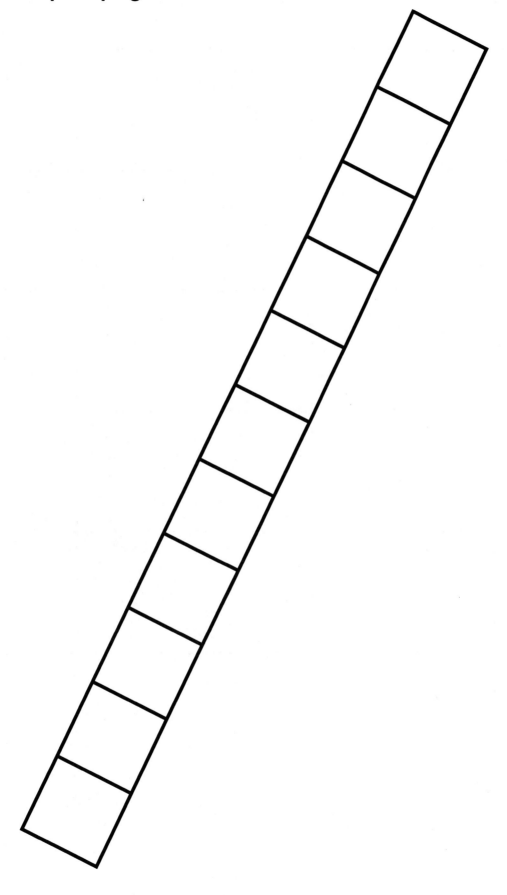

Sliding Block Puzzle Playing Board

Queen Bee Puzzle Playing Board

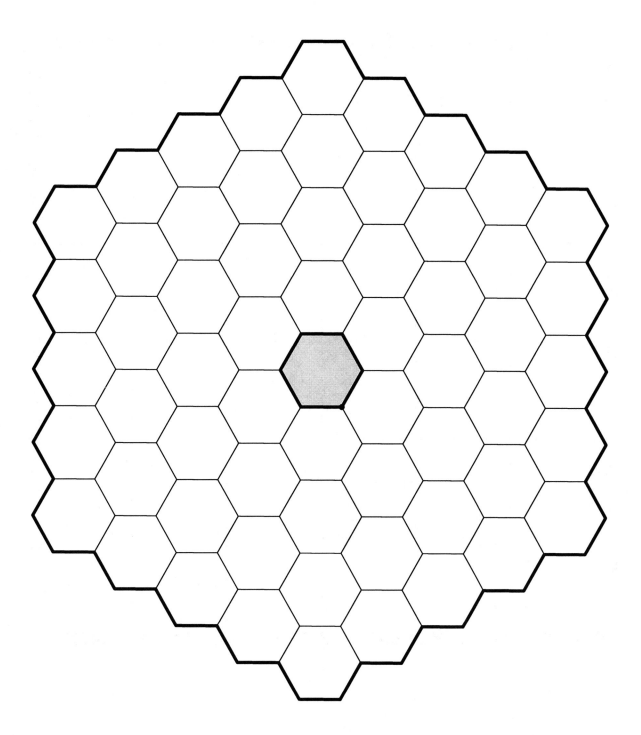

Mini Robot Puzzle Playing Board

Appendix 3: Properties of Algebra

Before you solve the algebra sequential reasoning puzzles in Chapter 6, you might wish to review some of the basic algebra properties shown below.

Properties of Arithmetic	Examples
For any numbers a, b, and c:	
Commutative Property of Addition $a + b = b + a$	$5 + 12 = 12 + 7$
Commutative Property of Multiplication $ab = ba$	$5 \cdot 12 = 12 \cdot 5$
Associative Property of Addition $(a + b) + c = a + (b + c)$	$(2 + 3) + 12 = 2 + (3 + 12)$
Associative Property of Multiplication $(ab)c = a(bc)$	$(2 \cdot 3)12 = 2(3 \cdot 12)$
Distributive Property $a(b + c) = ab + ac$	$2(3 + 12) = 2 \cdot 3 + 2 \cdot 12$

Order of Operations

What do you think the correct value for the following expression is: $8 \cdot 11 + 5 \cdot 12$?

If we calculate from left to right we get: $8 \cdot 11 + 5 \cdot 12 = 88 + 5 \cdot 12 = 93 \cdot 12 = 1116$.

If we calculate from right to left we get: $8 \cdot 11 + 5 \cdot 12 = 8 \cdot 11 + 60 = 5 \cdot 71 = 355$.

If we decide to do addition first we get: $8 \cdot 11 + 5 \cdot 12 = 8 \cdot 16 \cdot 12 = 128 \cdot 12 = 1536$.

This is not good! We would like to get the same result for the same arithmetic. The following, agreed upon Order of Operations makes the expression $8 \cdot 11 + 5 \cdot 12$ unambiguous.

Do operations within parentheses first. If an expression has powers, do them next. Then do all the multiplication and division in order, from left to right. Finally, do the addition and subtraction in order, from left to right.

Examples

- $8 \cdot 11 + 5 \cdot 12 = 88 + 60 = 148$

- $8 + 11 \cdot 5 + 12 = 8 + 55 + 12 = 75$

- $8 + 24 \cdot 5 \div 12 = 8 + 10 = 18$

- $8 \div 16 \cdot 50 + 13 = (1/2) \cdot 50 + 13 = 25 + 13 = 38$

- $5 + 34 \div 17 + 8(2 + 7) = 5 + 2 + 8 \cdot 9 = 5 + 2 + 72 = 79$

- $60 - 2(18 - 15)^3 = 60 - 2(3)^3 = 60 - 2 \cdot 27 = 60 - 54 = 6$

Properties of Equality	Examples
For any numbers a, b, c, and d:	
Reflexive property of Equality $a = a$ (Any number is equal to itself.)	$8 = 8$
Transitive Property of Equality If $a = b$ and $b = c$, then $a = c$. (This property is related to the substitution property, which says that if $b = c$, then c can be substituted for b.)	$35 = y$ $y = x + 5$, then $35 = x + 5$
Symmetric Property of Equality If $a = b$, then $b = a$.	If $y = x + 5$ then $x + 5 = y$
Addition Property of Equality If $a = b$, then $a + c = b + c$. (Also, if $a = b$ and $c = d$, then $a + c = b + d$.)	If $y = x$ then $y + 5 = x + 5$ if $x = 3$, $y = 5$, then $x + y = 8$
Subtraction Property of Equality If $a = b$, then $a - c = b - c$. (Also, if $a = b$ and $c = d$, then $a - c = b - d$.)	If $x + 3 = 5$, then $x = 2$ If $x = 3$, $y = 1$, then $x - y = 2$
Multiplication Property of Equality If $a = b$, then $ac = bc$. (Also, if $a = b$ and $c = d$, then $ac = bd$.)	If $x = 3$, then $2x = 6$ If $x = 3$, $y = 4$ then $xy = 12$
Division Property of Equality If $a = b$, then $a/c = b/c$ provided $c \neq 0$. (Also, if $a = b$ and $c = d$, then $a/c = b/d$) provided $c \neq 0$, $d \neq 0$.	If $6x = 30$, then $x = 5$ If $x = 12$, $y = 4$ then $x/y = 3$
Square Root Property of Equality If $a^2 = b$, then $a = \pm\sqrt{b}$.	If $x^2 = 49$, then $x = \pm\sqrt{49}$
Zero Product Property of Equality If $ab = 0$, then $a = 0$ or $b = 0$ or both $a = 0$ and $b = 0$.	If $(x - 5)(x + 1) = 0$, then $(x - 5) = 0$, $(x + 1) = 0$, or both.

Solving Equations in One Variable

Example A   Example B

Equation	Reason For Step	Equation	Reason For Step
$8x - 634 = 982$	starting equation	$y/6 + 51 = 931$	starting equation
$8x = 1616$	add 634 to both sides	$y/6 = 880$	subtract 51 from both sides
$x = 202$	divide both sides by 8	$y = 5{,}280$	multiply both sides by 6

Special Products and Factoring

Perfect Square Trinomial   Numerical Example

$x^2 \pm 2xy + y^2 = (x \pm y)^2$ $(17.8)^2 + 2(17.8)(2.2) + (2.2)^2 = (17.8 + 2.2)^2 = 20^2 = 400$

Difference of Squares   Numerical Example

$x^2 - y^2 = (x + y)(x - y)$ $37^2 - 36^2 = (37+36)(37-36) = (73)(1) = 73$

Solving Equations in Two Variables

Example A

Equations	Reason For Step
(a) $2x - 3y = 16$	equation (a)
(b) $3x + 2y = 11$	equation (b)
$4x - 6y = 32$	multiply (a) by 2
$9x + 6y = 33$	multiply (b) by 3
(c) $13x = 65$	add (a) and (b)
$x = 5$	divide (c) by 13
$2(5) - 3y = 16$	substitute 5 for x in (a)
$y = -2$	solve for y

Solution: $(5, -2)$

Example B

Equations	Reason For Step
(a) $2x - 3y = 7$	equation (a)
(b) $y = x - 5$	equation (b)
(c) $2x - 3[x - 5] = 7$	subst. $x - 5$ for y
$2x - 3x + 15 = 7$	simplify
$-x + 15 = 7$	simplify
$x = 8$	simplify
$y = (8) - 5$	subst. 8 for x in (b)
$y = 3$	solve for y

Solution: $(8, 3)$

Finding the Rule or Formula

Example A

Use the table to find a rule for the sum of measures of the interior angles in any polygon. What is the sum of the measures of the interior angles of a 50-sided polygon?

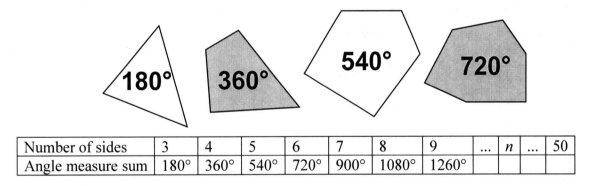

Number of sides	3	4	5	6	7	8	9	...	n	...	50
Angle measure sum	180°	360°	540°	720°	900°	1080°	1260°				

Solution

Notice when the number of sides increases by one, the angle measure sum increases by 180°. So the angle measure sum for a 10-gon is 1260° + 180°, or 1440°. This method gets the next term, but proceeding in this way, it will take awhile to get to a 50-gon. Also notice all the values (180, 360, 540, 720, ...) are multiples of 180°. Factor them to see a pattern.

Number of sides	3	4	5	6	7	8	9	...	n	...	50
Sum of the angle measures	1•180°	2•180°	3•180°	4•180°	5•180°	6•180°	7•180°				

The number multiplied by 180 is always 2 less than the number of sides. This can be written in functional notation as: $f(n) = (n - 2) \cdot 180°$, where n represents the number of sides. So the angle measure sum for a 50-gon is $(50 - 2) \cdot 180° = 48 \cdot 180° = 8,640°$.

Appendix 4: Properties of Geometry

Review of Basic Geometry

Before you attempt to solve some sequential reasoning puzzles in geometry, you might wish to review some of the basic geometry properties shown below.

Angle Properties

- If two angles are vertical angles then they are congruent.
- If two angles form a linear pair, then they are supplementary, and their sum is 180°.

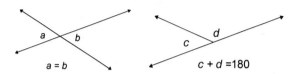

$a = b \qquad c + d = 180$

Parallel Properties

If two parallel lines are intercepted by a transversal, then

- corresponding angles are congruent.
- alternate interior angles are congruent.
- alternate exterior angles are congruent.

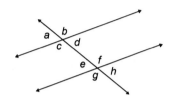

Corresponding angles: $a = e, b = f, c = g, d = h$
Alternate interior angles: $c = f, d = e$
Alternate exterior angles: $a = h, b = g$

Polygon Angle Sums

- The sum of the measures of the three angles of a triangle is 180°.
- The sum of the measures of the four angles of a quadrilateral is 360°.
- The sum of the measures of the five angles of a pentagon is 540°.
- In general, the sum of the measures of the n angles of an n-gon is $(n - 2) \cdot 180°$.
- In a triangle, the sum of the measures of two interior angles is equal to the measure of the remote exterior angle.
- In general, the sum of the measures of the n exterior angles of an n-gon is 360°.

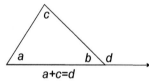

$a+b+c=180 \qquad a+b+c+d=360$

$a+b+c+d+e=540 \qquad a+c=d$

Isosceles Triangles and Trapezoids

- The base angles of an isosceles triangle are congruent.
- The base angles of an isosceles trapezoid are congruent.

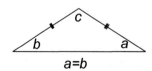

$a=b$

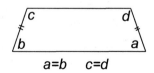

$a=b \qquad c=d$

Circle Properties

- The measure of an arc of a circle is equal to the measure of its central angle.
- The measure of an angle inscribed in a circle is equal to half the measure of its intercepted arc.

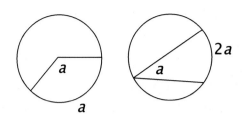

- Two or more angles in a circle that intercept the same arc are congruent.
- The measure of an angle inscribed in a semicircle is 90°.

180°

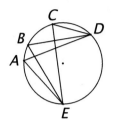

$m\angle A = m\angle B = m\angle C$

- The opposite angles of an inscribed quadrilateral (cyclic quadrilateral) are supplementary.
- Parallel lines intercept congruent arcs on a circle.

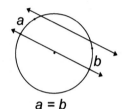

$a + c = 180°$ $a = b$
$b + d = 180°$

- A tangent is perpendicular to the radius drawn to the point of tangency.
- Two tangent segments from the same exterior point are congruent.

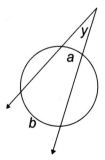

TN is tangent to circle O
$m\angle TAO = 90°$

$\overline{TA} = \overline{TN}$

- The measure of the angle formed by two chords or secants intersecting in the interior of a circle, is equal to the average of the two intercepted arcs.
- The measure of the angle formed by two secants intersecting in the exterior of a circle, is equal to half the difference of the two intercepted arcs.

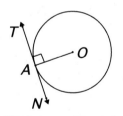
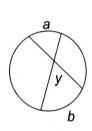

$y = (1/2)(a + b)$ $y = (1/2)(b - a)$

Hints for Chapter 1: Warm-Up Puzzles

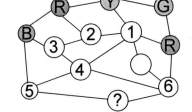

CN Puzzle 2 Circles 1, 2, 3, 4, and 5 can be found sequentially, one after the other. Circle 6 cannot be Red or the same color as circles 1, 4, or 5.

SR Puzzle 2 Start at 100 and work backwards:
$100 \rightarrow 97 \rightarrow 93 \rightarrow \ldots$

Container Puzzle 1 Fill the 8, pour into 5. Empty 5...

Container Puzzle 5 Fill the 5. From the 5 fill the 3. Empty the 3 back into the 8.

SM Puzzle 1 If a puzzle appears to be too difficult, try to solve easier but similar (analogous) puzzles first. Solving these puzzles may give you insight into solving the more challenging puzzles. So first try the *Tower of Hanoi* puzzle with two disks (it can be done in three moves), then try solving the puzzle using three disks (it should take seven moves). Here is a really big hint: when you are successful at moving all three disks in seven moves do it again and keep your eye on the smallest disk –observe how often it is moved and the pattern it makes.

SM Puzzle 2 Make a table and record the minimum number of moves it takes to solve the puzzle with 1, 2, 3, 4, 5, 6, and 7 disks.

SM Puzzle 6 Truck B needs to be below car X. So cars J and C need to be to the left of car A. Move cars I and K to the left so A can slide up...

Cryptarithm Puzzle 1 C = 1, therefore B = 2.

Cryptarithm Puzzle 2 C = 1, therefore E = 2 and B = 4.

Cryptarithm Puzzle 3 R = 1. A + A = __A, therefore A = 0.

Cryptarithm Puzzle 4 E × A4CD = A4CD, so E = 1. 3 × D = __4, therefore D = 8. If D = 8, then F = 0. If F = 0, then C = ?

Cryptarithm Puzzle 5 8 + 7 + A = __E, But 8 + 7 + A + (carry) = __D.
Also 8 + 7 + A + (a different carry) = __C. Therefore the first carry is 1 and the second carry is 2. A ≠ 0 because it is in a far left position, A ≠ 1 because 718 + 187 + 871 = 1776 (all four digits must be different. The same argument shows that A ≠ 2 and A ≠ 3.

Cryptarithm Puzzle 6 B × 7BC = 7BC, so B = 1. C × C = __C, therefore C = 5 or 6.

H.E. Dudeney's Send Money Puzzle Clearly M = 1. If M = 1 then S + M = 10 or 11. But it cannot be 11 since 1 is taken by M. Therefore O is 0 and S is 8 or 9. If S = 8 then E + 0 has a carry over. The only way for this to happen is if E = 9. But if E + 0 = N then N + R has a carry over. But N + R does not equal 19. Therefore, E ≠ 9 and S ≠ 8. Thus, S = 9.

Hints for Chapter 3: Movement Puzzles

CS Puzzle 4 If you successfully solved puzzles 1-3, you should notice a pattern.

CJ Puzzle 1 Try solving a similar, but easier puzzle on a 1×3 grid with a dime and a penny (3 moves). Then work a similar puzzle on a 1×5 grid with two dimes and two pennies (8 moves). After solving a similar puzzle on a 1×7 grid with three dimes and three pennies (15 moves), you should notice a pattern. You can use the pattern to solve a similar puzzle on a 1×9 grid with four dimes and four pennies (24 moves). After that you will be ready to solve the Coin Jump Puzzle on a 1×11 grid with five dimes and five pennies (35 moves).

SB Puzzle 3 You do not need to move any piece in the top two rows! Start with the 12.

SB Puzzle 14 Start with the Q up to the left.

SB Puzzle 17 Start with the 4 to the left.

SB Puzzle 20 Start with the 2 up.

SB Puzzle 27 Start with the 5 to the right then up.

QB Puzzle 7 Start with the 1 down to the right.

QB Puzzle 14 Start with the Q to the left then the 1 up.

MR Puzzle 1 Start by moving the 2-bot to the left then down.

MR Puzzle 6 Start by moving the 1-bot up then move the 3-bot.

MR Puzzle 9 Start by moving the 3-bot to the left then move the 4-bot.

Hints for Chapter 4: Tour Puzzles

RT Puzzle 3

RT Puzzle 8

RT Puzzle 14

RT Puzzle 24

KT Puzzle 2

KT Puzzle 11

KT Puzzle 17

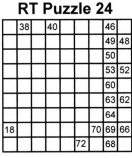

KT Puzzle 19

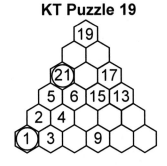

KT Puzzle 21

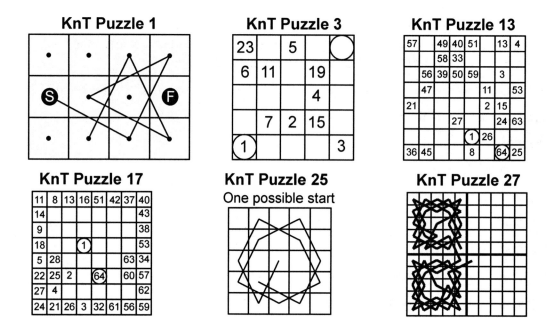

KnT Puzzle 1

KnT Puzzle 3

KnT Puzzle 13

KnT Puzzle 17

KnT Puzzle 25
One possible start

KnT Puzzle 27

Path Puzzle 2 Only three of the paths cannot be traveled. Five of them can only be traveled if you start at one of two points. Two of the networks can be traveled no matter where you start, and you end up back at the starting point.

Hints for Chapter 5: Magic Square Puzzles

MS Puzzle 2

12	7	
5		13
	11	6

MS Puzzle 8

9	7	
	11	3
15		

MS Puzzle 12

	8	12	
3	10		15
2	11		
16	5	9	4

MS Puzzle 27 Since the magic sum is 62, 13 goes in the remaining empty square in one of the diagonals. Notice there are 16 numbers from 8 through 23. So the remaining numbers you will use to fill in the empty squares are 9, 10, 12, 15, 16, 19, 20, 21, and 22. Next $a + b + 34 = 62$ so $a + b = 28$. Looking at the list of available numbers, (9, 19) and (12, 16) are the only pairs of numbers that work for a and b. Likewise $a + c + 27 = 62$ so $a + c = 35$. Looking at the list of available numbers, (15, 20) and (16, 19) are the only pairs of numbers that work for a and c. In the same manner, $d + e = 43$, $d + g = 32$, $e + f = 30$. From these clues you can determine the values of a, b, c, d, e, f, and g.

		17	b	18
		g	23	f
c		13	a	14
8	d	11	e	

MS Puzzle 41 Since the magic sum is 65, this means the magic square is a normal magic square and the numbers used are 1 through 25. If the magic sum is 65 then you can quickly fill in the numbers 4, 5, 6, 7, and 14. So the remaining numbers are 3, 9, 10, 17, 18, and 24. Next, $a + b + 39 = 65$, so $a + b = 26$. Looking at the list of available numbers, (9, 17) is the only pair of numbers that work for a and b. Likewise $a + c + 53 = 65$, so $a + c = 12$. From the list of available numbers, (3, 9) is the only pair of numbers that work for a and c. This tells us, since a is in both equations and 9 is in both solutions, $a = 9$.

8	16	4	12	25
14	22	d	f	1
20	c	11	e	7
21	a	b	5	13
2	15	23	6	19

MS Puzzle 42 Since the numbers are consecutive, the 25 numbers range from 16 to 40. Thus, the magic sum is $25 \cdot 56/10 = 140$. So you can fill in the empty cell in the second column with 36. The remaining numbers available are 19, 22, 24, 27, 30, 32, 33, 34, 37, and 39. Next, $a + d + 69 = 140$ so $a + d = 71$. Looking at the list of available numbers, (34, 37) and (32, 39) are the only pairs of numbers that work for a and d. Likewise $d + e + 70 = 140$, so $d + e = 70$. From the list, (33, 37) is the only pair of numbers that work for d and e. Since d is in both equations and 37 is in both solutions, $d = 37$.

d	29	16	e	25
31	23	40		
	17	a	21	38
	36	28	20	
18	35	b	c	26

MS Puzzle 48 Since this is a normal 8×8 magic square, the magic sum is $64 \cdot 65/2 \div 8 = 260$. Knowing the magic sum you can find the location for 30, 26, 34, 29, 20, 42, 18, 41 and 57 in quick succession. Notice there are only two even numbers left to be found: 16 and 64. A quick check locates their positions.

8		41	32	40	17	9	
58	15	23	34	26	47	55	2
	14	22	35	27	46	54	
5	52	44	29	37	20	12	61
4		45	28	36	21		60
62	11	19	38	30	43	51	6
63	10	18	39	31	42	50	7
	56	48	25	33	24		57

MS Puzzle 53 First using the knight's move locate the 2, 4, 5, 7, and 9. Then use the magic sum of 260 and half sum of 130 to find the numbers in the shaded squares.

1		31		33		63	
	51		3		19		
	2	49		15			
		4	45		61	36	13
5		25		9		21	
28		8	41	24			
43	6	55			10		
			7	58		38	

Hints for Chapter 6: Sequential Reasoning and Algebra

AMS Puzzle 1 Solve for x: $(x + 2) + x + (2x + 3) = (3x - 2) + 11 + (x - 4)$

AMS Puzzle 13 Solve for y: $(3x + 2) + y + (y + 4) + 41 = (2x - 1) + x + y + 45$
Solve for z: $(2x - 1) + x + y + 45 = (2x - 5) + (x - 4) + (y + 4) - 7z$

AMS Puzzle 20 $15 + x + (y + 3x) + (2y - 9) + (y - x)$
$= (y + 2) + (y - 2) + (y + 3x) + (20 - y) + y$

SS Puzzle 1 Express the side length of all the squares in terms of A. Then $B = A + 1$, $C = A + 2$, $D = A + 3$, $E = A + 7$, ...

SS Puzzle 4 Express the side length of all the squares in terms of A. Then $B = 177 - A$, $E = 176 - A$, $J = 2A - 177$, $F = 4A - 353$, ...

SS Puzzle 8 Since the side of the big square is 112 units and the side of square C is 50 units, the sides of squares A and B total 62. Thus, $A + B = 62$. But the sides of A and B differ in length by 4. So $B - A = 4$. Solve these two equations for A and B. A and E differ by 4. B and C also differ by 4. $B + C + D = 112$.

NC Puzzle 7
1. You are looking for two numbers that sum to 18 (half perimeter) and multiply to 56.

2. Solve for (C, D): $C + D = 31$ and $C - D = 15$.

3. From the Pythagorean theorem: $b^2 + 9^2 = c^2$.
   From the perimeter statement: $b + c + 9 = 36$.

4. $G + (G + 1) + (G + 2) = 57$.

5. $x + (x + 2) + (x + 4) + 6 = 21$.

6. From the perimeter statement: $x + x + x + b = 26$.
   From the area formula: $32 = (1/2)(4)(x + b)$.

NC Puzzle 8

1. $f(4) = 13 - 4 = 9$, therefore A = 9.

8. If $f(x) = 100 - 2x$, then find x so that $100 - 2x = 50$. Thus, $2x = 50$ or $x = 25$.

NC Puzzle 9

1. Surface area of body = surface area of palm × 100.
   Therefore, 1100 = 100(C) and 600 = 100(D).

2. A = 80% of (200 – 190). B = 75% of (200 – 184).

3. Miles from a thunderstorm = (number of seconds between thunder and lightning)/5.
   Therefore, E = 10/5 and F = 5/5.

4. (550' in elevation)/(boiling point falls 1° Fahrenheit) = (12,100' in elevation)/(boiling point falls G° Fahrenheit)
   (550' in elevation)/(boiling point falls 1° Fahrenheit) = (9,350' in elevation)/(boiling point falls H° Fahrenheit)

NC Puzzle 10

3. If $s(t) = (1/6)(t - 4)$, then E = $s(28) = (1/6)(28 - 4) = (1/6)(24) = 4$.

4. Temperature (°F) = (number of chirps/14 seconds) + 40. Therefore, 68° = G + 40.

5. Amount of ticket = $50 + 15(mph over limit)

8. Calories burned = 315 + (5 calories/minute)(minutes on eliptical trainer)

NC Puzzle 12

1. Distance traveled by Matt + distance traveled by Easton = total distance.
   (Matt's rate)(4 hrs) + (Easton's rate)(4 hrs) = total distance.
   (3.75 mph)(4 hrs) + (5 mph)(4 hrs) = A.

2. D = Diane's speed = 22.5 miles/2.25 hours.
   C = John's speed = 22.5 miles/(5/6) hour.

3. Distance traveled by Angie + distance traveled by Zack = total distance.
   (Angie's distance) + (Zack's distance) = 25. Therefore E + F = 25.
   (Zack's distance) – (Angie's distance) = 7. Therefore F – E = 7.

4. (Distance traveled by giraffe) – (distance traveled by elephant) = 2.5 miles.
   (Distance traveled by giraffe) + (distance traveled by elephant) = 13.5 miles.

5. Distance A to B = Distance B to A.
   Thus, (rate blimp + rate wind)(51 minutes) = (rate blimp – rate wind)(63 minutes).

Hints for Chapter 7: Sequential Reasoning and Geometry

AC Puzzle 3.1 Triangle is isosceles so $a + 55 + 55 = 180$.

AC Puzzle 9.1 Triangle is isosceles so $56 + n + n = 180$.

AC Puzzle 13.1 Each exterior angle of an equiangular hexagon = 360/6.
Each exterior angle of an equiangular octagon = 360/8.

AC Puzzle 15.1 Since a and b are right angles, $c + 56 = 180$.

ACPuzzle 18.1 $a = 102$, $b = 78$, $c = 78$, $d = 180 - 102$, $e = (1/2)a$, $f = (1/2)a$, ...

AC Puzzle 20.1 $20 = (1/2)a$, $a = b$, $63 = (1/2)(b + m)$, $n = 63$, ...

Answers for Chapter 1: Warm-Up Puzzles

CN Puzzle 1 The color is Yellow: Y.

CN Puzzle 2 The color is Blue: B.

SR Puzzle 1 1-3-8-6-30-28-14-19-95-100 **or** 1-5-3-8-6-30-28-14-19-95-100

SR Puzzle 2 1-2-5-7-9-27-54-52-55-58-29-31-93-95-97-100

Container Puzzle 1

	start	1	2	3	4	5
8-L	0	8	3	3	0	8
5-L	0	0	5	0	3	3

Container Puzzle 2

	start	1	2	3	4	5	6	7
9-L	0	0	4	4	8	8	9	0
4-L	0	4	0	4	0	4	3	3

Container Puzzle 3

	start	1	2	3	4	5	6	7	8	9	10	11
11-L	0	11	8	8	5	5	2	2	0	11	10	10
3-L	0	0	3	0	3	0	3	0	2	2	3	0

Container Puzzle 4

	start	1	2
6-L	6	3	3
3-L	0	3	2
1-L	0	0	1

Container Puzzle 5

	start	1	2	3	4	5	6	7
8-L	8	3	3	6	6	1	1	4
5-L	0	5	2	2	0	5	4	4
3-L	0	0	3	0	2	2	3	0

Container Puzzle 6 Start both timers. The 15 minutes begin when the 7-minute timer is finished. Four minutes later, your 11-minute timer is finished. Turn it over for an additional 11 minutes and when it is finished you've measured 15 minutes.

SM Puzzle 1 The solution to the *Tower of Hanoi* puzzle with seven disks will take 127 moves ($2^7 - 1$). It would take too long to describe all the steps. For three disks (7 moves) the solution would looks like this:
Let's start with the three disks on the far left peg (A). Move disk 1 to B, then disk 2 to C, then disk 1 to C, then move disk 3 to B. You are half way home. Move disk 1 to A, then disk 2 to B and finally disk 1 to B. Notice that the smallest disk (1) is moved every other time in the pattern A→B→C→A→B→C→A→B. The other moves are always forced. This same pattern is true no matter how many disks are in the puzzle.

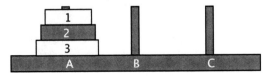

Starting Position

Final Position

SM Puzzle 2 The number of moves it takes to solve the *Tower of Hanoi* puzzle with 64 disks is $2^{64} - 1$ (See the table below). Assuming you could make a move every second, it would take about 5.28×10^{11} years or nearly six billion centuries.

The number of disks	1	2	3	4	5	6	7	...	n	64
The number of moves	1	3	7	15	31	63	127		$2^n - 1$	$2^{64} - 1$

SM Puzzle 3 CR1•HU2•GL2•EL3•AD2•BD2•XR5

SM Puzzle 4 JR1•AU3•IL1•EL1•FL2•GD2•BL1•CL1•KD2•XR4

SM Puzzle 5 FL1•EU1•GL3•CU4•HU1•AR3•BR3•GR3•ED3•XR6

SM Puzzle 6 IL1•KL1•AU1•JL2•CL3•AD2•BD3•GD1•EL1•FU1•XR6

Cryptarithm Puzzle 1

```
   9 2 1
 + 1 2 1
 -------
 1 0 4 2
```

Cryptarithm Puzzle 2

```
   7 4 4 1
 + 7 0 2 1
 ---------
 1 4 4 6 2
```

Cryptarithm Puzzle 3

```
    5 0
 +  5 0
 ------
 1 0 0
```

Cryptarithm Puzzle 4

```
   2468
 x   13
 ------
   7404
   2468
 ------
  32084
```

Cryptarithm Puzzle 5

```
    748
    487
 +  874
 ------
   2109
```

Cryptarithm Puzzle 6

```
     7 1 6
 x     1 6
 ---------
   4 2 9 6
   7 1 6
 ---------
 1 1 4 5 6
```

RP Puzzle 1 F8-TR-TR-F2-TR-F4-TL-F4-TR-TR-F3-TL

RP Puzzle 2 TR-F1-TR-F6-TL-F6-TL-F3-TL-F2-TR-F3-TR-F3-TL-F1

RP Puzzle 3 F9-TR-F1-CA-F9-TL-F3-TR-F3-CB-F2-TR-F9-TR-F11-CC-F4-TL-F3

RP Puzzle 4 F6-TL-F17-TL-F6-TL-F13-TL-F15-TL-F16-TL-F4-TL-F8-TL-F9-TL-F13-TL-F12-TL-F19-TL-F17-TL-F4-TL-F5-TL-F7-TL-F3

RP Puzzle 5 F2-TR-F11-TL-F16-CE-F2-TL-F22-CD-TR-TR-F11-TR-OE-F2-TL-F3-OD-F6-TR-F1-CC-F3-OD-F6-TR-F16-TR-F6-TL-F2-TL-F2-OC-F3-DE-DD-DC-CB-TR-TR-F7-OB-F3-TR-F5-CH-TR-TR-F5-TL-F5-TL-F6-TR-F7-TL-F3-TR-OB-F2-TR-F3-OH-F6-CF-TR-TR-F9-TL-F3-TR-F3-TL-F6-TL-F3-TL-OF-F2-DF-DH-CS-F1-CX-F1-OX-F3-OB-F3-OX-F4

Answers for Chapter 2: Racetrack

2.2 Mathematical Connections: Vectors

If the distance is 520 miles and the speed is 127.4 mph then, from the distance formula, $t = d/r$, we have 520/127.4, or about 4.1 hours.

Associative property for addition of vectors:

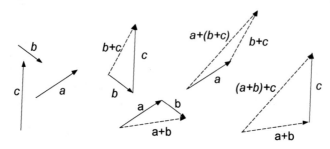

Answers for Chapter 3: Movement Puzzles

CS Puzzle 1 One solution is Wr-Wd-Bl2-Wu-Wr.

CS Puzzle 2 Wr2-Wd2-Wr3-Wd1-Bl5-Bl5-Wu1-Wr3-Wu2-Wr2

CS Puzzle 3 Wr3-Wd2-Wr4-Wd1-Bl6-Bl6-Bl6-Wu1-Wr5-Wu2-Wr4-Br4-Br4-Br4-Wr5-Wd1-Bl6-Bl6-Bl6-Wu1-Wr3

CS Puzzle 4 Wr3-Wd2-Wr4-Wd1-Bl7-Bl7-Bl7-Bl7-Wu1-Wr6-Wu2-Wr5-Br5-Br5-Br5-Br5-Wr5-Wd2-Wr6-Wd1-Bl7-Bl7-Bl7-Bl7-Wu1-Wr4-Wu2-Wr3

CJ Puzzle 1 The solutions below use symbols like those shown below.

Slide to the right   **Jump to the left**

One coin of each color: R L̂ R

Two coins of each color: R L̂ L̂ R R L̂ L̂ R

Three coins of each color: R L̂ L̂ R R R L̂ L̂ L̂ R R R L̂ L̂ R

Four coins of each color: R L̂ L̂ R R R L̂ L̂ L̂ L̂ R R R R L̂ L̂ L̂ L̂ R R R L̂ L̂ R

Five coins of each color: R L̂ L̂ R R R L̂ L̂ L̂ L̂ R R R R L̂ L̂ L̂ L̂ L̂ R R R R R L̂ L̂ L̂ L̂ L̂ R R R R L̂ L̂ L̂ L̂ R R R L̂ L̂ R

SB Puzzle 1 Four moves: 2-3-1-2

SB Puzzle 2 12 moves: 6-8-4-5-7-6-8-7-5-4-7-8

SB Puzzle 3 22 moves: 12-11-10-9-15-13-14-10-9-15-13-14-15-9-10-15-14-13-9-10-11-12

SB Puzzle 4

3 ↑ → 2 ↓ Q ← ↓

SB Puzzle 5

2 ← 3 ← 1 ↑ Q → ↑

SB Puzzle 6

1 ↑ → 3 ↑ 1 ← Q ← ↓

SB Puzzle 7

5 ↓ ← ↑ Q ↑ ← ↓

SB Puzzle 8

Q ↑ 2 ← 3 ↑ → ↑ Q ← ↓

SB Puzzle 9

5 ← 2 ↓ 4 ← ↑ Q ←

SB Puzzle 10

3 ↑ 4 ↓ Q ↑ →

SB Puzzle 11

4 ↑ → Q → ↓

SB Puzzle 12

3 → ↑ → Q ↑

SB Puzzle 13

3 ↑ 2 → Q ↑ ← ↓

SB Puzzle 14

Q ↑ 3 ↑ 2 → 4 ↑ Q →

SB Puzzle 15

1 ← ↓ Q ↓ ← ↓ →

SB Puzzle 16

Q → 1 ↓ 2 → Q ↓

SB Puzzle 17

4 ← 2 ← 3 ↑ Q → ↑

SB Puzzle 18

2 ← 4 ← ↑ 5 ← Q ←

SB Puzzle 19

1 → ↑ Q ← ↓ →

SB Puzzle 20

2 ↑ 4 ↑ Q → ↓ ←

SB Puzzle 21

4 → 3 → Q ↑ ← ↓

SB Puzzle 22

2 ↑ 4 ↑ Q → ↓ ←

SB Puzzle 23

1 ↓ Q → 2 ↓ 3 ← Q ↑ ←

SB Puzzle 24

4 → ↑ ← Q ↓ → ↓ ←

SB Puzzle 25

1 → ↓ ← Q → ↓ ←

SB Puzzle 26

Q → 5 ↓ 2 ↓ 4 ← 1 → Q ↓

SB Puzzle 27

5 → ↑ 2 ← 4 ↑ ← Q ↑

QB Puzzle 1

1 ↓ 3 ↘ ↗ Q ↓

QB Puzzle 2

1 ↓ Q ↗ ↑ ↗

QB Puzzle 3

2 ↘ 3 ↗ 5 ↓ Q ↓

QB Puzzle 4

Q ↗ 1 ↑ ↗ Q ↗ ↓

QB Puzzle 5

3 ↑ 5 ↗ ↘ Q ↗

QB Puzzle 6

4 ↑ ↗ 2 ↘ ↙ Q ↑ ↗

QB Puzzle 7

1 ↘ 3 ↑ ↘ ↗ Q ↓

QB Puzzle 8

Q ↗ ↖ 4 ↑ ↗ ↓ Q ↗

QB Puzzle 9

3 ↗ 5 ↗ 1 ↗ Q ↑ ↖

QB Puzzle 10

Q ↘ 5 ↗ 4 ↑ 3 ↘ Q ↑

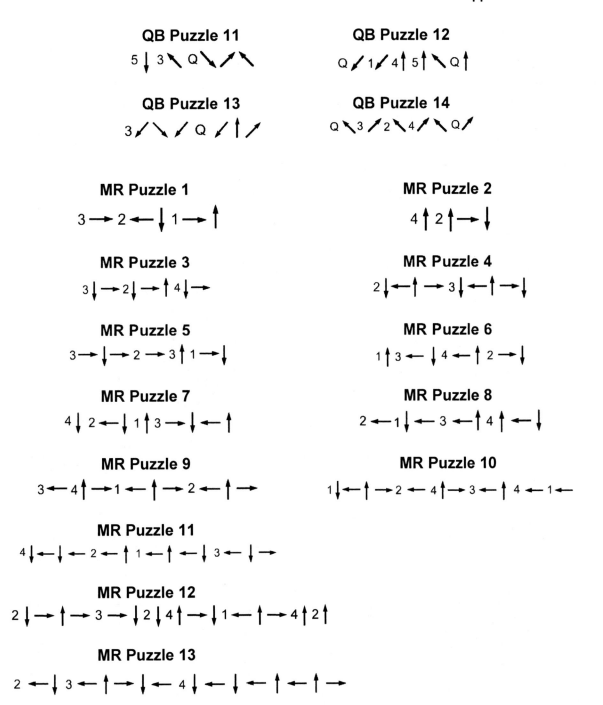

QB Puzzle 11

5 ↓ 3 ↘ Q ↘ ↗ ↖

QB Puzzle 12

Q ↗ 1 ↗ 4 ↑ 5 ↑ ↘ Q ↑

QB Puzzle 13

3 ↙ ↘ ↙ Q ↙ ↑ ↗

QB Puzzle 14

Q ↘ 3 ↗ 2 ↘ 4 ↗ ↘ Q ↗

MR Puzzle 1

3 → 2 ← ↓ 1 → ↑

MR Puzzle 2

4 ↑ 2 ↑ → ↓

MR Puzzle 3

3 ↓ → 2 ↓ → ↑ 4 ↓ →

MR Puzzle 4

2 ↓ ← ↑ → 3 ↓ ← ↑ → ↓

MR Puzzle 5

3 → ↓ → 2 → 3 ↑ 1 → ↓

MR Puzzle 6

1 ↑ 3 ← ↓ 4 ← ↑ 2 → ↓

MR Puzzle 7

4 ↓ 2 ← ↓ 1 ↑ 3 → ↓ ← ↑

MR Puzzle 8

2 ← 1 ↓ ← 3 ← ↑ 4 ↑ ← ↓

MR Puzzle 9

3 ← 4 ↑ → 1 ← ↑ → 2 ← ↑ →

MR Puzzle 10

1 ↓ ← ↑ → 2 ← 4 ↑ → 3 ← ↑ 4 ← 1 ←

MR Puzzle 11

4 ↓ ← ↓ ← 2 ← ↑ 1 ← ↑ ← ↓ 3 ← ↓ →

MR Puzzle 12

2 ↓ → ↑ → 3 → ↓ 2 ↓ 4 ↑ → ↓ 1 ← ↑ → 4 ↑ 2 ↑

MR Puzzle 13

2 ← ↓ 3 ← ↑ → ↓ ← 4 ↓ ← ↓ ← ↑ ← ↑ →

3.5 Mathematical Connections: Archimedean Tilings

The remaining five Archimedean tilings:

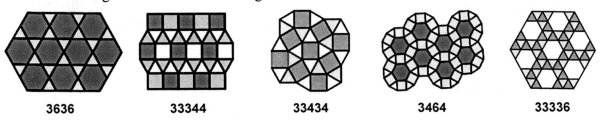

3636   33344   33434   3464   33336

Answers for Chapter 4: Tour Puzzles

RT Puzzle 1 The first two puzzles are possible, but the last three are not because the starting and ending squares are the same parity, either both odd or both even. If you start on an odd square, and there is an even number of squares, then you must end on an even square.

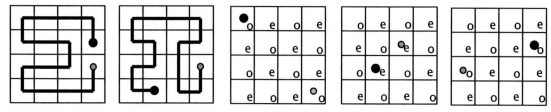

RT Puzzle 2 (Many possible answers)

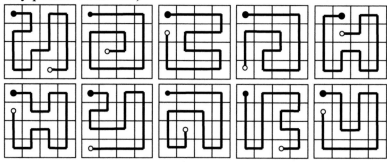

RT Puzzle 3

3	2	25	24	23	22
4	1	26	27	28	21
5	6	31	30	29	20
8	7	32	33	36	19
9	12	13	34	35	18
10	11	14	15	16	17

RT Puzzle 4

5	4	3	32	31	30
6	7	2	33	34	29
9	8	1	36	35	28
10	11	18	19	26	27
13	12	17	20	25	24
14	15	16	21	22	23

RT Puzzle 5

10	9	8	7	6	5
11	12	13	14	1	4
18	17	16	15	2	3
19	36	35	34	31	30
20	23	24	33	32	29
21	22	25	26	27	28

RT Puzzle 6

1	2	3	4	5	40	41
10	9	8	7	6	39	42
11	14	15	16	17	38	43
12	13	20	19	18	37	44
23	22	21	34	35	36	45
24	27	28	33	32	47	46
25	26	29	30	31	48	49

RT Puzzle 7

33	34	35	36	47	46	45
32	31	30	37	48	49	44
27	28	29	38	39	40	43
26	25	24	23	22	41	42
5	4	3	20	21	16	15
6	1	2	19	18	17	14
7	8	9	10	11	12	13

RT Puzzle 8

5	4	3	40	41	44	45
6	7	2	39	42	43	46
9	8	1	38	49	48	47
10	17	18	37	36	35	34
11	16	19	30	31	32	33
12	15	20	29	28	27	26
13	14	21	22	23	24	25

RT Puzzle 9

41	40	39	38	37	30	29
42	43	44	45	36	31	28
1	2	49	46	35	32	27
4	3	48	47	34	33	26
5	6	13	14	15	24	25
8	7	12	17	16	23	22
9	10	11	18	19	20	21

RT Puzzle 10

1	2	9	10	55	54	49	48
4	3	8	11	56	53	50	47
5	6	7	12	57	52	51	46
16	15	14	13	58	59	60	45
17	28	29	64	63	62	61	44
18	27	30	31	32	33	34	43
19	26	25	24	37	36	35	42
20	21	22	23	38	39	40	41

RT Puzzle 11

24	25	26	27	36	37	42	43
23	30	29	28	35	38	41	44
22	31	32	33	34	39	40	45
21	16	15	64	63	62	47	46
20	17	14	1	2	61	48	49
19	18	13	4	3	60	51	50
10	11	12	5	58	59	52	53
9	8	7	6	57	56	55	54

RT Puzzle 12

28	29	34	35	36	37	38	39
27	30	33	(64)	61	60	59	40
26	31	32	63	62	57	58	41
25	24	23	22	21	56	43	42
16	17	18	19	20	55	44	45
15	10	9	8	7	54	47	46
14	11	2	(1)	6	53	48	49
13	12	3	4	5	52	51	50

RT Puzzle 13

55	56	57	8	9	10	11	12
54	53	58	7	6	5	4	13
51	52	59	(64)	63	2	3	14
50	49	60	61	62	(1)	16	15
47	48	43	42	29	28	17	18
46	45	44	41	30	27	20	19
37	38	39	40	31	26	21	22
36	35	34	33	32	25	24	23

RT Puzzle 14

37	38	41	42	45	46	49
36	39	40	43	44	47	48
35	34	33	32	31	26	25
6	5	4	3	30	27	24
7	8	9	2	29	28	23
12	11	10	1	18	19	22
13	14	15	16	17	20	21

RT Puzzle 15

13	12	9	8	3	2	45	46
14	11	10	7	4	1	44	47
15	18	19	6	5	42	43	48
16	17	20	21	22	41	50	49
29	28	25	24	23	40	51	52
30	27	26	37	38	39	54	53
31	34	35	36	61	60	55	56
32	33	64	63	62	59	58	57

RT Puzzle 16

47	46	43	42	33	32	31	24	23
48	45	44	41	34	29	30	25	22
49	50	39	40	35	28	27	26	21
52	51	38	37	36	9	10	11	20
53	54	55	56	57	8	7	12	19
62	61	60	59	58	81	6	13	18
63	64	65	78	79	80	5	14	17
68	67	66	77	76	75	4	15	16
69	70	71	72	73	74	3	2	1

RT Puzzle 17

3	2	9	10	11	12	13	14	15
4	1	8	49	48	47	18	17	16
5	6	7	50	51	46	19	22	23
78	79	80	81	52	45	20	21	24
77	76	75	74	53	44	27	26	25
68	69	70	73	54	43	28	29	30
67	66	71	72	55	42	41	32	31
64	65	60	59	56	39	40	33	34
63	62	61	58	57	38	37	36	35

RT Puzzle 18

6	7	12	13	14	15	24	25
5	8	11	18	17	16	23	26
4	9	10	19	20	21	22	27
3	2	1	48	47	30	29	28
52	51	50	49	46	31	32	33
53	62	63	64	45	44	43	34
54	61	60	59	40	41	42	35
55	56	57	58	39	38	37	36

RT Puzzle 19

6	7	12	13	18	19	20	21
5	8	11	14	17	28	27	22
4	9	10	15	16	29	26	23
3	2	1	32	31	30	25	24
36	35	34	33	50	51	52	53
37	46	47	48	49	64	63	54
38	45	44	43	60	61	62	55
39	40	41	42	59	58	57	56

RT Puzzle 20

10	11	12	47	46	45	44	43
9	14	13	48	49	50	51	42
8	15	16	55	54	53	52	41
7	18	17	56	57	58	59	40
6	19	64	63	62	61	60	39
5	20	21	34	35	36	37	38
4	1	22	33	32	31	30	29
3	2	23	24	25	26	27	28

RT Puzzle 21

5	4	3	80	79	70	69	68	67
6	7	2	81	78	71	64	65	66
9	8	1	76	77	72	63	60	59
10	15	16	75	74	73	62	61	58
11	14	17	42	43	44	45	56	57
12	13	18	41	40	39	46	55	54
21	20	19	30	31	38	47	48	53
22	25	26	29	32	37	36	49	52
23	24	27	28	33	34	35	50	51

RT Puzzle 22

11	12	13	18	19	24	25	26	27
10	9	14	17	20	23	30	29	28
7	8	15	16	21	22	31	32	33
6	3	2	1	38	37	36	35	34
5	4	69	68	39	40	47	48	49
80	81	70	67	42	41	46	51	50
79	78	71	66	43	44	45	52	53
76	77	72	65	62	61	58	57	54
75	74	73	64	63	60	59	56	55

RT Puzzle 23

35	36	39	40	45	46	55	56	57
34	37	38	41	44	47	54	59	58
33	32	31	42	43	48	53	60	61
28	29	30	23	22	49	52	63	62
27	26	25	24	21	50	51	64	65
8	9	12	13	20	69	68	67	66
7	10	11	14	19	70	75	76	81
6	1	2	15	18	71	74	77	80
5	4	3	16	17	72	73	78	79

RT Puzzle 24

37	38	39	40	41	42	45	46	47
36	35	34	33	32	43	44	49	48
5	4	3	2	31	56	55	50	51
6	7	8	(1)	30	57	54	53	52
11	10	9	28	29	58	59	60	61
12	13	14	27	80	79	78	63	62
17	16	15	26	(81)	76	77	64	65
18	21	22	25	74	75	70	69	66
19	20	23	24	73	72	71	68	67

RT Puzzle 25

51	50	49	48	47	46	45	40	39
52	59	60	61	62	63	44	41	38
53	58	67	66	65	64	43	42	37
54	57	68	31	32	33	34	35	36
55	56	69	30	(1)	2	3	4	5
72	71	70	29	28	9	8	7	6
73	80	(81)	26	27	10	11	12	13
74	79	78	25	22	21	18	17	14
75	76	77	24	23	20	19	16	15

RT Puzzle 26

63	64	65	70	71	76	77	46	45
62	61	66	69	72	75	78	47	44
59	60	67	68	73	74	79	48	43
58	57	56	55	54	(81)	80	49	42
9	8	(1)	2	53	52	51	50	41
10	7	6	3	24	25	26	39	40
11	12	5	4	23	28	27	38	37
14	13	18	19	22	29	32	33	36
15	16	17	20	21	30	31	34	35

RT Puzzle 27

53	52	51	50	49	48	47	44	43
54	55	18	19	20	21	46	45	42
57	56	17	16	15	22	23	40	41
58	59	2	3	14	25	24	39	38
61	60	(1)	4	13	26	35	36	37
62	7	6	5	12	27	34	33	32
63	8	9	10	11	28	29	30	31
64	67	68	71	72	75	76	77	78
65	66	69	70	73	74	(81)	80	79

RT Puzzle 28

71	72	73	4	5	10	11	12	13
70	69	74	3	6	9	22	21	14
67	68	75	2	7	8	23	20	15
66	65	76	1	48	47	24	19	16
63	64	77	50	49	46	25	18	17
62	79	78	51	44	45	26	27	28
61	80	(81)	52	43	38	37	36	29
60	57	56	53	42	39	34	35	30
59	58	55	54	41	40	33	32	31

RT Puzzle 29

67	66	65	62	61	58	57	54	53
68	69	64	63	60	59	56	55	52
71	70	75	76	77	48	49	50	51
72	73	74	(81)	78	47	32	31	30
3	2	1	80	79	46	33	28	29
4	5	42	43	44	45	34	27	26
7	6	41	40	39	38	35	24	25
8	11	12	15	16	37	36	23	22
9	10	13	14	17	18	19	20	21

RT Puzzle 30

47	48	51	52	65	66	67	68	69
46	49	50	53	64	63	62	71	70
45	44	43	54	59	60	61	72	73
4	3	42	55	58	77	76	75	74
5	2	41	56	57	78	79	80	81
6	1	40	39	38	37	36	35	34
7	12	13	18	19	20	21	32	33
8	11	14	17	24	23	22	31	30
9	10	15	16	25	26	27	28	29

RT Puzzle 31

59	60	61	62	63	68	69	80	79
58	55	54	53	64	67	70	81	78
57	56	51	52	65	66	71	72	77
48	49	50	27	26	25	24	73	76
47	30	29	28	21	22	23	74	75
46	31	32	33	20	13	12	11	10
45	40	39	34	19	14	1	8	9
44	41	38	35	18	15	2	7	6
43	42	37	36	17	16	3	4	5

RT Puzzle 32

73	72	67	66	61	60	45	44	43
74	71	68	65	62	59	46	47	42
75	70	69	64	63	58	57	48	41
76	77	78	79	80	55	56	49	40
1	2	3	4	81	54	53	50	39
8	7	6	5	24	25	52	51	38
9	10	11	12	23	26	35	36	37
16	15	14	13	22	27	34	33	32
17	18	19	20	21	28	29	30	31

RT Puzzle 33

41	40	39	38	37	36	35	30	29
42	45	46	47	48	49	34	31	28
43	44	55	54	51	50	33	32	27
58	57	56	53	52	23	24	25	26
59	60	61	78	79	22	21	20	19
64	63	62	77	80	81	10	11	18
65	66	67	76	3	4	9	12	17
70	69	68	75	2	5	8	13	16
71	72	73	74	1	6	7	14	15

KT Puzzle 1

KT Puzzle 2

2	8	(9)
3	(1)	7
4	5	6

KT Puzzle 3

(1)	2	7
3	6	8
5	4	(9)

KT Puzzle 4

2	3	4
(1)	5	(9)
6	7	8

KT Puzzle 5

10	9	8	6
11	(16)	5	7
12	15	(1)	4
14	13	2	3

KT Puzzle 6

(16)	15	5	3
14	6	2	4
13	(1)	7	9
12	11	10	8

KT Puzzle 7

15	2	3	4
14	(16)	(1)	5
13	11	9	6
12	10	8	7

KT Puzzle 8

(1)	5	7	8	9
4	2	6	10	14
3	(25)	11	13	15
24	22	19	12	16
23	20	21	18	17

KT Puzzle 9

4	3	2	19	18
5	(1)	20	15	17
7	6	14	21	16
10	8	13	(25)	22
9	11	12	23	24

KT Puzzle 10

10	11	13	(25)	23
9	12	14	22	24
8	15	16	17	21
7	5	4	20	18
6	(1)	2	3	19

KT Puzzle 11

12	11	15	17	18	19
13	14	10	16	21	20
26	9	8	23	22	4
27	25	24	7	5	3
29	28	34	33	6	2
30	31	32	35	(36)	(1)

KT Puzzle 12

29	27	6	7	8	9
28	30	26	5	4	10
31	25	(1)	2	3	11
24	32	33	(36)	35	12
23	19	18	34	13	14
22	21	20	17	16	15

KT Puzzle 13

2	4	6	9	8	11
3	(1)	5	7	10	12
22	21	17	16	15	13
25	23	20	18	32	14
24	26	19	31	(36)	33
27	28	29	30	34	35

KT Puzzle 14

14	12	10	9	4	3
13	15	11	8	2	5
19	17	16	(1)	7	6
18	20	(36)	35	31	30
21	22	34	26	32	29
23	24	25	33	27	28

KT Puzzle 15

27	26	21	20	19		
(30)	28	25	22		18	
29	24	23		17	15	
4	3		(1)	14	16	
5		2	8	10	13	
	6	7	9	12	11	

KT Puzzle 16

		32	34			
	28	33	31	35		
27	26	29	30		(36)	
23	21	25		17	16	12	11
22	24	20	18		13	15	10
(1)		19	7	14	9	
	2	6	4	8		
	3	5				

KT Puzzle 17

		9	8	7	6		
		10	12	5	40		
31	30	11	4	13	39	41	42
29	32	3			14	38	43
28	2	33			37	15	(44)
(1)	27	34	35	36	18	17	16
		26	23	19	20		
		24	25	22	21		

KT Puzzle 18

		9	8	7	6		
		10	12	40	5		
31	30	11	41	13	39	4	3
29	32	42			14	38	2
28	43	33			37	15	(1)
(44)	27	34	35	36	18	17	16
		26	23	19	20		
		24	25	22	21		

KT Puzzle 19

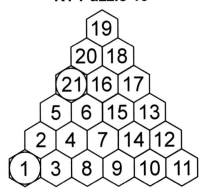

KT Puzzle 20

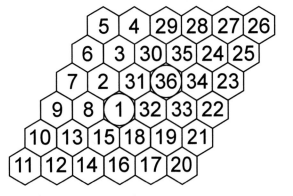

KT Puzzle 21

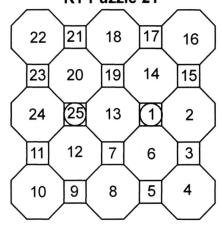

KT Puzzle 22

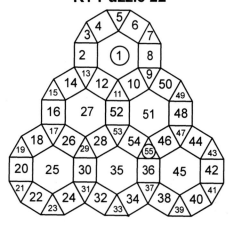

KnT Puzzle 1

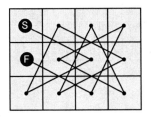

KnT Puzzle 2

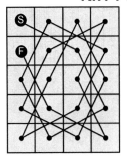

KnT Puzzle 3

23	18	5	10	(25)
6	11	24	19	14
17	22	13	4	9
12	7	2	15	20
(1)	16	21	8	3

KnT Puzzle 4

3	22	9	14	(1)
10	15	2	23	18
21	4	17	8	13
16	11	6	19	24
5	20	(25)	12	7

KnT Puzzle 5

3	10	21	16	5
20	15	4	11	22
9	2	23	6	17
14	19	8	(25)	12
(1)	24	13	18	7

KnT Puzzle 6

32	25	30	21	34	23
29	18	33	24	9	20
26	31	28	19	22	35
17	4	(1)	10	13	8
2	27	6	15	(36)	11
5	16	3	12	7	14

KnT Puzzle 7

13	26	21	30	19	28
22	(1)	12	27	6	31
25	14	23	20	29	18
(36)	11	2	5	32	7
15	24	9	34	17	4
10	35	16	3	8	33

KnT Puzzle 8

28	11	24	5	26	35
23	6	27	34	17	4
10	29	12	25	36	33
7	22	9	16	3	18
30	13	20	1	32	15
21	8	31	14	19	2

KnT Puzzle 9

(1)	22	19	44	35	40	37
20	43	24	41	38	45	34
23	2	21	18	47	36	39
4	17	42	25	8	33	46
11	14	3	32	29	48	27
16	5	12	9	26	7	30
13	10	15	6	31	28	(49)

KnT Puzzle 10

(1)	46	21	36	3	48	19
22	37	2	47	20	31	4
45	12	35	38	29	18	(49)
34	23	44	11	32	5	30
13	10	33	42	39	28	17
24	43	8	15	26	41	6
9	14	25	40	7	16	27

KnT Puzzle 11

17	6	33	46	15	4	25
32	47	16	5	26	45	14
7	18	43	34	39	24	3
42	31	48	27	44	13	38
19	8	35	40	(49)	2	23
30	41	10	21	28	37	12
9	20	29	36	11	22	(1)

KnT Puzzle 12

49	12	23	42	3	14	25
22	39	2	13	24	41	4
11	48	45	40	43	26	15
38	21	32	(1)	46	5	34
31	10	47	44	33	16	27
20	37	8	29	18	35	6
9	30	19	36	7	28	17

KnT Puzzle 13

57	32	49	40	51	60	13	4
48	41	58	33	12	5	52	61
31	56	39	50	59	54	3	14
42	47	34	55	6	11	62	53
21	30	43	38	23	2	15	10
46	35	22	27	18	7	24	63
29	20	37	44	(1)	26	9	16
36	45	28	19	8	17	(64)	25

KnT Puzzle 14

40	43	38	33	22	29	24	27
37	34	41	44	9	26	21	30
42	39	36	5	32	23	28	25
35	6	45	10	(1)	8	31	20
46	57	2	7	4	19	(64)	61
51	54	49	58	11	62	13	16
56	47	52	3	18	15	60	63
53	50	55	48	59	12	17	14

KnT Puzzle 15

3	28	9	24	5	30	11	18
8	23	4	29	10	17	14	31
27	2	21	6	25	12	19	16
22	7	26	(1)	20	15	32	13
45	(64)	47	52	33	58	39	54
48	51	44	57	38	53	34	59
63	46	49	42	61	36	55	40
50	43	62	37	56	41	60	35

KnT Puzzle 16

37	(64)	45	58	39	62	43	52
46	57	38	63	44	51	40	61
(1)	36	55	48	59	42	53	50
56	47	2	35	54	49	60	41
9	28	17	22	3	34	15	24
18	21	10	27	16	23	4	33
29	8	19	12	31	6	25	14
20	11	30	7	26	13	32	5

KnT Puzzle 17

11	8	13	16	51	42	37	40
14	17	10	7	36	39	52	43
9	12	15	48	45	50	41	38
18	47	6	(1)	30	35	44	53
5	28	19	46	49	54	63	34
22	25	2	29	(64)	31	60	57
27	4	23	20	55	58	33	62
24	21	26	3	32	61	56	59

KnT Puzzle 18

3	48	57	8	5	12	59	10
56	31	4	49	58	9	6	13
47	2	51	32	7	60	11	22
52	55	30	(1)	50	21	14	61
29	46	53	18	33	62	23	20
54	43	28	39	(64)	19	34	15
45	38	41	26	17	36	63	24
42	27	44	37	40	25	16	35

KnT Puzzle 19

28	3	22	9	30	5	24	15
21	10	29	4	23	16	31	6
2	27	12	19	8	25	14	17
11	20	(1)	26	13	18	7	32
(64)	39	50	45	58	33	52	43
49	46	57	40	51	44	59	34
38	63	48	55	36	61	42	53
47	56	37	62	41	54	35	60

KnT Puzzle 20

(1)	38	57	44	63	40	59	50
56	45	(64)	39	58	51	62	41
37	2	47	54	43	60	49	52
46	55	36	3	48	53	42	61
29	10	21	16	35	4	23	14
20	17	28	11	22	15	34	5
9	30	19	26	7	32	13	24
18	27	8	31	12	25	6	33

KnT Puzzle 21

75	58	45	32	77	60	47	34	79
44	31	76	59	46	33	78	61	48
57	74	21	12	7	2	23	80	35
30	43	6	17	22	13	8	49	62
73	56	11	20	(1)	24	3	36	(81)
42	29	16	5	18	9	14	63	50
55	72	19	10	15	4	25	66	37
28	41	70	53	26	39	68	51	64
71	54	27	40	69	52	65	38	67

KnT Puzzle 22

13	76	15	20	11	74	25	22	9
16	19	12	75	26	21	10	67	24
77	14	17	28	73	56	23	8	69
18	81	78	43	60	27	68	57	66
79	44	29	2	55	72	59	70	7
30	51	80	61	42	3	36	65	58
45	48	41	52	1	54	71	6	35
50	31	46	39	62	33	4	37	64
47	40	49	32	53	38	63	34	5

KnT Puzzle 23

86	91	88	69	84	71	80	67	64	61
89	4	85	98	81	68	77	62	79	66
92	87	90	3	70	83	72	65	60	63
5	2	97	82	99	76	57	78	73	44
96	93	8	(1)	50	25	74	45	56	59
9	6	95	24	75	(100)	51	58	43	46
94	23	28	7	26	49	32	47	52	55
13	10	15	22	33	20	53	40	37	42
16	29	12	27	18	31	48	35	54	39
11	14	17	30	21	34	19	38	41	36

KnT Puzzle 24

71	84	41	12	69	82	39	10	67	96
42	13	70	83	40	11	68	97	38	9
85	72	79	50	81	74	77	4	95	66
14	43	52	73	78	5	98	75	8	37
57	86	49	80	51	76	3	6	65	94
44	15	56	53	26	(1)	30	99	36	7
87	58	25	48	55	28	23	2	93	64
16	45	54	27	24	31	(100)	29	22	35
59	88	47	18	61	90	33	20	63	92
46	17	60	89	32	19	62	91	34	21

KnT Puzzle 25
Answers will vary, two possible answers.

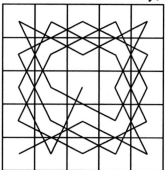
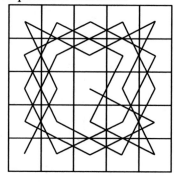

KnT Puzzle 26
Answers will vary, two possible answers.

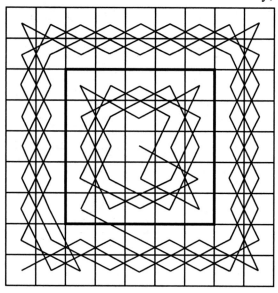
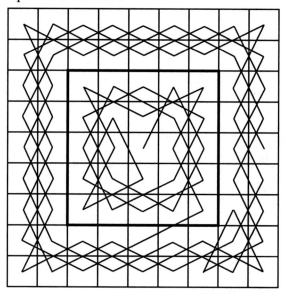

KnT Puzzle 27
KnT Puzzle 28

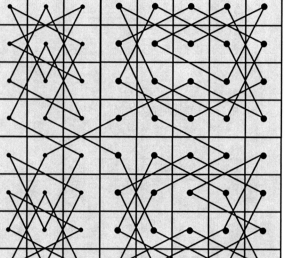

Path Puzzle 1

Path Puzzle 2

    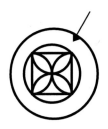

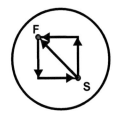 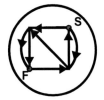  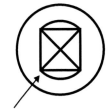

NO

Start anywhere and end in the same spot

 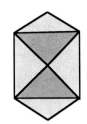 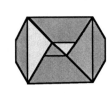  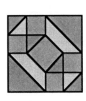

NO

NO

Path Puzzle 3

| CBT | Euler Circuit | Euler Path | Euler Path | Euler Path | Euler Circuit |

Path Puzzle 4

One possible solution.

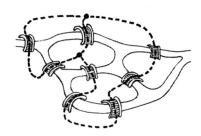

Path Puzzle 5

One possible solution.

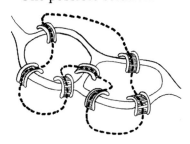

Answers for Chapter 5: Magic Square Puzzles

MS Puzzle 1

4	9	2
3	5	7
8	1	6

MS Puzzle 2

12	7	8
5	9	13
10	11	6

MS Puzzle 3

4	14	12
18	10	2
8	6	16

MS Puzzle 4

11	1	15
13	9	5
3	17	7

MS Puzzle 5

23	8	11
2	14	26
17	20	5

MS Puzzle 6

-3	11	1
7	3	-1
5	-5	9

MS Puzzle 7

19	4	7
-2	10	22
13	16	1

MS Puzzle 8

9	7	17
19	11	3
5	15	13

MS Puzzle 9

13	18	17
20	16	12
15	14	19

MS Puzzle 10

48	58	44
46	50	54
56	42	52

MS Puzzle 11

A few possible solutions.

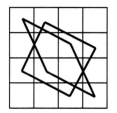 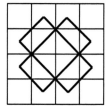 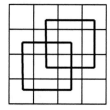 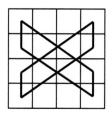

MS Puzzle 12

13	8	12	1
3	10	6	15
2	11	7	14
16	5	9	4

MS Puzzle 13

7	2	16	9
12	13	3	6
1	8	10	15
14	11	5	4

MS Puzzle 14

13	3	2	16
8	10	11	5
12	6	7	9
1	15	14	4

MS Puzzle 15

10	15	8	1
5	4	11	14
3	6	13	12
16	9	2	7

MS Puzzle 16

4	14	15	1
9	7	6	12
5	11	10	8
16	2	3	13

MS Puzzle 17

2	14	11	7
1	13	8	12
15	3	10	6
16	4	5	9

MS Puzzle 18

4	14	15	1
5	11	10	8
9	7	6	12
16	2	3	13

MS Puzzle 19

8	10	5	11
13	3	16	2
12	6	9	7
1	15	4	14

MS Puzzle 20

1	2	16	15
13	14	4	3
12	7	9	6
8	11	5	10

MS Puzzle 21

34	4	1	43
31	13	16	22
19	25	28	10
-2	40	37	7

MS Puzzle 22

25	15	23	1
5	19	11	29
3	21	13	27
31	9	17	7

MS Puzzle 23

19	5	6	16
12	10	9	15
8	14	13	11
7	17	18	4

MS Puzzle 24

10	0	-1	13
9	3	4	6
5	7	8	2
-2	12	11	1

MS Puzzle 25

19	9	8	22
14	16	17	11
18	12	13	15
7	21	20	10

MS Puzzle 26

0	11	10	-3
5	2	3	8
1	6	7	4
12	-1	-2	9

MS Puzzle 27

15	17	12	18
20	10	23	9
19	13	16	14
8	22	11	21

MS Puzzle 28

19	9	8	22
14	16	17	11
18	12	13	15
7	21	20	10

MS Puzzle 29

32	6	4	26
10	20	22	16
18	12	14	24
8	30	28	2

MS Puzzle 30

1	22	20	19	3
2	10	17	12	24
18	15	13	11	8
21	14	9	16	5
23	4	6	7	25

MS Puzzle 31

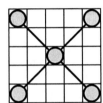

MS Puzzle 32

17	24	1	8	15
23	5	7	14	16
4	6	13	20	22
10	12	19	21	3
11	18	25	2	9

MS Puzzle 33

13	11	18	7	16
8	19	4	12	22
5	20	17	21	2
25	6	23	1	10
14	9	3	24	15

MS Puzzle 34

18	21	4	8	14
11	3	23	19	9
25	22	5	7	6
1	17	20	15	12
10	2	13	16	24

MS Puzzle 35

3	21	25	7	9
23	6	15	20	1
16	13	10	14	12
5	8	11	22	19
18	17	4	2	24

MS Puzzle 36

15	11	3	17	19
13	9	18	5	20
7	23	21	2	12
24	14	1	16	10
6	8	22	25	4

MS Puzzle 37

5	14	23	7	16
22	6	20	4	13
19	3	12	21	10
11	25	9	18	2
8	17	1	15	24

MS Puzzle 38

23	6	19	2	15
10	18	1	14	22
17	5	13	21	9
4	12	25	8	16
11	24	7	20	3

MS Puzzle 39

23	6	19	2	15
4	12	25	8	16
10	18	1	14	22
11	24	7	20	3
17	5	13	21	9

MS Puzzle 40

24	16	13	2	10
12	15	20	17	1
6	7	5	22	25
9	19	23	3	11
14	8	4	21	18

MS Puzzle 41

8	16	4	12	25
14	22	10	18	1
20	3	11	24	7
21	9	17	5	13
2	15	23	6	19

MS Puzzle 42

37	29	16	33	25
31	23	40	27	19
30	17	34	21	38
24	36	28	20	32
18	35	22	39	26

MS Puzzle 43

22	48	14	40	6
34	10	26	42	18
46	12	38	4	30
8	24	50	16	32
20	36	2	28	44

MS Puzzle 44

6	32	3	34	35	1
7	11	27	28	8	30
19	14	16	15	23	24
18	20	22	21	17	13
25	29	10	9	26	12
36	5	33	4	2	31

MS Puzzle 45

22	42	31	6	43	20	11
40	33	10	9	44	24	15
7	1	30	49	21	32	35
39	14	25	47	4	12	34
23	38	46	2	3	26	37
36	18	28	45	19	13	16
8	29	5	17	41	48	27

MS Puzzle 46

43	47	2	26	1	45	37	59
54	18	63	17	14	16	58	20
40	36	35	44	50	21	9	25
10	22	42	12	53	32	38	51
24	23	52	15	27	46	11	62
28	34	4	49	60	64	13	8
30	19	5	41	48	33	55	29
31	61	57	56	7	3	39	6

MS Puzzle 47

25	17	52	36	19	48	59	4
43	33	5	47	38	57	21	16
49	31	24	53	11	54	10	28
1	60	46	39	64	12	35	3
37	8	30	7	45	20	51	62
22	32	50	23	6	13	56	58
41	18	9	40	63	29	26	34
42	61	44	15	14	27	2	55

MS Puzzle 48

8	49	41	32	40	17	9	64
58	15	23	34	26	47	55	2
59	14	22	35	27	46	54	3
5	52	44	29	37	20	12	61
4	53	45	28	36	21	13	60
62	11	19	38	30	43	51	6
63	10	18	39	31	42	50	7
1	56	48	25	33	24	16	57

MS Puzzle 49

43	47	2	26	1	45	37	59
54	18	63	17	14	16	58	20
40	36	35	44	50	21	9	25
10	22	42	12	53	32	38	51
24	23	52	15	27	46	11	62
28	34	4	49	60	64	13	8
30	19	5	41	48	33	55	29
31	61	57	56	7	3	39	6

MS Puzzle 50

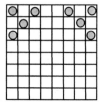 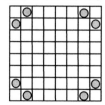 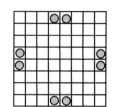

MS Puzzle 51

29	44	52	28	5	45	53	4
30	43	51	27	6	46	54	3
31	42	50	26	7	47	55	2
32	41	16	40	57	17	56	1
33	24	49	25	8	48	9	64
34	23	15	39	58	18	10	63
35	22	14	38	59	19	11	62
36	21	13	37	60	20	12	61

MS Puzzle 52

36	37	21	20	13	12	60	61
35	22	38	19	14	59	11	62
34	39	23	18	15	10	58	63
33	40	24	17	16	9	57	64
32	25	41	48	49	56	8	1
31	26	42	47	50	55	7	2
30	43	27	46	51	6	54	3
29	28	44	45	52	53	5	4

MS Puzzle 53

1	48	31	50	33	16	63	18
30	51	46	3	62	19	14	35
47	2	49	32	15	34	17	64
52	29	4	45	20	61	36	13
5	44	25	56	9	40	21	60
28	53	8	41	24	57	12	37
43	6	55	26	39	10	59	22
54	27	42	7	58	23	38	11

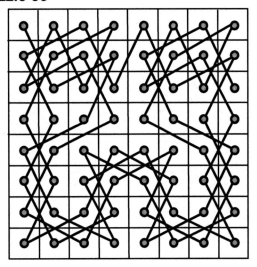

MS Puzzle 54

47	2	49	32	15	34	17	64
30	51	46	3	62	19	14	35
1	48	31	50	33	16	63	18
52	29	4	45	20	61	36	13
5	44	25	56	9	40	21	60
28	53	8	41	24	57	12	37
43	6	55	26	39	10	59	22
54	27	42	7	58	23	38	11

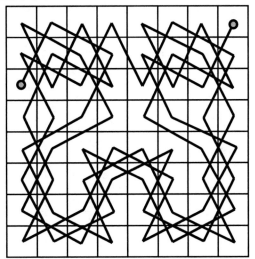

MS Puzzle 55

50	11	24	63	14	37	26	35
23	62	51	12	25	34	15	38
10	49	64	21	40	13	36	27
61	22	9	52	33	28	39	16
48	7	60	1	20	41	54	29
59	4	45	8	53	32	17	42
6	47	2	57	44	19	30	55
3	58	5	46	31	56	43	18

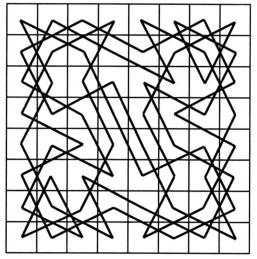

MS Puzzle 56

38	35	62	25	60	23	10	7
63	26	37	34	11	8	59	22
36	39	28	61	24	57	6	9
27	64	33	40	5	12	21	58
50	29	4	13	48	41	56	19
1	14	49	32	53	20	47	44
30	51	16	3	42	45	18	55
15	2	31	52	17	54	43	46

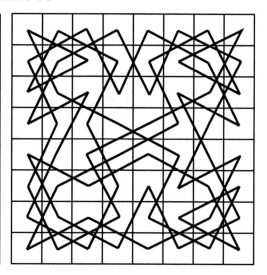

MS Puzzle 57 (Rajah of Mysore)

91	126	53	20	93	124	51	22	107	110	35	38
54	19	92	125	52	21	94	123	34	37	108	111
127	90	17	56	121	96	23	50	109	106	39	36
18	55	128	89	24	49	122	95	40	33	112	105
87	130	57	16	97	120	45	28	101	116	41	32
58	15	88	129	48	25	100	117	44	29	104	113
131	86	13	60	119	98	27	46	115	102	31	42
14	59	132	85	26	47	118	99	30	43	114	103
83	12	61	136	79	138	67	6	69	144	73	2
62	133	84	9	66	7	78	139	76	3	70	143
11	82	135	64	137	80	5	68	141	72	1	74
134	63	10	81	8	65	140	77	4	75	142	71

MS Puzzle 58 (Awani Kumar)

1	70	107	112	5	66	103	116	9	64	99	118
108	111	2	69	104	115	6	65	100	117	10	63
71	106	109	4	113	102	67	8	61	98	119	12
110	3	72	105	68	7	114	101	120	11	62	97
73	142	35	40	77	140	17	60	93	122	13	58
36	39	74	141	32	41	92	121	16	59	96	123
143	34	37	76	139	78	51	18	129	94	57	14
38	75	144	33	42	31	130	91	52	15	124	95
81	136	29	44	79	138	19	50	89	128	21	56
28	45	80	137	30	43	90	131	20	53	88	125
135	82	47	26	133	84	49	24	127	86	55	22
46	27	134	83	48	25	132	85	54	23	126	87

Answers for Chapter 6: Sequential Reasoning and Algebra

AMS Puzzle 1
$x = 7$

9	7	17
19	11	3
5	15	13

AMS Puzzle 2
$x = 9$

25	5	9
-3	13	29
17	21	1

AMS Puzzle 3
$x = 25$

20	45	10
15	25	35
40	5	30

AMS Puzzle 4
$x = 21$, $y = 9$

12	9	24
27	15	3
6	21	18

AMS Puzzle 5
$x = 6, y = 9$

21	6	9
0	12	24
15	18	3

AMS Puzzle 6
$x = 6, y = -8$

-2	8	-6
-4	0	4
6	-8	2

AMS Puzzle 7
$x = 8$

1	8	15	10
14	11	4	5
12	13	6	3
7	2	9	16

AMS Puzzle 8
$x = 24$

28	2	24	14
22	16	26	4
10	20	6	32
8	30	12	18

AMS Puzzle 9
$x = 36$

45	9	18	30
48	12	27	15
6	42	21	33
3	39	36	24

AMS Puzzle 10
$x = 16, y = 18$

22	11	15	10
8	17	13	20
9	16	12	21
19	14	18	7

AMS Puzzle 11
$x = 7, y = 12$

7	18	14	19
21	12	16	9
20	13	17	8
10	15	11	22

AMS Puzzle 12
$x = 10, y = 24$

2	26	24	16
4	28	14	22
32	8	18	10
30	6	12	20

AMS Puzzle 13
$x = 17, y = -3, z = -7$

5	45	49	-7
25	17	13	37
9	33	29	21
53	-3	1	41

AMS Puzzle 14
$x = 19, y = 7, z = 4$

43	1	4	34
22	16	13	31
10	28	25	19
7	37	40	-2

AMS Puzzle 15
$x = 9, y = 5, z = 3$

-1	19	21	-7
1	13	11	7
9	5	3	15
23	-5	-3	17

AMS Puzzle 16
$x = 12$

17	23	4	10	11
24	5	6	12	18
1	7	13	19	25
8	14	20	21	2
15	16	22	3	9

AMS Puzzle 17
$x = 12, y = 8$

10	1	25	11	18
2	17	22	3	21
13	20	5	23	4
16	15	7	19	8
24	12	6	9	14

AMS Puzzle 18
$x = 16, y = 24$

20	2	50	22	36
4	34	44	6	42
26	40	10	46	8
32	30	14	38	16
48	24	12	18	28

AMS Puzzle 19
$x = 3, y = 7$

14	8	4	21	18
9	19	23	3	11
6	7	5	22	25
12	15	20	17	1
24	16	13	2	10

AMS Puzzle 20
$x = 1, y = 14,$

15	10	2	22	16
24	1	21	12	7
3	23	17	4	18
9	6	20	19	11
14	25	5	8	13

AMS Puzzle 21
$x = 6, y = 7, z = 21$

11	18	25	2	9
10	12	19	21	3
4	6	13	20	22
23	5	7	14	16
17	24	1	8	15

AMS Puzzle 22
$x = 10, y = 6, z = 17$

7	13	5	25	15
11	17	16	18	3
19	24	14	6	2
20	10	9	4	22
8	1	21	12	23

AMS Puzzle 23
$x = 15, y = 24, z = 11$

13	4	28	14	21
5	20	25	6	24
16	23	8	26	7
19	18	10	22	11
27	15	9	12	17

AMS Puzzle 24
$w = 13, x = 18,$
$y = 9, z = 8$

22	16	15	9	28
10	29	23	17	11
18	12	6	30	24
26	25	19	13	7
14	8	27	21	20

SS Puzzle 1

Square	A	B	C	D	E	F	G	Rectangle
Edge Length	7	8	9	10	14	18	15	32×33

SS Puzzle 2

Square	A	B	C	D	E	F	G	H	K
Edge Length	36	25	16	28	33	9	7	5	2

SS Puzzle 3

Square	A	B	C	D	E	F	G	H	X
Edge Length	24	19	22	25	17	23	11	6	3

SS Puzzle 4

Square	A	B	C	D	E	F	G	H	I	J	K
Edge Length	99	78	57	41	77	43	34	25	16	21	9

SS Puzzle 5

Square	B	C	E	F	G	I	J	K	L	M	Rectangle
Edge Length	31	42	24	19	36	14	11	9	5	3	75×112

SS Puzzle 6

Square	A	B	C	D	E	F	G	H	I	J	K	L	M
Edge Length	56	55	38	39	18	20	16	14	9	5	4	3	1

SS Puzzle 7

Square	A	B	C	D	E	F	G	H	I	J	K
Edge Length	81	51	43	35	33	64	31	30	29	8	2

SS Puzzle 8

Square	A	B	C	D	E	F	H	I	J	K	L	M	N	O	P	Q	R	S	U
Edge Length	27	35	50	29	33	37	24	19	25	16	18	17	15	9	7	11	8	6	2

NC Puzzle 1

5	7	-3
-5	3	11
9	-1	1

NC Puzzle 2

7	8	12	19
17	14	10	5
18	13	9	6
4	11	15	16

NC Puzzle 3

5	22	19	11	8
14	6	3	25	17
23	20	12	9	1
7	4	21	18	15
16	13	10	2	24

NC Puzzle 4

21	20	19	18	11	10
22	23	36	17	12	9
25	24	35	16	13	8
26	33	34	15	14	7
27	32	31	2	1	6
28	29	30	3	4	5

NC Puzzle 5

7	6	5	40	39	38	37
8	9	4	41	42	43	36
11	10	3	46	45	44	35
12	(1)	2	47	32	33	34
13	14	(49)	48	31	28	27
16	15	20	21	30	29	26
17	18	19	22	23	24	25

NC Puzzle 6

17	16	15	14	9
18	12	13	10	8
21	19	11	6	7
20	22	(25)	2	5
23	24	3	4	(1)

NC Puzzle 7

3	20	9	14	1
10	15	2	19	22
25	4	21	8	13
16	11	6	23	18
5	24	17	12	7

NC Puzzle 8

11	12	13	14	33	35
8	10	15	32	(36)	34
9	7	16	18	31	30
6	5	17	20	19	29
4	(1)	21	23	26	28
2	3	22	25	24	27

NC Puzzle 9

1	16	21	8	3
12	7	2	15	20
17	22	13	4	9
6	11	24	19	14
23	18	5	10	25

NC Puzzle 10

9	3	22	16	15
2	21	20	14	8
25	19	13	7	1
18	12	6	5	24
11	10	4	23	17

NC Puzzle 11

9	30	19	36	7	28	17
20	37	8	29	18	35	6
31	10	47	44	33	16	27
38	21	32	1	46	5	34
11	48	45	40	43	26	15
22	39	2	13	24	41	4
49	12	23	42	3	14	25

NC Puzzle 12

35	26	5	24	11	28
4	17	34	27	6	23
33	(36)	25	12	29	10
18	3	16	9	22	7
15	32	(1)	20	13	30
2	19	14	31	8	21

Answers for Chapter 7: Sequential Reasoning and Geometry

AC Puzzle 1.1

a	b	c	d	e	f	g	h	i	j	k	m	n	p	q	r	s	t	u	v
105	11	108	72	72	108	72	108	72	108	64	116	64	116	116	64	79	90	101	119

AC Puzzle 1.2

a	b	c	d	e	f	g	h	i	j	k	m	n	p	r	s	t	u
104	168	108	72	72	108	72	108	72	108	64	116	64	116	64	78	90	120

AC Puzzle 2.1

a	b	c	d	e	f	g	h	i	j	k	m	n	p	r	s	t
152	28	28	152	76	28	152	152	14	14	90	62	62	118	36	36	166

AC Puzzle 2.2

a	b	c	d	e	f	g	h	i	j	k	m	n	p	r	s	t
148	32	32	148	74	32	148	148	16	16	90	58	58	122	60	120	164

AC Puzzle 3.1

a	b	c	d	e	f	g	h	j	k	m	n	p	r	s
70	40	140	40	140	20	160	140	40	50	125	55	70	55	160

AC Puzzle 3.2

a	b	c	d	e	f	g	h	j	k	m	n	p	r	s
72	36	144	36	144	18	162	144	36	54	126	54	54	54	162

AC Puzzle 4.1

a	b	c	d	e	f	g	h	j	k	m	n	p	r	s
128	128	52	76	52	104	76	52	104	70	110	40	70	70	70

AC Puzzle 4.2

a	b	c	d	e	f	g	h	j	k	m	n	p	r	s
130	130	50	80	50	100	80	50	100	68	112	44	68	68	68

AC Puzzle 5.1

a	b	c	d	e	f	g	h	i	j	k	m	n	p	r	s	t	u	v	w
58	61	61	122	58	64	116	52	49	64	64	105	75	75	64	151	29	61	58	122

AC Puzzle 5.2

a	b	c	d	e	f	g	h	i	j	k	m	n	p	r	s	t	u	v	w	x
56	62	56	124	56	52	128	76	34	52	52	72	72	108	52	152	28	62	56	124	128

AC Puzzle 6.1

a	b	c	d	e	f	g	h	i	j	k	m	n	p	q	r	s	t	u	v	w	x
52	128	52	128	128	26	154	52	128	52	76	76	26	78	76	26	64	58	64	58	58	136

AC Puzzle 6.2

a	b	c	d	e	f	g	h	i	j	k	m	n	p	q	r	s	t	u	v	w	x
56	124	56	124	124	28	152	56	124	56	68	68	28	84	124	28	62	59	62	59	59	143

AC Puzzle 7.1

a	b	c	d	e	f	g	h	k	m	n	p	r	s	t
108	108	18	46	134	68	44	68	44	46	116	64	52	60	120

AC Puzzle 7.2

a	b	c	d	e	f	g	h	k	m	n	p	r	s	t	u
104	104	14	52	128	71	38	71	76	52	114	66	64	45	90	45

AC Puzzle 8.1

a	b	c	d	e	f	g	h	k	m	n	p	r	s	t
37	143	37	58	37	53	48	84	96	26	127	69	111	69	32

AC Puzzle 8.2

a	b	c	d	e	f	g	h	k	m	n	p	r	s	t
36	144	36	57	36	87	47	54	94	29	47	64	116	64	28

AC Puzzle 9.1

a	b	c	d	e	f	g	h	k	m	n	p	r	s	t
50	50	130	142	38	92	88	38	142	58	62	118	65	150	80

AC Puzzle 9.2

a	b	c	d	e	f	g	h	k	m	n	p	r	s	t
50	50	130	140	40	90	90	40	140	68	62	84	56	152	78

AC Puzzle 10.1

a	b	c	d	e	f	g	h	k	m	n	p	r	s	t	u	v	w	x
74	74	74	74	74	32	32	148	32	58	58	58	64	48	42	64	26	61	77

AC Puzzle 10.2

a	b	c	d	e	f	g	h	k	m	n	p	r	s	t	u	v	w	x
73	73	73	73	73	34	34	146	34	56	56	56	39	51	39	68	22	62	79

AC Puzzle 11.1

a	b	c	d	e	f	g	h	k	m	n	p	r	s	t	u	v	w
114	18	104	59	31	37	42	40	80	66	48	114	24	100	40	34	58	48

AC Puzzle 11.2

a	b	c	d	e	f	g	h	k	m	n	p	r	s	t	u	v	w
112	120	102	64	26	37	46	40	80	68	44	112	22	80	40	32	58	53

AC Puzzle 12.1

a	b	c	d	e	f	g	h	k	m	n	p	r	s
64	116	90	82	99	99	88	150	56	118	136	68	112	81

AC Puzzle 12.2

a	b	c	d	e	f	g	h	k	m	n	p	q	r	s	t
65	115	90	83	99	99	88	115	139	116	136	78	56	102	70	136

AC Puzzle 13.1

a	b	c	d	e	f	g	h	k	m	n	p	r	s
135	135	90	120	105	90	45	60	60	105	37.5	60	45	90

AC Puzzle 13.2

a	b	c	d	e	f	g
108	60	24	78	144	144	18

AC Puzzle 14.1

a	b	c	d	e	f	g	h	k	m	n	p	q	r	s	t
60	60	85	85	85	55	80	43	137	68	137	69	107	140	38	47

AC Puzzle 14.2

a	b	c	d	e	f	g	h	k	m	n	p	q	r	s	t
60	60	96	84	84	58	75	45	135	70	135	146	96	158	36	45

AC Puzzle 15.1

a	b	c	d	e	f	g	h	k	m	n	p
90	90	124	124	28	28	34	68	56	56	56	124

AC Puzzle 15.2

a	b	c	d	e	f	g	h	k	m	n	p	r
90	90	64	58	29	29	32	64	58	58	58	122	58

AC Puzzle 16.1

a	b	c	d	e	f	g	h	k	m	n	p	r	s	t
19	142	38	38	38	38	142	90	104	38	38	52	90	104	52

AC Puzzle 16.2

a	b	c	d	e	f	g	h	k	m	n	p	r	s	t
21	138	42	42	42	42	138	90	96	42	42	48	90	96	48

AC Puzzle 17.1

a	b	c	d	e	f	g	h	k	m
68	68	112	22	34	90	56	22	68	44

AC Puzzle 17.2

a	b	c	d	e	f	g	h	k	m
66	66	114	114	33	90	57	24	66	48

AC Puzzle 18.1

a	b	c	d	e	f	g	h	k	m	n	p	r	s
102	78	78	78	51	51	52	26	77	103	26	90	39	25

AC Puzzle 18.2

a	b	c	d	e	f	g	h	k	m	n	p	r
74	74	90	106	106	64	10	37	106	27	54	27	126

AC Puzzle 19.1

a	b	c	d	e	f	g	h	k	m	n	p	r	s	t	u
50	50	50	50	80	50	50	25	119	94	36	94	86	40	40	105

AC Puzzle 19.2

a	b	c	d	e	f	g	h	k	m	n	p	r	s	t	u
48	48	48	48	132	24	24	24	70	86	46	46	44	44	42	42

AC Puzzle 20.1

a	b	c	d	e	f	g	h	k	m	n	p	r	s	t	u	v	w
40	40	40	124	56	56	56	56	72	86	63	117	61	61	99	43	61	99

AC Puzzle 20.2

a	b	c	d	e	f	g	h	k	m	n	p	r	s	t	u	v
53	53	70	20	40	40	40	57	57	57	57	70	33	74	66	90	100

AC Puzzle 21.1

a	b	c	d	e	f	g	h	k	m	n	p	r	s	t	u	v
66	33	33	57	90	123	24	54	54	108	36	72	72	54	54	66	108

AC Puzzle 21.2

a	b	c	d	e	f	g	h	k	m	r	s	t	u
35	35	55	55	90	125	76	52	90	67	38	104	76	58

AC Puzzle 22.1

a	b	c	d	e	f	g	h	k	m	n	p	r	s	t	u	v	w	x	y	z
47	133	133	80	55	55	90	43	86	43	110	55	78	102	22	44	22	25	50	35	110

AC Puzzle 22.2

a	b	c	d	e	f	g	h	k	m	n	p	r	s	t	u	v	w	x	y	z
112	34	56	124	25	65	56	68	56	112	56	68	112	59	22	43	90	25	43	86	44

Section 4.3

Proof: There can be no open knight's tour on a 4×4 grid.

Let's look at some smaller boards as a warm up. Certainly there is no knight's tour on any 1×*n* board since the knight travels the diagonal of a 2×3 rectangle. We can also see that there is no knight's tour on any 2×*n* board because the knight needs another row in order to turn back and travel other squares.

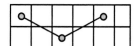  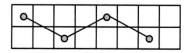

In Chapter 4, you have already seen that a knight's tour on a 3×3 grid is also impossible but 3×4 and 4×5 boards permit knight's tours. Now, let's look at a 4×4 grid.

Suppose there is a tour on a 4×4 board, and the squares marked with 1's only connect to 2's (see Figure 1 below). This means one of the 1-squares must be an end of the tour. If neither of the 1-squares are ends of the tour, then to cover both the 1-squares, you have to start at a 2-square. This forces a closed loop 2-1-2-1-2, which is not possible since you cannot land on the same square twice.

Likewise, the squares marked with 3's only connect to squares with 4's. By the same argument, this means one of the 3-squares must be an end of the tour. So there are only three possible paths connecting 1-2 and three possible paths connecting 3-4 (see Figure 2).

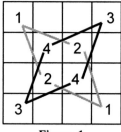 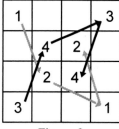 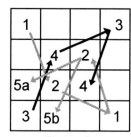 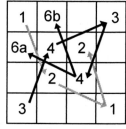

| Figure 1 | Figure 2 | Figure 3 | Figure 4 |

This implies there are only two possible paths from the end of the path ending at 2 (2 ⇒ 5a or 2 ⇒ 5b), and only two possible paths from the end of the path ending at 4 (4 ⇒ 6a or 4 ⇒ 6b) (see Figures 3 and 4). Suppose we pick the path 1-2-1-2-5a. This forces the remaining moves into the loop ABC (or CBA), and we end at C or A. Similarly, suppose we pick the path 1-2-1-2-5b. This forces the remaining moves into the loop DEF (or FED), and we end at F or D (see Figures 5 and 6).

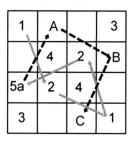 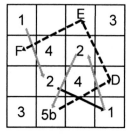 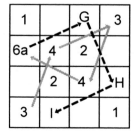 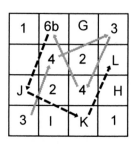

| Figure 5 | Figure 6 | Figure 7 | Figure 8 |

In like manner, suppose we pick the path 3-4-3-4-6a. This forces the remaining moves into the loop GHI (or IHG), and we end at I or G. The same is true if we pick the path 3-4-3-4-6b. This path forces the remaining moves into the loop JKL (or LKJ), and ends at J or L (see Figures 7 and 8).

So what do we have? We must start at one of the corner squares containing a 1 and we must end at one of the corner squares containing a 3. Yet any path we choose forces us to end on F, D, J, or L. Therefore, there can be no open knight's tour on a 4×4 grid.

Proof: There can be no closed tour on an *m×n* grid when *m* and *n* are both odd.

A closed knight's tour is a sequence of moves in which the last move leaves the knight one move from its starting square. Picture a grid of squares like a chessboard, with alternating colors, say red and white. When a knight moves from one square to another, it always lands on a different color from its previous position; if it starts on white then it will end on red. After an even number of moves, it will end on the same color on which it started. After an odd number of moves, it will end on the opposite color on which it started. For example, if the grid has 25 squares, it would take 24 moves to land on every other square, and the knight would end on the same color on which it started.

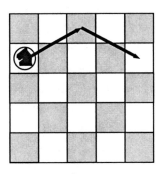

If *m* and *n* are both odd numbers, then an *m×n* grid has an odd number of squares. As in the section 4.3 example, it will then take *m×n* − 1 moves (since you start on square number one) to land on every square. This is an even number of moves and the knight will end its tour on the same color from which it started. But this square cannot be one move from the starting point because the knight must change colors in the move. Therefore, there cannot be a closed tour on an *m×n* grid where *m* and *n* are both odd.

It is possible to have an open tour on an odd grid as shown in the figure on the right.

Section 4.4

Proof: The Seven Bridges of Königsberg cannot be traveled.

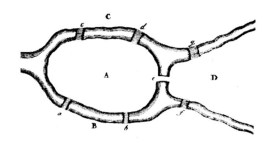

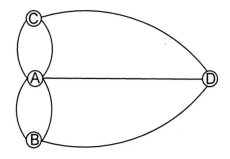

Euler's insight was to recognize that there are two different types of points, or vertices, in this problem. The difference is vertices can have either an odd or an even number of paths connected to them. In the *Seven Bridges of Königsberg* puzzle, all the vertices are odd. Passing in and out of an odd vertex is like switching a light switch on and off an odd number of times. If a light switch starts out off, after switching it three or five times, it will be on.

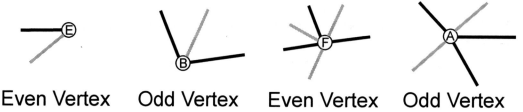

| Even Vertex | Odd Vertex | Even Vertex | Odd Vertex |

Consider the islands, A and D, and the land on the two sides of the river, B and C. Each has an odd number of paths or bridges coming onto it. Both sides B and C have three bridges connecting to them, island A has five paths connecting to it, and island D has three paths connecting to it.

Suppose you do not start on island D and in order to travel over the other paths connecting to D, you must enter the island over one of the bridges, leave it over another bridge, and return to it over the third bridge. So, if you do not start on island D you must end there.

Odd Vertex

By a similar argument, if you do not start on island A, then in order to travel over the other paths connecting to A, you must enter the island, leave it, enter it, leave it, and return to it, traveling over all five bridges. So, if you do not start on island A, you must end there.

In the same way, if you do not start on side B, then in order to travel over the three paths connecting to B you must enter side B over one of the bridges, leave it over another bridge, and return to it over the third. So, if you do not start on side B you must end there.

Odd Vertex

The same argument applies for side C. If you do not start on side C you must end there.

Now we have reached a contradiction! No matter where you start, if you are to travel over all the paths, there are three other vertices where you must end. For example, if you start at vertex A, then vertices B, C, and D must be stopping points. But we can only end at one vertex. Therefore, the network cannot be traveled.

A closer look at some questions posed in Section 4.4

If all the vertices of a network are even, can the network be traveled? Why? When can the network be traveled so that the traveler ends at the starting point? If a network has exactly two odd vertices can it be traveled? Why?

Claim: If all the vertices of a network are even then it can be traveled.

If all the vertices of a network are even then consider starting at any vertex and label it A. If you leave vertex A along one of the edges connected to it, then there are an odd number of edges left at A. If there are three edges remaining, you will return, leave, and return. If there are five edges remaining, you will return, leave, return, leave, and finally return. Therefore, for any odd number of edges, you will have to return, leave, return, leave, return and so on, until the remaining edges have been traveled. An odd number of paths remaining always requires you to return to the starting point, A. Since all the other vertices are even, you will enter, leave, enter, leave, and so on, until each edge has been covered. Therefore, if all vertices are even, you can start at any one of them, pass in and out of all the others until each connecting edge has been covered, and return to the starting vertex.

Even/Start & End   Even/Start & End   Even/Start & End

Claim: Every network with exactly two odd vertices can be traveled.

In the analysis of the *Seven Bridges of Königsberg* puzzle we saw if there were more than two odd vertices, there would be too many vertices vying to be the ending vertex. If there are exactly two odd vertices, one odd vertex can be a starting point, and traveling the edges connected to it you will leave, return,…leave. The other odd vertex must be the end point, and traveling the edges connected to it you will enter, leave,…, enter. The final edge travelled to enter the point will end the path.

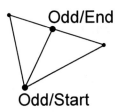
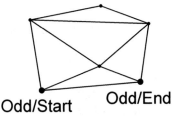
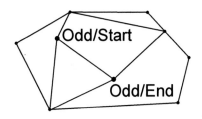

What did you notice about the number of odd vertices in a network?

To explore this we begin with an interesting theorem.

Theorem: The sum of the degrees of the vertices of a network is equal to twice the number of edges.

What does this mean? Let's look at an example of this theorem, then we will prove it. Network ABCDE has seven edges and five vertices. The degree of a vertex is the number of edges that connect to it, so the degree of each of the vertices in network ABCDE is A = 2, B = 3, C = 3, D = 2, and E = 4. The sum of the degrees is 14, which is twice the number of edges. To explain why, let's continue with the example.

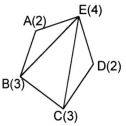

The degree of each vertex is the number of edges connected to it. Edge AB, for example, has two endpoints, A and B. If we sum these degrees, we will count each edge twice since each edge is connected to two vertices. So the number of edges is half the sum of the degrees of the vertices.

This illustrates one part of the theorem. It demonstrates the sum of the degrees of the vertices of any network is twice the number of edges.

After Path Puzzle 3 in Section 4.4, you were asked to find a graph with an odd number of odd vertices. You were most likely unsuccessful. Isn't that odd! Now we are ready to answer the question, "What did you notice about the number of odd vertices in a network?" We can prove, with the help of the above theorem, it is impossible for a network to have an odd number of odd vertices. Let's take a look.

First we do a quick review of odd and even sums.

Claim: The sum of any two odd numbers is even.

Proof: Let n and m be any numbers. Then $(2n + 1) + (2m + 1) = 2n + 2m + 2 = 2(n + m + 1)$

Claim: The sum of an odd and even number is odd.

Proof: Let n and m be any numbers. Then $(2n + 1) + 2m = (2n + 2m) + 1 = 2(n + m) + 1$

Claim: The sum of an odd number of odd numbers is odd.

Proof: Let $a_1, a_2, a_3, a_4, \ldots a_k$ be k odd numbers where k is odd. (Then $k - 1$ is even.)
Then the sum: $a_1 + a_2 + a_3 + a_4 + \ldots + a_k = (a_1 + a_2) + (a_3 + a_4) + \ldots + (a_{k-2} + a_{k-1}) + a_k$
But the sum of each pair of odd numbers $(a_i + a_{i+1})$ is an even number.
Therefore $(a_1 + a_2) + (a_3 + a_4) + \ldots + (a_{k-2} + a_{k-2})$ is even.
Therefore $(a_1 + a_2) + (a_3 + a_4) + \ldots + (a_{k-2} + a_{k-2}) + a_k$ is odd.

Suppose there exists a network that has an odd number of odd vertices. This would mean that the sum of the degrees is odd. But this contradicts the theorem above, which states the sum of the degrees of all the vertices of a network is twice the number of edges, an even number. Therefore, if there are odd vertices in a network there must be an even number of odd vertices.

Section 5.2

Proof: How to determine the magic sum of a normal magic square.

A normal magic square is an arrangement of n^2 consecutive numbers in an $n{\times}n$ square grid such that each row, column, and main diagonal has the same sum, called the magic sum. For example, consider the 4×4 normal magic square. It is an arrangement of the numbers 1 through 16. Let's begin by assigning letters to the numbers in a 4×4 magic square grid, as shown to the right. Let's assume the numbers are correctly placed so the sum of the numbers in each row is the same. This means:
$(a + b + c + d) = (e + f + g + h) = (i + j + k + l) = (m + n + o + p)$

a	b	c	d
e	f	g	h
i	j	k	l
m	n	o	p

The sum of all the numbers is: $a + b + c + d + e + f + g + h + i + j + k + l + m + n + o + p$.

How do you find the sum of 16 consecutive numbers? We could simply add them or we could add them in a clever way:

$$1 + 2 + 3 + 4 + 5 + 6 + 7 + 8 + 9 + 10 + 11 + 12 + 13 + 14 + 15 + 16$$
$$16 + 15 + 14 + 13 + 12 + 11 + 10 + 9 + 8 + 7 + 6 + 5 + 4 + 3 + 2 + 1$$
$$\overline{17 + 17 + 17 + 17 + 17 + 17 + 17 + 17 + 17 + 17 + 17 + 17 + 17 + 17 + 17 + 17}$$

By pairing the first number (1) with the last number (16) and the second number (2) with the next to last number (15), and so on, we get 16 pairs of numbers that each add to 17. This is twice what we want however, so the sum is half of 17 times 16, or 136.

From this method we can create a general rule for adding k consecutive numbers: add the first and last number and multiply by the number of numbers (k) then take half. As a formula it would look like sum $= (a + l) \cdot k/2$ (where a is the first number, l is the last number, and k is the number of numbers). Thus, the sum of the numbers 1 through k would be $(1 + k) \cdot k/2$, where the first number is 1 and the last number is k.

Once you have calculated the sum of all the numbers, notice the sum in each row must be one-fourth of the total. Thus, for a 4×4 magic square, the sum of all 16 numbers is 136 and the sum in each row (and therefore each column or main diagonal) is one-fourth of 136, or 34.

a	b	c	d	— (one-fourth the total sum)
e	f	g	h	— (one-fourth the total sum)
i	j	k	l	— (one-fourth the total sum)
m	n	o	p	— (one-fourth the total sum)

In general, in an $n \times n$ magic square, the magic sum is the sum of the n^2 numbers divided by the number of rows. So the formula for the magic sum of an $n \times n$ magic square is $(1 + n^2)(n^2)/2n$ or $(1 + n^2)(n)/2$. For a 5×5 magic square the magic sum would be the sum of 1 through 25 divided by 5. The sum of the numbers 1 through 25 is $(26)(25)/2 = 325$, so the magic sum is $325/5 = 65$.

Proof: The 3×3 magic square is unique.

To prove the 3×3 magic square is unique means we must show, disregarding the possible reflections and rotations, the arrangement of the numbers is the only possible one. First, we determine the magic sum. The sum of the numbers 1 through 9 is $(10)(9)/2 = 45$, so the magic sum is $45/3 = 15$.

4	9	2
3	5	7
8	1	6

The next step is to look at all the possible combinations of three numbers from the set 1 through 9 that add to 15, our magic sum. A thorough search gives us:

$1 + 5 + 9$ $\quad$ $2 + 4 + 9$ $\quad$ $3 + 4 + 8$ $\quad$ $4 + 5 + 6$
$1 + 6 + 8$ $\quad$ $2 + 5 + 8$ $\quad$ $3 + 5 + 7$ $\quad$ $2 + 6 + 7$

There are exactly eight different possible sums of three numbers, using 1 through 9, which sum to 15. There are three row sums, three column sums, and two diagonal sums, or 8 different sums in the 3×3 magic square, as shown on the right. Can we match the eight possible sums of 15 with the eight possible sums in the magic square? Let's take a look.

Notice that the center square is part of four different sums: one column sum, one row sum, and both diagonal sums. How many numbers appear in exactly four sums? Only the number 5 appears four times $(1 + 5 + 9, 2 + 5 + 8, 3 + 5 + 7,$ and $4 + 5 + 6)$. Therefore, the 5 must be placed in the center square (see Figure 9 on the next page).

Each of the four corner squares a, c, g, and i occurs in exactly three sums. What numbers occur in exactly three sums? Looking back at our list we see each of the numbers 2, 4, 6, and 8 occur in a sum three times. Therefore, 2, 4, 6, and 8 are at the four corners of the magic square. Since the center square is 5 and the magic sum is 15 then the opposite corners must add to 10. Thus 2 and 8 are opposite ends of one diagonal and 4 and 6 are opposite ends of the other.

Each of the four middle squares on the sides b, d, f, and h occurs in exactly two sums. What numbers occur in exactly two sums? Looking at our list we see that each of the numbers 1, 3, 7, and 9 occur in a sum twice. Therefore, 1, 3, 7, and 9 are at the four side positions of the magic square. Again, since the center square is 5 and the magic sum is 15 then the numbers in the opposite squares must add to 10. Thus, 1 and 9 are opposite each other, and 3 and 7 are opposite each other (see Figure 12).

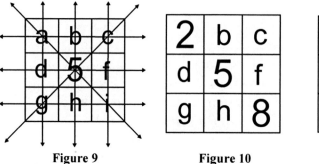

| Figure 9 | Figure 10 | Figure 11 | Figure 12 |

Since we are not counting rotations or reflections, we could have initially placed the 2 in any one of the four corners. This forces the 8 into the opposite corner. In the example above, we chose to place the 2 in position a (see Figure 10). If we had placed the 2 in the c, g, or i positions, it would just be a rotation of our final magic square.

Similarly, we next placed the 4 into one of the remaining corners, but either corner would work since one is just a reflection of the other. We chose position c, which then forced the 6 into the opposite corner (see Figure 11). Finally, the remaining numbers were forced into their positions (see Figure 12). This reasoning also produces the eight possible arrangements shown below.

The Eight Possible Arrangements

2	9	4
7	5	3
6	1	8

6	7	2
1	5	9
8	3	4

8	1	6
3	5	7
4	9	2

4	3	8
9	5	1
2	7	6

4	9	2
3	5	7
8	1	6

2	7	6
9	5	1
4	3	8

6	1	8
7	5	3
2	9	4

8	3	4
1	5	9
6	7	2

Footnotes

1. *(4)* An internationally know inventor of puzzles, Yoshigahara (1936 – 2004), affectionately known as "Nob", was perhaps Japan's most famous puzzle inventor and collector. He authored over 80 puzzle books and contributed to monthly puzzles columns. He also invented the game Lunar Lockout®, which is featured later in this book.

2. *(5)* The earliest known cryptarithms were created in China.

3. *(7)* Prior to the 1970s, flowcharts were a popular means for describing computer algorithms and are still occasionally used for this purpose.

4. *(11)* Martin Gardner was a prolific mathematics and science writer. In addition to writing for *Scientific American* and the *Skeptical Inquirer*, he authored over 70 books including *Mathematics Magic and Mystery* and *Mathematical Circus*. He introduced Solomon Golomb's *Polyominoes,* John H. Conway's *Game of Life*, and Roger Penrose's non-periodic tilings to the general public. Martin Gardner also helped popularize the works of M. C. Escher, the artist known for woodcuts and lithographs of impossible constructions and tessellations of recognizable figures. One comment from an article in *The Economist* magazine (6/3/2010) sums it up best, "No wonder it is sometimes said that Mr. Gardner made mathematicians out of children and children out of mathematicians."

5. *(18)* Matrix algebra is another mathematical system where the elements are matrices but unfamiliar results can occur in this mathematical system. For example, in matrix algebra, the commutative property of multiplication does not hold. Boolean algebra, another abstract mathematical system, has a number of different forms. In the Boolean algebra of circuits, the elements are switches and the operations are "parallel" or "series" connections. In Boolean logic, the elements are sentences and the binary operations are "and" and "or."

6. *(23)* Sam Loyd did not actually create the puzzle. The latest research by Slocum and Sonneveld gives credit to Noyes Chapman as the creator of the original 15-Puzzle. Sam Loyd did offer the prize of $1,000 for a solution. Of course the puzzle was impossible.

7. *(23)* In 1998, the puzzle was introduced as *UFO* at the third Gathering for Gardner. It was played on a 9×9 board. The commercial version was released in 2000.

8. *(39)* Abraham de Moivre (1667-1754) was the French mathematician most noted for the formula that bears his name, which is: $(\cos x + i\sin x)^n = \cos nx + i\sin nx$. According to legend, near the end of his life, de Moivre noticed he required a quarter of an hour more sleep than the previous day. When the pattern reached 24 hours, he passed away.

9. *(39)* Legendre (1752-1833) was one of the great teachers of mathematics. His geometry textbook was the model for geometry textbooks in America from 1819 to the mid 1960's.

Footnotes

10. *(39)* Math historians consider Leonhard Euler (1707-1783) the most prolific mathematician of all time. Euler (pronounced "Oyler") made discoveries in all branches of mathematics. His name is given to the amazing relationship that connects the five most important numbers in mathematics: $e^{i\pi} + 1 = 0$. In geometry there is the Euler line: the line containing the centroid, circumcenter, and the orthocenter of a triangle. In the theory of equations, Euler's method is a numerical procedure for solving ordinary differential equations. In topology, the Euler equation $V + F = E + 2$ relates the vertices, faces, and edges of any simple, closed polyhedron.

11. *(51)* When every vertex of a regular polygon tessellation has the same combination of regular polygons in the same order, the tiling is called a 1-uniform tiling or an Archimedean tiling. For more information on Archimedean Tilings, see Chapter 3 Section 5.

12. *(61)* The Hampton court maze in England was planted in 1690, and is perhaps the world's oldest continuously used hedge maze. There are corn field mazes, mirror mazes, water mazes, 3D mazes, trap door mazes, and logic mazes. Mazes are also an integral part of video game design. The video game player must advance from one level of the maze to the next, solving intricate mini-puzzles within the larger puzzle.

13. *(76)* David Bergamini displays this unique semi-magic square on page 69 of the Time-Life Books series Life Science Library, *Mathematics*. He attributes it to Euler. This special magic square also appears in *The Zen of Magic Squares, Circles, and Stars* by Clifford Pickover. Pickover also attributes this magic square to Euler. However, another prominent magic square enthusiast and researcher, George Jelliss, claims Euler did not create the 8x8 knight's tour semi-magic square.

14. *(85)* The problem of "squaring the circle" is to construct a square with a perimeter that is equal to the circumference of a given circle, using only a compass and straightedge (also stated as "constructing a square with an area equal to that of the area of a given circle"). It was proven to be impossible by Ferdinand von Lindemann in 1882.

15. *(85)* Sherman Stein, in his text, *Mathematics The Man-Made Universe,* has a nice series of theorems with proofs on this topic. They include: *A rectangle whose sides are rational can be tiled with congruent squares* and *A rectangle whose dimensions are L by W, with L/W irrational, cannot be tiled with congruent squares.*

16. *(85)* A Golden Rectangle is a rectangle in which the length (l) and width (w) satisfy the proportion: $w/l = l/(w + l)$.

17. *(85)* Mathematician Tutte was also a code breaker during World War II and was instrumental in breaking a German code, which helped the Allies in their invasion plans.

Illustration and Photo Credits

The author and publisher would like to thank the following for permission to reproduce their work.

Introduction: Page ix – photos of fifth graders playing Racetrack and tenth graders solving Coin Jump puzzles by Angela Snead

Chapter 1: Page 3 – Hourglass illustrations by Tamar Chestnut, photo of high school students solving the Tower of Hanoi puzzle by Angela Snead

Page 7, 8 – Robot © photos by Julien Tromeur/iStockphoto

Chapter 2: All Racetrack illustrations by Tamar Chestnut

Page 11 – Martin Gardner © photo, used with permission, Estate of Martin Gardner

Page 12 – Vintage Racecar © David Mingay/ScribblyMotor.co.uk/iStockphoto

Page 16 – Four Forces on an Airplane© Tom Benson NASA Glenn Research Center and NASA Langley

Chapter 3: Page 21,22 – photos of students working on Coin Slide puzzles and Coin Jump puzzles by Angela Snead

Page 23 – Lunar Lockout ® game, courtesy of Thinkfun

Page 28 – Honeycomb and Bee © JulyVelchev/iStockphoto

Page 33 – Ricochet Robots ® cover, courtesy of Rio Grande Games

Chapter 5: Page 65 – 3×3 Magic Square Sculpture, Eaton Fine Art, West Palm Beach, Florida, Title: Magic Square, 1967-2005 (date of artwork) Artist: Brian O'Doherty/Patrick Ireland, Photo by Diana Snider

Chapter 6: Page 81 – Mathematics Student© Andres Rodriguez/iStockphoto/andresrodriguez.co.uk

Page 95 – Tom Serra Bowling courtesy of Betty Jane Serra

Page 96 – Teenage Girl Receiving a Speeding Ticket © Rich Legg/iStockphoto/ Legacy One Photography

Page 98 – Sunrise © David Davis/iStockphoto

Page 98 – Airship © Vectorbot/iStockphoto

Back Cover: Michael Serra by Rick Der Photography

CPSIA information can be obtained at www.ICGtesting.com
Printed in the USA
BVOW040033021112

304462BV00004B/1/P